THE URANTIA BOOK WORKBOOKS

URANTIA®

URANTIA FOUNDATION
533 WEST DIVERSEY PARKWAY
CHICAGO, ILLINOIS 60614
U.S.A.

URANTIA®

®: Registered Mark of URANTIA Foundation

THE URANTIA BOOK WORKBOOKS

VOLUME VIII

Worship and Wisdom

This series of workbooks originally was published in the 1950s and 1960s to assist those early students who wanted to pursue an in-depth study of *The Urantia Book*. The workbook creators recognized that the materials were imperfect and were far from being definitive works on these subjects. Current students may be able to make more exhaustive analyses due to advances in knowledge and computerization of the text that are available today. Nevertheless, we recognize the enormous effort that went into this attempt to enhance understanding of *The Urantia Book* by some of its earliest students. We think these materials will be of interest to many and are therefore republishing them for their historic and educational value.

FIRST PRINTING 2003

THE URANTIA BOOK WORKBOOKS
VOLUME VIII
WORSHIP AND WISDOM

The Urantia Book Workbooks

Volume I: Transcripts of Lecture and Discussion of the Foreword and An Analytic Study of Part One of *The Urantia Book*
Volume II: Science in *The Urantia Book*
Volume III: Topical Studies in *The Urantia Book* and A Short Course in Doctrine
Volume IV: The Teachings of Jesus in *The Urantia Book*, The Life of Jesus Compared to the Four Gospels
Volume V: Urantia Doctrine: The Theology of *The Urantia Book*
Volume VI: History of The Bible and A Detailed Study of the Books of The Bible.
Volume VII: Quick Reference Dictionary, Terms and Defined in *The Urantia Book*, and A Keyword Index to the Table of Contetnts
Volume VIII: Worship and Wisdom: Gems from *The Urantia Book*

"URANTIA", "URANTIAN", "THE URANTIA BOOK", and ⓧ are the trademarks, service marks, and collective membership marks of URANTIA Foundation.

© 1959, 2003 URANTIA Foundation

All rights reserved, including translation, under the Berne Convention, Universal Copyright Convention, and other international copyright conventions.

To request permission to translate or to reproduce material contained in *The Urantia Book Workbooks* or the *The Urantia Book* by any means (including electronic, mechanical, or other—such as photocopying, recording, or any information storage and retrieval system), please contact Urantia Foundation. Copies of Urantia Foundation's current Copyright and Trademark Policies are available upon request.

ISBN:
0-942430-92-1

PUBLISHED BY URANTIA FOUNDATION
Original Publisher since 1955
533 Diversey Parkway
Chicago, Illinois 60614 U.S.A.
Telephone: +1 (773) 525-3319
Fax: +1 (773) 525-7739
Website: http://www.urantia.org
E-mail: urantia@urantia.org

Information

URANTIA Foundation has Representatives in Argentina, Belgium, Brazil, Bulgaria, Colombia, Ecuador, Estonia, Greece, Indonesia, Korea, Lithuania, México, Norway, Perú, Senegal, Spain, Uruguay, and Venezuela. If you require information on study groups, where you can obtain *The URANTIA Book*, or a Representative's telephone number, please contact the office nearest you or the head office in Chicago, Illinois.

International Offices:

Head Office
533 West Diversey Parkway
Chicago, Illinois 60614 U.S.A.
Tel.: +(773) 525-3319
Fax: +(773) 525-7739
Website: www.urantia.org
E-mail: urantia@urantia.org

Canada—English
PO Box 92006
West Vancouver, BC Canada V7V 4X4
Tel: +(604) 926-5836
Fax: +(604) 926-5899
E-mail: urantia@telus.net

Finland/Estonia/Sweden
PL 18,
15101 Lahti Finland
Tel./Fax: +(358) 3 777 8191
E-mail: urantia-saatio@urantia.fi

Great Britain/Ireland
Tel./Fax: +(44) 1491 641-922
E-Mail: urantia@easynet.co.uk

Australia/New Zealand/Asia
Tel./Fax: +(61) 2 9970-6200
E-mail: urantia@urantia.org.au

Canada—French
C. P. 233
Cap-Santé (Québec) Canada G0A 1L0
Tel.: +(418) 285-3333
Fax: +(418) 285-0226
E-mail: fondation@urantia-quebec.org

St. Petersburg, Russia
Tel./Fax: +(7) 812-580-3018
E-Mail: vitgen@peterlink.ru

Other books available from URANTIA Foundation:

The URANTIA Book	hard cover		ISBN 0-911560-02-5
The URANTIA Book	leather collector ($7^{5}/_{8}$" x $5^{3}/_{4}$")		ISBN 0-911560-75-0
The URANTIA Book	small hard cover ($8^{7}/_{16}$" x $5^{1}/_{2}$")		ISBN 0-911560-07-6
The URANTIA Book	paperback ($8^{7}/_{16}$" x $5^{1}/_{2}$")		ISBN 0-911560-51-3
The URANTIA Book	gift-box leather ($8^{7}/_{16}$" x $5^{1}/_{2}$")		ISBN 0-911560-08-4
The URANTIA Book	softcover ($8^{7}/_{16}$" x $5^{1}/_{2}$")		ISBN 0-911560-50-5
Le Livre d'URANTIA	hard cover	French	ISBN 0-911560-05-X
Le Livre d'URANTIA	soft cover	French	ISBN 0-911560-53-X
El libro de URANTIA	paperback ($8^{7}/_{16}$" x $5^{1}/_{2}$")	Spanish	ISBN 1-883395-02-X
El libro de URANTIA	hard cover ($8^{7}/_{16}$" x $5^{1}/_{2}$")	Spanish	ISBN 1-883395-03-8
URANTIA-kirja	hard cover	Finnish	ISBN 0-911560-03-3
URANTIA-kirja	soft cover	Finnish	ISBN 0-911560-52-1
The URANTIA Book Concordance		English Index	ISBN 0-911560-00-9
The URANTIA Book	Audio	English	ISBN 0-911560-30-0
The URANTIA Book	CD ROM	English, Finnish, French	ISBN 0-911560-63-7

The URANTIA Book Workbooks

Title	Format	Language	ISBN
Forward and Part I	Paperback	English	ISBN 0-942430-99-9
Science	Paperback	English	ISBN 0-942430-98-0
Topical and Doctrinal Study	Paperback	English	ISBN 0-942430-97-2
Jesus	Paperback	English	ISBN 0-942430-96-4
Theology	Paperback	English	ISBN 0-942430-95-6
Bible Study	Paperback	English	ISBN 0-942430-94-8
Terminology	Paperback	English	ISBN 0-942430-93-X
Worship and Wisdom	Paperback	English	ISBN 0-942430-92-1

Dutch, Korean, Portuguese, and Russian translations also available from Urantia Foundation.

WORSHIP AND WISDOM:
GEMS FROM THE URANTIA BOOK

Quotations from *The Urantia Book* are
with the permission of the owner of
the copyright of *The Urantia Book*.

© 1959, WILLIAM S. SADLER

Part I
THE CENTRAL AND SUPERUNIVERSES

                                                                                 PAGE

1. URANTIA'S PLACE IN THE COSMOS 25
2. SOUL AND PERSONALITY DEFINED 25
3. MAN'S SPIRITUAL ENDOWMENT 25
4. WORLDS CREATED TO BE INHABITED 26
5. GOD'S SUPREME MANDATE: "BE YOU PERFECT" 26
6. PORTRAIT OF THE REALITY OF GOD 26
7. MYSTERY OF THE DIVINE INDWELLING 27
8. THE PERSONALITY OF GOD 27
9. DIFFERING VIEWS OF GOD 28
10. THE EXPERIENCE OF KNOWING GOD 28
11. REALITY OF MAN'S IDENTITY 28
12. THE ONLY WAY TO KNOW GOD 29
13. THE ETERNAL PURPOSE OF GOD 29
14. THE DIVINE MERCY 29
15. THE FATHER'S AFFECTION 29
16. THE FORGIVING HEAVENLY FATHER 30
17. FAITHFUL GUIDANCE BY THE INDWELLING SPIRIT 30
18. GOD'S GOODNESS TO ERRING MAN 30
19. GOD NOT A DIVIDED PERSONALITY 30
20. THE NEW PHILOSOPHY OF GOD 31
21. GOD'S UNFAILING OVERCARE 31
22. THE FATHER KNOWS ALL ABOUT US 31
23. WE CAN FEEL GOD'S UNKNOWABLE LOVE 32
24. THE AMAZING INEVITABILITIES 32
25. CONTRASTIVE EXPERIENCE ON HAVONA 33
26. DON'T HUMANIZE OR MECHANIZE GOD 33
27. THE FATHER SHARES OUR AFFLICTIONS 33
28. GOD IS ALL THIS—AND MUCH MORE 34
29. THE URANTIA BENEDICTION 34
30. UNLIMITED FORCES OF SURVIVAL 34
31. GOD GRIEVES OVER OUR FAILURES 34
32. GOD IS ALWAYS A LOVING FATHER 35
33. REVELATION PRESENTS A GOD OF SALVATION 35
34. GOD IS NOT IN HIDING 35

Table of Contents

		Page
35.	God's Spirit Indwells Us	35
36.	The Father Wants to See Us on Paradise	36
37.	The Dynamic Religion of Love	36
38.	Diverse Views of God	36
39.	Satisfactions of Religious Experience	36
40.	Human Limitations Do Not Prevent Survival	37
41.	Man's Will Is Sovereign as Regards Survival	37
42.	Worship Can Go Direct to the Father	37
43.	Mandates of Eternal Son Keyed in Tones of Mercy	38
44.	The Spiritual Gravity Circuit	38
45.	The Divine Perfection Plans	38
46.	When the God of Action Functioned	39
47.	The Love, Mercy, and Ministry of Deity	40
48.	The Anxiety of Animal Fear	40
49.	The Living Ladder from Chaos to Glory	40
50.	God's Self-Distribution	40
51.	How All Things Work Together for Good	41
52.	The Omnipotent Gravity Pull	41
53.	Paradise Destiny of the Sons of God	41
54.	Undiscovered Galaxies of Space	41
55.	God Is a Freewill Personality	42
56.	God's Love Is Individualized	42
57.	God Is Always with Us	42
58.	Matter Is the Shadow of Spirit Reality	43
59.	Love Is the Secret of Personal Relations	43
60.	Science Does Not Explain Everything	43
61.	Death Starts the Eternal Voyage of Discovery	44
62.	Autocracy and Democracy Meet on Uversa	44
63.	We Never Escape the Badge of Our Nativity	44
64.	Innate Responses of the Cosmic Mind	44
65.	Personality Can Look before It Leaps	45
66.	Innate Scope of the Cosmic Mind	45
67.	The Creation of Majeston	45
68.	Only-Begotten Sons	46
69.	Rebellion-Tested Mortals—Mighty Messengers	46
70.	Purpose of Trials and Troubles	47

Table of Contents

		Page
71.	How a Census Director Functions	47
72.	Grandfanda Discovers Havona	47
73.	Affection for Our Morontia Companions	48
74.	Pilgrim Arrivals in Havona	48
75.	Battle Cry of Havona Pilgrims	49
76.	Finding God on Paradise	49
77.	Graduation from Havona	50
78.	Last Resurrection on Paradise	50
79.	Learning How to Worship	50
80.	The Mercy Trial Balance	51
81.	The Celestial Vocation Guiders	51
82.	Power Centers Never Play	52
83.	The Master Force Organizers	52
84.	Diverse Functions of God	52
85.	Our Status from Death to Resurrection	52
86.	Arriving in Havona	53
87.	Composition of Mortal Corps of the Finality	53
88.	The Master Architects	53
89.	The Mortal Finality Corps	54

Part II
THE LOCAL UNIVERSE

		Page
90.	Evolutionary Origin Not a Stigma	57
91.	The Father's Magnanimous Self Bestowal	57
92.	The Father's Eternal Purpose	57
93.	The Race for Eternity Is On	58
94.	Michael Is Just as Efficient as the Eternal Son	58
95.	The Gift of High Spiritual Forces	58
96.	The Need for Living Truth	59
97.	The Refreshing Water of Life	59
98.	Man's Dual Nature	59
99.	The Spirit Leads—But Never Drives	60
100.	The Fruits of the Spirit	60
101.	The Sure Guidance of the Spirit	60
102.	Conflicts of the Flesh and the Spirit	60
103.	The Hairs of Our Heads Are Numbered	61
104.	How God Lives with Us	61
105.	We Are Really the Sons of God	61
106.	Five Reasons for Sonship	62
107.	Calcium Escaping from the Sun	62
108.	Energy Is Eternal but Not Infinite	63
109.	The Endless Energy Changes	63
110.	Size of the Electron	64
111.	Atomic Internal Space	64
112.	Seven Groups of Chemical Elements	64
113.	Relation of Mind, Matter, and Spirit	64
114.	Confusion about the Most Highs	65
115.	Botanical Beauties of Eden	65
116.	Morontia Music	65
117.	Beauty, Rhythm, and Harmony	66
118.	Satania Probation Nursery	66
119.	First Mansion World	66
120.	Take Up Where We Leave Off Down Here	67
121.	Mansion World Arrivals	67
122.	Details of the Morontia Life	68
123.	On Mansion World No. Five	68
124.	The Time of Adjuster Fusion	68
125.	Departure for Jerusem	69

TABLE OF CONTENTS

		PAGE
126.	JOHN HAD A VISION OF THESE EVENTS	69
127.	THE MORONTIA LIFE	70
128.	MORONTIAL RELAXATION	70
129.	SUPERHUMAN HUMOR	70
130.	HUMOR PREVENTS EXALTATION OF EGO	71
131.	BENEFICIAL INFLUENCE OF HUMOR	71
132.	THE TWENTY-THIRD PSALM	72
133.	HUMAN PHILOSOPHY CONTRASTED WITH MORONTIA MOTA	72
134.	MAN NOT AN EVOLUTIONARY ACCIDENT	75
135.	COMPENSATION FOR URANTIA ISOLATION	75
136.	THE AGONDONTERS	75
137.	RACE IMPROVEMENT	76
138.	MIXING GOOD AND BAD STOCKS	76
139.	THE NEW AND LIVING WAY	76
140.	HIGH STATUS OF NORMAL WORLDS	77
141.	LIFE ON A PROGRESSIVE WORLD	77
142.	LIFE ON A RENOVATED PLANET	77
143.	MANOTIA IN THE LUCIFER REBELLION	77
144.	MORTAL CONSTANCY IN THE LUCIFER REBELLION	78
145.	TRUE AND FALSE LIBERTY	79
146.	THE THEFT OF LIBERTY	79
147.	THE TIME LAG OF JUSTICE	80
148.	THE MERCY TIME LAG	80
149.	TIME DELAY IN PUNISHING LUCIFER	81
150.	OUR SALVATION UNAFFECTED BY ANOTHER'S SIN	81
151.	COMPENSATIONS FOR REBELLION	81
152.	NET RESULTS OF THE LUCIFER REBELLION	82
153.	THE MORONTIA TEMPLE	82
154.	TRANSLATION FROM THE LIVING	83
155.	WORLD STATUS IN LIGHT AND LIFE	84
156.	THE EVOLUTIONARY GOAL	84
157.	GRAND UNIVERSE SETTLED IN LIGHT AND LIFE	85
158.	UNIVERSAL UNITY	85
159.	THE CEASELESS MARCH OF CREATIVE FORCE	85
160.	PURSUIT OF TRUTH, BEAUTY, AND GOODNESS	85
161.	SCOPE OF TRUTH, BEAUTY, AND GOODNESS	86

Part III
THE HISTORY OF URANTIA

PAGE

162. FIRST ANDRONOVER SUN 89
163. BIRTH OF OUR SUN 89
164. SUNSPOT CYCLES 89
165. CHEMICAL TYPE OF URANTIA LIFE 89
166. LIFE IS NOT AN ACCIDENT 90
167. TRANSITION FROM VEGETABLE TO ANIMAL LIFE 90
168. THE GEOLOGIC STONE RECORD BOOK 91
169. TIME OF BIOLOGIC TRIBULATION 91
170. THE ORIGIN OF MAMMALS 91
171. THE DAWN MANNALS 92
172. THE MID-MAMMALS 92
173. THE PRIMATES 92
174. THE FIRST HUMAN BEINGS 93
175. SPIRIT OF WORSHIP 95
176. URANTIA AN INHABITED WORLD 95
177. ANDON AND FONTA 95
178. SURVIVAL OF ANDON AND FONTA 97
179. HEROIC STRUGGLES OF PRIMITIVE MEN 98
180. MAN'S ASCENT FROM SEAWEED TO LORDSHIP 98
181. THE ANCESTRAL FROG 98
182. SCIENTIFIC SELECTION VS. NATURAL SELECTION 98
183. URANTIA A LIFE-EXPERIMENT WORLD 99
184. PHYSICS AND CHEMISTRY CAN'T EXPLAIN EVOLUTION 100
185. LENGTH OF LIFE THE YARDSTICK OF TIME 100
186. SUDDEN MENTAL AND SPIRITUAL TRANSFORMATIONS 100
187. FREE-WILL SUPREMACY 101
188. THE FORTITUDE OF VAN 101
189. AMADON WAS THE HERO OF REBELLION 101
190. WE DO NOT SPIRITUALLY SUFFER FROM ANOTHER'S SIN .. 101
191. THE STEADFAST AMADON 102
192. CULTURE IS NOT HEREDITARY 102
193. THE DELUSION OF "BACK TO NATURE" 103
194. DANGERS OF VANITY AND PLEASURE-SEEKING 103
195. SAFEGUARDS OF SOCIETY 103

Table of Contents

		Page
196.	Basic Human Institutions	103
197.	Capital and Modern Society	104
198.	Care about Social Changes	104
199.	Natural Rights	104
200.	Governmental Responsibilities	105
201.	"Golden Rulers" Must Protect Themselves	105
202.	The Ideal State	105
203.	The Profit Motive	105
204.	Arrival of Adam and Eve	106
205.	Handicaps of Adam and Eve	106
206.	Default of Adam and Eve	106
207.	Disillusionment of Eve	107
208.	Adam and Eve Lose Some of Their Children	108
209.	Humanity Profited Much from Adam and Eve	108
210.	The Folly of Impatience	108
211.	Adam's Body Cells Resistant to Disease	109
212.	Misfortunes and Compensations of Urantia	109
213.	Survival of Adam and Eve	109
214.	Contribution of Adam and Eve	109
215.	Adamson and Ratta	110
216.	Value of Racial Mixtures	111
217.	The Tools of Civilization	111
218.	Family, the Master Civilizer	111
219.	Supreme Value of Marriage	112
220.	Dangers of Self-Gratification	112
221.	Enjoying Wholesome Pleasures	113
222.	Mission of Primitive Religion	113
223.	Magic, the Cocoon of Science	113
224.	Sin Redefined	113
225.	Forgiveness of Sin	113
226.	Evolution Achieves Its End	114
227.	Prayer and the Alter Ego	114
228.	Prayer Does Not Change God	114
229.	Prayer and Civilization	114
230.	Thoughts about Praying	115
231.	Conditions of Effective Prayer	115

Table of Contents

		Page
232.	Primitive Religion and Civilization	116
233.	The Urantia Revelation	116
234.	The Sage of Salem	116
235.	The Salem Religion	117
236.	Melchizedek and Abraham	118
237.	Urantia Is Waiting for Michael's Message	119
238.	Mistakes of Melchizedek Missionaries	119
239.	Moses and Ikhnaton	119
240.	The Matchless Moses	120
241.	The Book of Psalms	121
242.	The Prophet Samuel	121
243.	Amos and Hosea	122
244.	Isaiah the Second	122
245.	Purpose of Christ's Bestowal	123
246.	Religion and Social Reconstruction	123
247.	Institutional Religion	123
248.	Religion and the Religionist	124
249.	Sectarianism	125
250.	Religious Growth	126
251.	The Believer's Surety	126
252.	Problems of Spiritual Growth	127
253.	Marks of Religious Living	128
254.	Jesus' Religious Experience	129
255.	Thinking Vs. Feeling	130
256.	The Marks of Faith	131
257.	Faith Vs. Belief	132
258.	From Darkness to Light	132
259.	In the Presence of the Eternal	133
260.	The Discovery of God	133
261.	Knowing a God of Salvation	133
262.	Diverse Views of God	134
263.	Gone Are Guilt and Isolation	134
264.	How We Get Our Idealism	134
265.	Reason and Faith	135
266.	The Transcendence of Religious Experience	135
267.	How God Lives within Us	135

TABLE OF CONTENTS

PAGE

268. THE DIVINE "PILOT LIGHT" 136
269. THOUGHT ADJUSTERS AND HUMAN WILL 136
270. MISSION OF THOUGHT ADJUSTERS 136
271. TIME OF ADJUSTER TRANSIT 136
272. AGE AT THE ADJUSTER'S ARRIVAL 136
273. ADJUSTERS CONSERVE ALL TRUE VALUES 137
274. HOW THE ADJUSTERS HELP US 137
275. ADJUSTERS LIKE TO TALK WITH US 138
276. TRIUMPHANT FAITH 138
277. POSSIBILITY OF HEARING THE ADJUSTER 138
278. PERSONALIZED ADJUSTERS 138
279. HOW THE ADJUSTERS WORK WITHIN US 138
280. CARE OF THE ADJUSTER'S EARTHLY TABERNACLE 139
281. THE SUPERB GAME OF THE AGES 139
282. TOO MUCH THOUGHT ON THE TRIFLES OF LIVING 140
283. HOW ADJUSTERS WORK WITH THE MIND 140
284. RELATION OF ADJUSTER TO CONSCIENCE 141
285. INTELLECTUAL AND SPIRITUAL DEVELOPMENT 141
286. GREAT DAYS FOR THE ADJUSTER 141
287. ADJUSTER SOUL PARTNERSHIP 142
288. MESSAGE OF ADJUSTER TO ITS SOUL 142
289. THE MYSTERY OF THE EVOLVING SOUL 143
290. SCOPE OF THE MATERIAL MIND 143
291. THE ADJUSTER IS OUR SHIP'S PILOT 143
292. VALUES OF THE INNER AND OUTER WORLDS 143
293. THE CONSECRATION OF WILL 144
294. CO-OPERATION WITH THE ADJUSTER 144
295. ADJUSTER HANDICAPS 145
296. HOW ADJUSTER GAINS PERSONALITY 145
297. IS THERE PROBATION AFTER DEATH? 146
298. THE GREAT MORONTIA CHANGE 146
299. ADJUSTER FUSION 146
300. GRANDEUR OF MORTAL DESTINY 147
301. GUARDIAN ANGELS NOT A MYTH 147
302. THE RESERVE CORPS OF DESTINY 148
303. URANTIA NOT A COSMIC ORPHAN 148

Table of Contents

		Page
304.	Finite and Evolutionary Deity	147
305.	Spirit Dominance	149
306.	Grand Universe a Living Organism	149
307.	God the Supreme	150
308.	Our Relation to the Supreme Being	150
309.	The Finite God	151
310.	We Are a Part of the Supreme	151
311.	The Oversoul of Creation	151
312.	Finaliter Transcendation	152
313.	God the Supreme Our Evolutionary Mother	152
314.	Our Relation to the Supreme	152
315.	God the Supreme, Then God the Ultimate	153
316.	Truth Is Timeless	153
317.	God's Omnipotence and Omnificence	153
318.	God the Supreme and Providence	154
319.	Misconceptions of Providence	155
320.	The Bestowals of Michael	156
321.	Urantia a Sentimental Shrine	156

PART IV
THE LIFE AND TEACHINGS OF JESUS

		PAGE
322.	MYSTERY OF THE INCARNATION	159
323.	JESUS' HEREDITY	159
324.	BIRTH OF JESUS	160
325.	JESUS GETS HIS ADJUSTER	160
326.	TROUBLE ABOUT JESUS' PRAYERS	160
327.	TROUBLE OVER JESUS' ARTISTIC EFFORTS	160
328.	JESUS' UNWILLINGNESS TO FIGHT	161
329.	JESUS A DIFFICULT CHILD TO REAR	161
330.	JESUS' FIRST VIEW OF THE TEMPLE	162
331.	JESUS' REACTIONS TO THE TEMPLE SERVICES	162
332.	JESUS AND HIS FATHER DISCUSS SACRIFICES	163
333.	JESUS' MEDITATIONS ARE TROUBLED	163
334.	NOTHING EXTRAORDINARY HAPPENED	164
335.	ORIGIN OF "THE LORD'S PRAYER"	164
336.	SHOCKS, CONFLICTS, AND DISAPPOINTMENTS	165
337.	JESUS' ADOLESCENT RESPONSIBILITIES	165
338.	ABOUT JOINING THE ZEALOTS	166
339.	THE DEATH OF LITTLE AMOS	167
340.	THE FIRST BLOODLESS PASSOVER	167
341.	JESUS MASTERING THE ART OF LIVING	168
342.	THE HUMANITY OF JESUS	169
343.	THE DIVINITY OF JESUS	169
344.	JESUS' LOVE FOR CHILDREN	170
345.	JESUS MEETS GONAD AND GANID	170
346.	PURPOSE OF THE TRIP TO ROME	170
347.	JESUS KNOWS ALL ABOUT US	171
348.	"OUR RELIGION"	172
349.	THE STORY ABOUT WEALTH	173
350.	GANID WANTS TO MAKE A NEW RELIGION	174
351.	SAYING GOODBY TO THE INDIANS	174
352.	JESUS' TALKS AT URMIA	175
353.	WINNING THE SOVEREIGNTY OF A UNIVERSE	176
354.	JESUS LAYS DOWN HIS TOOLS	176
355.	BAPTISM OF JESUS	176

Table of Contents

		Page
356.	Jesus and His Adjuster	177
357.	Just after the Baptism	178
358.	Jesus Refuses to Be a Wonder-Worker	178
359.	Philip Leads Nathaniel to Jesus	179
360.	Mary on the Way to Cana	179
361.	The Water and the Wine	180
362.	Jesus Realizes That He Must Be on Guard	181
363.	Banquet at Matthew's House	181
364.	The Wednesday Play Day	182
365.	Warning against Religion about Jesus	182
366.	The Apostles Believed in Jesus	183
367.	Faith Vs. Works	183
368.	Jesus' Respect for the Individual	183
369.	Characteristics of the Apostles	184
370.	From the Ordination Sermon	184
371.	Fatherly Vs. Brotherly Love	186
372.	The Futility of Hate and Vengeance	186
373.	Jesus' Attitude toward Society	186
374.	Wrong Ideas of Jesus and His Religion	187
375.	Growth Vs. Self-Examination	187
376.	Jesus Not a Social Reformer	187
377.	Jesus' Life an Inspirational Ideal	188
378.	All Men Are Sons of God	188
379.	Jesus Craved Family Affection	188
380.	Jesus Was a Commanding Personality	189
381.	Warnings against Creeds	189
382.	The Story of Teherma	190
383.	Jesus' Unperturbed Character	190
384.	The Heroic and Militant Gospel	191
385.	Self-Mastery	192
386.	First Statement of His Divinity	193
387.	The Lord's Prayer	193
388.	The Steadfastness of Ruth	194
389.	Hate Is the Shadow of Fear	194
390	Spontaneous Healing	194
391.	Evil Is Not Sin	195

Table of Contents

		Page
392.	Affliction Not Punishment	195
393.	The Liberation of Women	196
394.	The Secret of Happiness	196
395.	Love in the Place of Fear	197
396.	What Shall We Do to Be Saved?	197
397.	Mission of Adversity	198
398.	The Religion of the Spirit	198
399.	Doing the Will of God	198
400.	The Faintest Flicker of Faith	199
401.	This Life Is Only a Bridge	199
402.	Humor and Faith	199
403.	Leadership and Human Frailties	200
404.	Certainty of Salvation	200
405.	The Keys of the Kingdom	200
406.	Judgment Belongs to the Group	201
407.	Avoid Frightening People	201
408.	Jesus Not a Man of Sorrows	201
409.	Dangers of False Sympathy	201
410.	We Are Always Unafraid	202
411.	How to Look at the Bible	202
412.	On Being "Second Milers"	202
413.	Mastering the Art of Living	203
414.	Worship and Spiritual Strength	203
415.	Learning How to Fail Gracefully	203
416.	True Success	203
417.	Transcendence of the Religion of Jesus	204
418.	The Water of Life	204
419.	Love of Riches	204
420.	Jesus Thankful for His Associates	204
421.	Of More Value than Many Sparrows	205
422.	Why Tarry in the Valley of Decision?	205
423.	We Can Have the Kingdom	205
424.	Prosperity Not a Token of Divine Favor	205
425.	Meaning of Health and Disease	206
426.	Woman with Spirit of Infirmity	206
427.	The Pharisee and the Publican	207

Table of Contents

		Page
428.	Jesus Concerned Only with Religion	207
429.	At the Tomb of Lazarus	207
430.	Lazarus Is Resurrected	207
431.	How We Can Know God	208
432.	Knowing God as a Father	208
433.	Jesus' Methods of Ministry	208
434.	"As Jesus Passed By"	209
435.	How We Should Carry On	209
436.	One Day with God in the Hills	210
437.	Dual Citizenship	211
438.	Not to Be Mystics or Ascetics	212
439.	How We Should Live	212
440.	Washing the Apostles' Feet	213
441.	Establishing the Remembrance Supper	213
442.	The New Commandment	214
443.	Let Not Your Hearts Be Troubled	215
444.	Words of Comfort	215
445.	The Old and the New Religion	215
446.	The Mansion Worlds	216
447.	More Words of Comfort	216
448.	Jesus' Titles	216
449.	Jesus' Suffering in the Garden	217
450.	"Behold the Man"	217
451.	The Trial of Jesus	217
452.	Jesus Lays Down His Life	218
453.	At the Crucifixion	218
454.	The Thief on the Cross	219
455.	Last Hour on the Cross	219
456.	Jesus' Burial	220
457.	Meaning of the Cross	220
458.	Resurrection of Jesus	221
459.	Disposing of Jesus' Body	222
460.	The Women at the Tomb	223
461.	David Zebedee Heralds the Resurrection	223
462.	Jesus Appearing to Thomas	224
463.	Jesus' Last Appearance	225

Table of Contents

		Page
464.	Jesus' Religion	225
465.	Endurance of Christianity	226
466.	The Materialistic Panic	226
467.	Inconsistencies of the Mechanist	226
468.	Weakness of Secularism	227
469.	The Needs of Christianity	227
470.	The Hope of Christiantiy	228
471.	The Faith of Jesus	229
472.	Prayer Life of Jesus	229
473.	Jesus Wants Us to Believe WITH Him	230
474.	The Religion about Jesus	230
475.	Jesus a Wholehearted Religionist	230
476.	Jesus' Faith in Men	231
477.	Man's Divine Indwelling	231
478.	True Nobility Spurns Mere Success	231
479.	Father Idea the Highest Concept of God	231

Part I

THE CENTRAL AND SUPERUNIVERSES

1. URANTIA'S PLACE IN THE COSMOS

"Your world, Urantia, is one of many similar inhabited planets which comprise the local universe of *Nebadon*. This universe, together with similar creations, makes up the superuniverse of *Orvonton*, from whose capital, Uversa, our commission hails. Orvonton is one of the seven evolutionary superuniverses of time and space which circle the never-beginning, never-ending creation of divine perfection—the central universe of *Havona*. At the heart of this eternal and central universe is the stationary Isle of Paradise, the geographic center of infinity and the dwelling place of the eternal God." *P. 1.*

2. SOUL AND PERSONALITY DEFINED

"The soul of man is an experiential acquirement. As a mortal creature chooses to 'do the will of the Father in heaven,' so the indwelling spirit becomes the father of a *new reality* in human experience. The mortal and material mind is the mother of this same emerging reality. The substance of this new reality is neither material nor spiritual—it is *morontial*. This is the emerging and immortal soul which is destined to survive mortal death and begin the Paradise ascension.

"*Personality*. The personality of mortal man is neither body, mind, nor spirit; neither is it the soul. Personality is the one changeless reality in an otherwise ever-changing creature experience; and it unifies all other associated factors of individuality. The personality is the unique bestowal which the Universal Father makes upon the living and associated energies of matter, mind, and spirit, and which survives with the survival of the morontial soul.

"*Morontia* is a term designating a vast level intervening between the material and the spiritual. It may designate personal or impersonal realities, living or nonliving energies. The warp of morontia is spiritual; its woof is physical." *Pp. 8, 9.*

3. MAN'S SPIRITUAL ENDOWMENT

"We are fully cognizant of the difficulties of our assignment; we recognize the impossibility of fully translating the language of the concepts of divinity and eternity into the symbols of the language of the finite concepts of the mortal mind. But we know that there dwells within the human mind a fragment of God, and that there sojourns with the human soul the Spirit of Truth;

and we further know that these spirit forces conspire to enable material man to grasp the reality of spiritual values and to comprehend the philosophy of universe meanings. But even more certainly we know that these spirits of the Divine Presence are able to assist man in the spiritual appropriation of all truth contributory to the enhancement of the ever-progressing reality of personal religious experience—God-consciousness." *P. 17.*

4. WORLDS CREATED TO BE INHABITED

"The myriads of planetary systems were all made to be eventually inhabited by many different types of intelligent creatures, beings who could know God, receive the divine affection, and love him in return. The universe of universes is the work of God and the dwelling place of his diverse creatures. 'God created the heavens and formed the earth; he established the universe and created this world not in vain; he formed it to be inhabited.'" *P. 21.* **Isa. 45:18.**

5. GOD'S SUPREME MANDATE: "BE YOU PERFECT"

"The enlightened worlds all recognize and worship the Universal Father, the eternal maker and infinite upholder of all creation. The will creatures of universe upon universe have embarked upon the long, long Paradise journey, the fascinating struggle of the eternal adventure of attaining God the Father. The transcendent goal of the children of time is to find the eternal God, to comprehend the divine nature, to recognize the Universal Father. God-knowing creatures have only one supreme ambition, just one consuming desire, and that is to become, as they are in their spheres, like him as he is in his Paradise perfection of personality and in his universal sphere of righteous supremacy. From the Universal Father who inhabits eternity there has gone forth the supreme mandate, 'Be you perfect, even as I am perfect.' In love and mercy the messengers of Paradise have carried this divine exhortation down through the ages and out through the universes, even to such lowly animal-origin creatures as the human races of Urantia.

"This magnificent and universal injunction to strive for the attainment of the perfection of divinity is the first duty, and should be the highest ambition, of all the struggling creature creation of the God of perfection. This possibility of the attainment of divine perfection is the final and certain destiny of all man's eternal spiritual progress." *Pp. 21, 22.* **Matt. 5:48.**

6. PORTRAIT OF THE REALITY OF GOD

"God is primal reality in the spirit world; God is the source of truth in the mind spheres; God overshadows all throughout the material realms. To all created intelligences God is a personality, and to the universe of universes he is the First Source and Center of eternal reality. God is neither manlike nor machine-like. The First Father is universal spirit, eternal truth, infinite reality, and father personality.

"The eternal God is infinitely more than reality idealized or the universe personalized. God is not simply the supreme desire of man, the mortal quest objectified. Neither is God merely a concept, the power-potential of righteousness. The Universal Father is not a synonym for nature, neither is he natural law personified. God is a transcendent reality, not merely man's traditional concept of supreme values. God is not a psychological focalization of spiritual meanings, neither is he 'the noblest work of man.' God may be any or all of these concepts in the minds of men, but he is more. He is a saving person and a loving Father to all who enjoy spiritual peace on earth, and who crave to experience personality survival in death." *Pp. 23, 24.*

7. MYSTERY OF THE DIVINE INDWELLING

"The infinity of the perfection of God is such that it eternally constitutes him mystery. And the greatest of all the unfathomable mysteries of God is the phenomenon of the divine indwelling of mortal minds. The manner in which the Universal Father sojourns with the creatures of time is the most profound of all universe mysteries; the divine presence in the mind of man is the mystery of mysteries." *P. 26.*

"When you are through down here, when your course has been run in temporary form on earth, when your trial trip in the flesh is finished, when the dust that composes the mortal tabernacle 'returns to the earth whence it came'; then, it is revealed, the indwelling 'Spirit shall return to God who gave it.' There sojourns within each moral being of this planet a fragment of God, a part and parcel of divinity. It is not yet yours by right of possession, but it is designedly intended to be one with you if you survive the mortal existence." *P. 26.* **Eccl. 12:7.**

8. THE PERSONALITY OF GOD

"Do not permit the magnitude of God, his infinity, either to obscure or eclipse his personality. 'He who planned the ear, shall he not hear? He who formed the eye, shall he not see?' The Universal Father is the acme of divine personality; he is the origin and destiny of personality throughout all creation. God is both infinite and personal; he is an infinite personality. The Father is truly a personality, notwithstanding that the infinity of his person places him forever beyond the full comprehension of material and finite beings." *P. 27.*

"Even though material mortals cannot see the person of God, they should rejoice in the assurance that he is a person; by faith accept the truth which portrays that the Universal Father so loved the world as to provide for the eternal spiritual progression of its lowly inhabitants; that he 'delights in his children.' *God is lacking in none of those superhuman and divine* attributes which constitute a perfect, eternal, loving, and infinite Creator personality." *P. 28*. **Prov. 8:31. Isa. 62:4.**

9. DIFFERING VIEWS OF GOD

"God is to science a cause, to philosophy an idea, to religion a person, even the loving heavenly Father. God is to the scientist a primal force, to the philosopher a hypothesis of unity, to the religionist a living spiritual experience. Man's inadequate concept of the personality of the Universal Father can be improved only by man's spiritual progress in the universe and will become truly adequate only when the pilgrims of time and space finally attain the divine embrace of the living God on Paradise." *P. 30.*

10. THE EXPERIENCE OF KNOWING GOD

"The more completely man understands himself and appreciates the personality values of his fellows, the more he will crave to know the Original Personality, and the more earnestly such a God-knowing human will strive to become like the Original Personality. You can argue over opinions about God, but experience with him and in him exists above and beyond all human controversy and mere intellectual logic. The God-knowing man describes his spiritual experiences, not to convince unbelievers, but for the edification and mutual satisfaction of believers." *P. 30.*

"God is spirit—spirit personality; man is also a spirit—potential spirit personality. Jesus of Nazareth attained the full realization of this potential of spirit personality in human experience; therefore his life of achieving the Father's will becomes man's most real and ideal revelation of the personality of God. Even though the personality of the Universal Father can be grasped only in actual religious experience, in Jesus' earth life we are inspired by the perfect demonstration of such a realization and revelation of the personality of God in a truly human experience." *P. 30.* **John 4:24.**

11. REALITY OF MAN'S IDENTITY

"Man does not achieve union with God as a drop of water might find unity with the ocean. Man attains divine union by progressive reciprocal spiritual communion, by personality intercourse with the personal God, by increasingly attaining the divine nature through wholehearted and intelligent *conformity to*

12. THE ONLY WAY TO KNOW GOD

"Ultimate universe reality cannot be grasped by mathematics, logic, or philosophy, only by personal experience in progressive conformity to the divine will of a personal God. Neither science, philosophy, nor theology can validate the personality of God. Only the personal experience of the faith sons of the heavenly Father can effect the actual spiritual realization of the personality of God." *P. 31*.

13. THE ETERNAL PURPOSE OF GOD

"The reactions of a changeless God, in the execution of his eternal purpose, may seem to vary in accordance with the changing attitude and the shifting minds of his created intelligences; that is, they may apparently and superficially vary; but underneath the surface and beneath all outward manifestations, there is still present the changeless purpose, the everlasting plan, of the eternal God." *P. 36*. **Eph. 3:11**.

14. THE DIVINE MERCY

"Mercy is simply justice tempered by that wisdom which grows out of perfection of knowledge and the full recognition of the natural weaknesses and environmental handicaps of finite creatures. 'Our God is full of compassion, gracious, long-suffering, and plenteous in mercy.' Therefore 'whosoever calls upon the Lord shall be saved,' 'for he will abundantly pardon.' 'The mercy of the Lord is from everlasting to everlasting'; yes, 'his mercy endures forever.' 'I am the Lord who executes loving-kindness, judgment, and righteousness in the earth, for in these things I delight.' 'I do not afflict willingly nor grieve the children of men,' for I am 'the Father of mercies and the God of all comfort.'" *P. 38*. **Ps. 86:15. Rom. 10:13. Isa. 55:7. Ps. 103:17. 1 Chron. 16:34. Jer. 9:24. Lam. 3:33. 2 Cor. 1:3**.

15. THE FATHER'S AFFECTION

"It is wrong to think of God as being coaxed into loving his children because of the sacrifices of his Sons or the intercession of his subordinate creatures, 'for the Father himself loves you.' It is in response to this paternal affection that God sends the marvelous Adjusters to indwell the minds of men. God's love is universal; 'whosoever will may come.' He would 'have all men be saved by coming into the knowledge of the truth.' He is 'not willing that any should perish.'

"The Creators are the very first to attempt to save man from the disastrous results of his foolish transgression of the divine laws. God's love is by nature a fatherly affection; therefore does he sometimes 'chasten us for our own profit, that we may be partakers of his holiness.' Even during your fiery trials remember that 'in all our afflictions he is afflicted with us.'" P. 39. **John 16:27. Rev. 22:17. 1 Tim. 2:4. 2 Peter 3:9. Heb. 12:9,10. Isa. 63:9.**

16. THE FORGIVING HEAVENLY FATHER

"God is divinely kind to sinners. When rebels return to righteousness, they are mercifully received, 'for our God will abundantly pardon.' 'I am he who blots out your transgressions for my own sake, and I will not remember your sins.' 'Behold what manner of love the Father has bestowed upon us that we should be called the sons of God.'" P. 39. **Isa. 55:7; 43:25. 1 John 3:1.**

17. FAITHFUL GUIDANCE BY THE INDWELLING SPIRIT

"After all, the greatest evidence of the goodness of God and the supreme reason for loving him is the indwelling gift of the Father—the Adjuster who so patiently awaits the hour when you both shall be eternally made one. Though you cannot find God by searching, if you will submit to the leading of the indwelling spirit, you will be unerringly guided, step by step, life by life, through universe upon universe, and age by age, until you finally stand in the presence of the Paradise personality of the Universal Father." P. 39. **Job 11:7.**

18. GOD'S GOODNESS TO ERRING MAN

"The 'richness of the goodness of God leads erring man to repentance.' 'Every good gift and every perfect gift comes down from the Father of lights.' 'God is good; he is the eternal refuge of the souls of men.' 'The Lord God is merciful and gracious. He is long-suffering and abundant in goodness and truth.' 'Taste and see that the Lord is good! Blessed is the man who trusts him.' 'The Lord is gracious and full of compassion. He is the God of salvation.' 'He heals the brokenhearted and binds up the wounds of the soul. He is man's all-powerful benefactor.'" P. 41. **Rom. 2:4. Jas. 1:17. Ps. 73:1. Deut. 33:27. Ps. 103:8. Ex. 34:6. Ps. 34:8; 111:4. Ps. 68:20. Isa. 61:1.**

19. GOD NOT A DIVIDED PERSONALITY

"The affectionate heavenly Father, whose spirit indwells his children on earth, is not a divided personality—one of justice and one of mercy—neither does it require a mediator to secure the Father's favor or forgiveness. Divine righteousness is not dominated by strict retributive justice; God as a father transcends God as a judge." P. 41.

20. THE NEW PHILOSOPHY OF GOD

"The religious challenge of this age is to those farseeing and forward-looking men and women of spiritual insight who will dare to construct a new and appealing philosophy of living out of the enlarged and exquisitely integrated modern concepts of cosmic truth, universe beauty, and divine goodness. Such a new and righteous vision of morality will attract all that is good in the mind of man and challenge that which is best in the human soul. Truth, beauty, and goodness are divine realities, and as man ascends the scale of spiritual living, these supreme qualities of the Eternal become increasingly co-ordinated and unified in God, who is love." *P. 43.* **1 John 4:8.**

21. GOD'S UNFAILING OVERCARE

"The Universal Father is not a transient force, a shifting power, or a fluctuating energy. The power and wisdom of the Father are wholly adequate to cope with any and all universe exigencies. As the emergencies of human experience arise, he has foreseen them all, and therefore he does not react to the affairs of the universe in a detached way but rather in accordance with the dictates of eternal wisdom and in consonance with the mandates of infinite judgment. Regardless of appearances, the power of God is not functioning in the universe as a blind force." *P. 47.*

22. THE FATHER KNOWS ALL ABOUT US

"The Universal Father is the only personality in all the universe who does actually know the number of the stars and planets of space. All the worlds of every universe are constantly within the consciousness of God. He also says: 'I have surely seen the affliction of my people, I have heard their cry, and I know their sorrows.' For 'the Lord looks from heaven; he beholds all the sons of men; from the place of his habitation he looks upon all the inhabitants of the earth.' Every creature child may truly say: 'He knows the way I take, and when he has tried me, I shall come forth as gold.' 'God knows our downsittings and our uprisings; he understands our thoughts afar off and is acquainted with all our ways.' 'All things are naked and open to the eyes of him with whom we have to do.' And it should be a real comfort to every human being to understand that 'he knows your frame; he remembers that you are dust.' Jesus, speaking of the living God, said, 'Your Father knows what you have need of even before you ask him.'" *P. 49.* **Ex. 3:7. Ps. 33:13,14; 139:2,3. Heb. 4:13. Ps. 103:14. Matt. 6:8.**

23. WE CAN FEEL GOD'S UNKNOWABLE LOVE

"Mortal man cannot possibly know the infinitude of the heavenly Father. Finite mind cannot think through such an absolute truth or fact. But this same finite human being can actually *feel*—literally experience—the full and undiminished impact of such an infinite Father's LOVE. Such a love can be truly experienced, albeit while quality of experience is unlimited, quantity of such an experience is strictly limited by the human capacity for spiritual receptivity and by the associated capacity to love the Father in return." *P. 50.*

24. THE AMAZING INEVITABILITIES

"The uncertainties of life and the vicissitudes of existence do not in any manner contradict the concept of the universal sovereignty of God. All evolutionary creature life is beset by certain *inevitabilities*. Consider the following:

"1. Is *courage*—strength of character—desirable? Then must man be reared in an environment which necessitates grappling with hardships and reacting to disappointments.

"2. Is *altruism*—service of one's fellows—desirable? Then must life experience provide for encountering situations of social inequality.

"3. Is *hope*—the grandeur of trust—desirable? Then human existence must constantly be confronted with insecurities and recurrent uncertainties.

"4. Is *faith*—the supreme assertion of human thought—desirable? Then must the mind of man find itself in that troublesome predicament where it ever knows less than it can believe.

"5. Is the *love of truth* and the willingness to go wherever it leads, desirable? Then must man grow up in a world where error is present and falsehood always possible.

"6. Is *idealism*—the approaching concept of the divine—desirable? Then must man struggle in an environment of relative goodness and beauty, surroundings stimulative of the irrepressible reach for better things.

"7. Is *loyalty*—devotion to highest duty—desirable? Then must man carry on amid the possibilities of betrayal and desertion. The valor of devotion to duty consists in the implied danger of default.

"8. Is *unselfishness*—the spirit of self-forgetfulness—desirable? Then must mortal man live face to face with the incessant clamoring of an inescapable self for recognition and honor. Man could not dynamically choose the divine life if there were no self-life to forsake. Man could never lay saving hold on righteousness if there were no potential evil to exalt and differentiate the good by contrast.

"9. Is *pleasure*—the satisfaction of happiness—desirable? Then must man live in a world where the alternative of pain and the likelihood of suffering are ever-present experiential possibilities." *P. 51.*

25. CONTRASTIVE EXPERIENCE ON HAVONA

"The creatures of Havona are naturally brave, but they are not courageous in the human sense. They are innately kind and considerate, but hardly altruistic in the human way. They are expectant of a pleasant future, but not hopeful in the exquisite manner of the trusting mortal of the uncertain evolutionary spheres. They have faith in the stability of the universe, but they are utter strangers to that saving faith whereby mortal man climbs from the status of an animal up to the portals of Paradise. They love the truth, but they know nothing of its soul-saving qualities. They are idealists, but they were born that way; they are wholly ignorant of the ecstasy of becoming such by exhilarating choice. They are loyal, but they have never experienced the thrill of whole-hearted and intelligent devotion to duty in the face of temptation to default. They are unselfish, but they never gained such levels of experience by the magnificent conquest of a belligerent self. They enjoy pleasure, but they do not comprehend the sweetness of the pleasure escape from the pain potential." *P. 52.*

26. DON'T HUMANIZE OR MECHANIZE GOD

"It is a great blunder to humanize God, except in the concept of the indwelling Thought Adjuster, but even that is not so stupid as completely to *mechanize* the idea of the First Great Source and Center." *P. 53.*

27. THE FATHER SHARES OUR AFFLICTIONS

"Does the Paradise Father suffer? I do not know. The Creator Sons most certainly can and sometimes do, even as do mortals. The Eternal Son and the Infinite Spirit suffer in a modified sense. I think the Universal Father does, but I cannot understand *how*; perhaps through the personality circuit or through the individuality of the Thought Adjusters and other bestowals of his eternal nature. He has said of the mortal races, 'In all your afflictions I am afflicted.' He unquestionably experiences a fatherly and sympathetic understanding; he may truly suffer, but I do not comprehend the nature thereof." *P. 53.* **Isa. 63:9.**

28. GOD IS ALL THIS — AND MUCH MORE

"The infinite and eternal Ruler of the universe of universes is power, form, energy, process, pattern, principle, presence, and idealized reality. But he is more; he is personal; he exercises a sovereign will, experiences self-consciousness of divinity, executes the mandates of a creative mind, pursues the satisfaction of the realization of an eternal purpose, and manifests a Father's love and affection for his universe children. And all these more personal traits of the Father can be better understood by observing them as they were revealed in the bestowal life of Michael, your Creator Son, while he was incarnated on Urantia." P. 53.

29. THE URANTIA BENEDICTION

"God the Father loves men; God the Son serves men; God the Spirit inspires the children of the universe to the ever-ascending adventure of finding God the Father by the ways ordained by God the Sons through the ministry of the grace of God the Spirit." P. 53.

30. UNLIMITED FORCES OF SURVIVAL

"There is no limitation of the forces and personalities which the Father may use to uphold his purpose and sustain his creatures. 'The eternal God is our refuge, and underneath are the everlasting arms.' 'He who dwells in the secret place of the Most High shall abide under the shadow of the Almighty.' 'Behold, he who keeps us shall neither slumber nor sleep.' 'We know that all things work together for good to those who love God,' 'for the eyes of the Lord are over the righteous, and his ears are open to their prayers.'" P. 55. **Deut. 33:27. Ps. 91:1; 121:4. Rom. 8:28. Ps. 34:15.**

31. GOD GRIEVES OVER OUR FAILURES

"The Universal Father never does anything that causes subsequent sorrow or regret, but the will creatures of the planning and making of his Creator personalities in the outlying universes, by their unfortunate choosing, sometimes occasion emotions of divine sorrow in the personalities of their Creator parents. But though the Father neither makes mistakes, harbors regrets, nor experiences sorrows, he is a being with a father's affection, and his heart is undoubtedly grieved when his children fail to attain the spiritual levels they are capable of reaching with the assistance which has been so freely provided by the spiritual-attainment plans and the mortal-ascension policies of the universes." P. 58. **Eph. 4:30. Heb. 3:10,17.**

32. GOD IS ALWAYS A LOVING FATHER

"In God the Father freewill performances are not ruled by power, nor are they guided by intellect alone; the divine personality is defined as consisting in spirit and manifesting himself to the universes as love. Therefore, in all his personal relations with the creature personalities of the universes, the First Source and Center is always and consistently a loving Father. God is a Father in the highest sense of the term. He is eternally motivated by the perfect idealism of divine love, and that tender nature finds its strongest expression and greatest satisfaction in loving and being loved." *P. 59*.

33. REVELATION PRESENTS A GOD OF SALVATION

"In science, God is the First Cause; in religion, the universal and loving Father; in philosophy, the one being who exists by himself, not dependent on any other being for existence but beneficently conferring reality of existence on all things and upon all other beings. But it requires revelation to show that the First Cause of science and the self-existent Unity of philosophy are the God of religion, full of mercy and goodness and pledged to effect the eternal survival of his children on earth." *P. 59*.

34. GOD IS NOT IN HIDING

"Our Father is not in hiding; he is not in arbitrary seclusion. He has mobilized the resources of divine wisdom in a never-ending effort to reveal himself to the children of his universal domains. There is an infinite grandeur and an inexpressible generosity connected with the majesty of his love which causes him to yearn for the association of every created being who can comprehend, love, or approach him; and it is, therefore, the limitations inherent in you, inseparable from your finite personality and material existence, that determine the time and place and circumstances in which you may achieve the goal of the journey of mortal ascension and stand in the presence of the Father at the center of all things." *Pp. 62, 63*.

35. GOD'S SPIRIT INDWELLS US

"Although the approach to the Paradise presence of the Father must await your attainment of the highest finite levels of spirit progression, you should rejoice in the recognition of the ever-present possibility of immediate communion with the bestowal spirit of the Father so intimately associated with your inner soul and your spiritualizing self." *P. 63*.

"However Urantia mortals may differ in their intellectual, social, economic, and even moral opportunities and endowments, forget not that their spiritual endowment is uniform and unique. They all enjoy the same divine presence of the gift from the Father, and they are all equally privileged to seek intimate personal communion with this indwelling spirit of divine origin, while they may all equally choose to accept the uniform spiritual leading of these Mystery Monitors." *P. 63.*

"Man is spiritually indwelt by a surviving Thought Adjuster. If such a human mind is sincerely and spiritually motivated, if such a human soul desires to know God and become like him, honestly wants to do the Father's will, there exists no negative influence of mortal deprivation nor positive power of possible interference which can prevent such a divinely motivated soul from securely ascending to the portals of Paradise." *P. 63.* **Rom. 8:35, 38, 39.**

36. THE FATHER WANTS TO SEE US ON PARADISE

"The Father desires all his creatures to be in personal communion with him. He has on Paradise a place to receive all those whose survival status and spiritual nature make possible such attainment. Therefore settle in your philosophy now and forever: To each of you and to all of us, God is approachable, the Father is attainable, the way is open; the forces of divine love and the ways and means of divine administration are all interlocked in an effort to facilitate the advancement of every worthy intelligence of every universe to the Paradise presence of the Universal Father." *P. 63.*

37. THE DYNAMIC RELIGION OF LOVE

"The morality of the religions of evolution *drives* men forward in the God quest by the motive power of fear. The religions of revelation *allure* men to seek for a God of love because they crave to become like him. But religion is not merely a passive feeling of 'absolute dependence' and 'surety of survival'; it is a living and dynamic experience of divinity attainment predicated on humanity service." *P. 66.* **Rom. 2:4.**

38. DIVERSE VIEWS OF GOD

"The fact-seeking scientist conceives of God as the First Cause, a God of force. The emotional artist sees God as the ideal of beauty, a God of aesthetics. The reasoning philosopher is sometimes inclined to posit a God of universal unity, even a pantheistic Deity. The religionist of faith believes in a God who fosters survival, the Father in heaven, the God of love." *P. 68.*

39. SATISFACTIONS OF RELIGIOUS EXPERIENCE

"Mortal man secures three great satisfactions from religious experience, even in the days of his temporal sojourn on earth:

"1. *Intellectually* he acquires the satisfactions of a more unified human consciousness.

"2. *Philosophically* he enjoys the substantiation of his ideals of moral values.

"3. *Spiritually* he thrives in the experience of divine companionship, in the spiritual satisfactions of true worship." P. 69.

40. HUMAN LIMITATIONS DO NOT PREVENT SURVIVAL

"Eternal survival of personality is wholly dependent on the choosing of the mortal mind, whose decisions determine the survival potential of the immortal soul. When the mind believes God and the soul knows God, and when, with the fostering Adjuster, they all *desire* God, then is survival assured. Limitations of intellect, curtailment of education, deprivation of culture, impoverishment of social status, even inferiority of the human standards of morality resulting from the unfortunate lack of educational, cultural, and social advantages, cannot invalidate the presence of the divine spirit in such unfortunate and humanly handicapped but believing individuals. The indwelling of the Mystery Monitor constitutes the inception and insures the possibility of the potential of growth and survival of the immortal soul." Pp. 69, 70.

41. MAN'S WILL IS SOVEREIGN AS REGARDS SURVIVAL

"Having thus provided for the growth of the immortal soul and having liberated man's inner self from the fetters of absolute dependence on antecedent causation, the Father stands aside. Now, man having thus been liberated from the fetters of causation response, at least as pertains to eternal destiny, and provision having been made for the growth of the immortal self, the soul, it remains for man himself to will the creation or to inhibit the creation of this surviving and eternal self which is his for the choosing. No other being, force, creator, or agency in all the wide universe of universes can interfere to any degree with the absolute sovereignty of the mortal free will, as it operates within the realms of choice, regarding the eternal destiny of the personality of the choosing mortal. As pertains to eternal survival, God has decreed the sovereignty of the material and mortal will, and that decree is absolute." P. 71.

42. WORSHIP CAN GO DIRECT TO THE FATHER

"As all gravity is circuited in the Isle of Paradise, as all mind is circuited in the Conjoint Actor and all spirit in the Eternal Son, so is all personality circuited in the personal presence of the Universal Father, and this circuit unerringly transmits the worship of all personalities to the Original and Eternal Personality." P. 71.

43. MANDATES OF ETERNAL SON KEYED IN TONES OF MERCY

"The Eternal Son is the great mercy minister to all creation. Mercy is the essence of the Son's spiritual character. The mandates of the Eternal Son, as they go forth over the spirit circuits of the Second Source and Center, are keyed in tones of mercy." *P. 75.*

44. THE SPIRITUAL GRAVITY CIRCUIT

"The spiritual-gravity pull of the Eternal Son constitutes the inherent secret of the Paradise ascension of surviving human souls. All genuine spirit values and all bona fide spiritualized individuals are held within the unfailing grasp of the spiritual gravity of the Eternal Son. The mortal mind, for example, initiates its career as a material mechanism and is eventually mustered into the Corps of the Finality as a well-nigh perfected spirit existence, becoming progressively less subject to material gravity and correspondingly more responsive to the inward pulling urge of spirit gravity during this entire experience. The spirit-gravity circuit literally pulls the soul of man Paradiseward.

"The spirit-gravity circuit is the basic channel for transmitting the genuine prayers of the believing human heart from the level of human consciousness to the actual consciousness of Deity. That which represents true spiritual value in your petitions will be seized by the universal circuit of spirit gravity and will pass immediately and simultaneously to all divine personalities concerned. Each will occupy himself with that which belongs to his personal province.

Therefore, in your practical religious experience, it is immaterial whether, in addressing your supplications, you visualize the Creator Son of your local universe or the Eternal Son at the center of all things." *P. 84.*

"But how much more perfect is the superb technique of the spiritual world: If anything originates in your consciousness that is fraught with supreme spiritual value, when once you give it expression, no power in the universe can prevent its flashing directly to the Absolute Spirit Personality of all creation." *P. 84.*

45. THE DIVINE PERFECTION PLANS

"This divine plan of perfection attainment embraces three unique, though marvelously correlated, enterprises of universal adventure:

"1. *The Plan of Progressive Attainment.* This is the Universal Father's plan of evolutionary ascension, a program unreservedly accepted by the Eternal Son when he concurred in the Father's proposal, 'Let us make mortal creatures in our own image.' This provision for upstepping the creatures of time involves the Father's bestowal of the Thought Adjusters and the endowing of material creatures with the prerogatives of personality.

"2. *The Bestowal Plan.* The next universal plan is the great Father-revelation enterprise of the Eternal Son and his co-ordinate Sons. This is the proposal of the Eternal Son and consists of his bestowal of the Sons of God upon the evolutionary creations, there to personalize and factualize, to incarnate and make real, the love of the Father and the mercy of the Son to the creatures of all universes. Inherent in the bestowal plan, and as a provisional feature of this ministration of love, the Paradise Sons act as rehabilitators of that which misguided creature will has placed in spiritual jeopardy. Whenever and wherever there occurs a delay in the functioning of the attainment plan, if rebellion, perchance, should mar or complicate this enterprise, then do the emergency provisions of the bestowal plan become active forthwith. The Paradise Sons stand pledged and ready to function as retrievers, to go into the very realms of rebellion and there restore the spiritual status of the spheres. And such a heroic service a co-ordinate Creator Son did perform on Urantia in connection with his experiential bestowal career of sovereignty acquirement.

"3. *The Plan of Mercy Ministry.* When the attainment plan and the bestowal plan had been formulated and proclaimed, alone and of himself, the Infinite Spirit projected and put in operation the tremendous and universal enterprise of mercy ministry. This is the service so essential to the practical and effective operation of both the attainment and the bestowal undertakings, and the spiritual personalities of the Third Source and Center all partake of the spirit of mercy ministry which is so much a part of the nature of the Third Person of Deity. Not only in creation but also in administration, the Infinite Spirit functions truly and literally as the conjoint executive of the Father and the Son." *P. 85.* **Gen. 1:26, 27.**

46. WHEN THE GOD OF ACTION FUNCTIONED

"The God of Action functions and the dead vaults of space are astir. One billion perfect spheres flash into existence. Prior to this hypothetical eternity moment the space-energies inherent in Paradise are existent and potentially operative, but they have no actuality of being; neither can physical gravity be measured except by the reaction of material realities to its incessant pull. There is no material universe at this (assumed) eternally distant moment, but the very instant that one billion worlds materialize, there is in evidence gravity sufficient and adequate to hold them in the everlasting grasp of Paradise.

"There now flashes through the creation of the Gods the second form of energy and this outflowing spirit is instantly grasped by the spiritual gravity of the Eternal Son. Thus the twofold gravity-embraced universe is touched with the energy of infinity and immersed in the spirit of divinity. In this way is the soil of life prepared for the consciousness of mind made manifest in the associated intelligence circuits of the Infinite Spirit.

"Upon these seeds of potential existence, diffused throughout the central creation of the Gods, the Father acts, and creature personality appears. Then does the presence of the Paradise Deities fill all organized space and begin effectively to draw all things and beings Paradiseward." *P. 91*.

47. THE LOVE, MERCY, AND MINISTRY OF DEITY

"God is love, the Son is mercy, the Spirit is ministry—the ministry of divine love and endless mercy to all intelligent creation. The Spirit is the personification of the Father's love and the Son's mercy; in him are they eternally united for universal service. The Spirit is *love applied* to the creature creation, the combined love of the Father and the Son." *P. 94*.

48. THE ANXIETY OF ANIMAL FEAR

"Too often, all too often, you mar your minds by insincerity and sear them with unrighteousness; you subject them to animal fear and distort them by useless anxiety. Therefore, though the source of mind is divine, mind as you know it on your world of ascension can hardly become the object of great admiration, much less of adoration or worship. The contemplation of the immature and inactive human intellect should lead only to reactions of humility." *P. 103*.

49. THE LIVING LADDER FROM CHAOS TO GLORY

"The spirit personalities of the vast family of the Divine and Infinite Spirit are forever dedicated to the service of the ministry of the love of God and the mercy of the Son to all the intelligent creatures of the evolutionary worlds of time and space. These spirit beings constitute the living ladder whereby mortal man climbs from chaos to glory." *P. 107*.

50. GOD'S SELF-DISTRIBUTION

"It would seem that the Father, back in eternity, inaugurated a policy of profound self-distribution. There is inherent in the selfless, loving, and lovable nature of the Universal Father something which causes him to reserve to himself the exercise of only those powers and that authority which he apparently finds it impossible to delegate or to bestow." *P. 108*.

51. HOW ALL THINGS WORK TOGETHER FOR GOOD

"The mortal mind can immediately think of a thousand and one things—catastrophic physical events, appalling accidents, horrific disasters, painful illnesses, and world-wide scourges—and ask whether such visitations are correlated in the unknown maneuvering of this probable functioning of the Supreme Being. Frankly, we do not know; we are not really sure. But we do observe that, as time passes, all these difficult and more or less mysterious situations *always* work out for the welfare and progress of the universes. It may be that the circumstances of existence and the inexplicable vicissitudes of living are all interwoven into a meaningful pattern of high value by the function of the Supreme and the over-control of the Trinity." *P. 115.* **Rom. 8:28.**

52. THE OMNIPOTENT GRAVITY PULL

"The inescapable pull of gravity effectively grips all the worlds of all the universes of all space. Gravity is the all-powerful grasp of the physical presence of Paradise. Gravity is the omnipotent strand on which are strung the gleaming stars, blazing suns, and whirling spheres which constitute the universal physical adornment of the eternal God, who is all things, fills all things, and in whom all things consist." *P. 125.* **Col. 1:17.**

53. PARADISE DESTINY OF THE SONS OF GOD

"After all, to mortals the most important thing about eternal Paradise is the fact that this perfect abode of the Universal Father is the real and far-distant destiny of the immortal souls of the mortal and material sons of God, the ascending creatures of the evolutionary worlds of time and space. Every God-knowing mortal who has espoused the career of doing the Father's will has already embarked upon the long, long Paradise trail of divinity pursuit and perfection attainment. And when such an animal-origin being does stand, as countless numbers now do, before the Gods on Paradise, having ascended from the lowly spheres of space, such an achievement represents the reality of a spiritual transformation bordering on the limits of supremacy." *P. 127.*

54. UNDISCOVERED GALAXIES OF SPACE

"In the not-distant future, new telescopes will reveal to the wondering gaze of Urantian astronomers no *less than 375 million new galaxies* in the remote stretches of outer space. At the same time these more powerful telescopes will disclose that many island universes formerly believed to be in outer space are really a part of the galactic system of Orvonton. The seven superuniverses are still growing; the periphery of each is gradually expanding;

new nebulae are constantly being stabilized and organized; and some of the nebulae which Urantian astronomers regard as extragalactic are actually on the fringe of Orvonton and are traveling along with us." Pp. 130, 131.

55. GOD IS A FREEWILL PERSONALITY

"And all this steadfastness of conduct and uniformity of action is personal, conscious, and highly volitional, for the great God is not a helpless slave to his own perfection and infinity. God is not a self-acting automatic force; he is not a slavish law-bound power. God is neither a mathematical equation nor a chemical formula. He is a freewill and primal personality. He is the Universal Father, a being surcharged with personality and the universal fount of all creature personality." P. 138.

56. GOD'S LOVE IS INDIVIDUALIZED

"The love of the Father absolutely individualizes each personality as a unique child of the Universal Father, a child without duplicate in infinity, a will creature irreplaceable in all eternity. The Father's love glorifies each child of God, illuminating each member of the celestial family, sharply silhouetting the unique nature of each personal being against the impersonal levels that lie outside the fraternal circuit of the Father of all. The love of God strikingly portrays the transcendent value of each will creature, unmistakably reveals the high value which the Universal Father has placed upon each and every one of his children from the highest creator personality of Paradise status to the lowest personality of will dignity among the savage tribes of men in the dawn of the human species on some evolutionary world of time and space." P. 138. **John 16:27.**

57. GOD IS ALWAYS WITH US

"It is a mystery that God is a highly personal self-conscious being with residential headquarters, and at the same time personally present in such a vast universe and personally in contact with such a well-nigh infinite number of beings. That such a phenomenon is a mystery beyond human comprehension should not in the least lessen your faith. Do not allow the magnitude of the infinity, the immensity of the eternity, and the grandeur and glory of the matchless character of God to overawe, stagger, or discourage you; for the Father is not very far from any one of you; he dwells within you, and in him do we all literally move, actually live, and veritably have our being.

"Even though the Paradise Father functions through his divine creators and his creature children, he also enjoys the most intimate inner contact with you, so sublime, so highly personal, that it is even beyond my comprehension—that mysterious communion of the Father fragment with the human soul and with the mortal mind of its actual indwelling. Knowing what you do of these gifts of God, you therefore know that the Father is in intimate touch, not only with his divine associates, but also with his evolutionary mortal children of time. The Father indeed abides on Paradise, but his divine presence also dwells in the minds of men.

"Even though the spirit of a Son be poured out upon all flesh, even though a Son once dwelt with you in the likeness of mortal flesh, even though the seraphim personally guard and guide you, how can any of these divine beings of the Second and Third Centers ever hope to come as near to you or to understand you as fully as the Father, who has given a part of himself to be in you, to be your real and divine, even your eternal, self?" P. 139.

58. MATTER IS THE SHADOW OF SPIRIT REALITY

"In cosmic evolution matter becomes a philosophic shadow cast by mind in the presence of spirit luminosity of divine enlightenment, but this does not invalidate the reality of matter-energy. Mind, matter, and spirit are equally real, but they are not of equal value to personality in the attainment of divinity. Consciousness of divinity is a progressive spiritual experience." Pp. 140, 141.

59. LOVE IS THE SECRET OF PERSONAL RELATIONS

"Love is the secret of beneficial association between personalities. You cannot really know a person as the result of a single contact. You cannot appreciatingly know music through mathematical deduction, even though music is a form of mathematical rhythm. The number assigned to a telephone subscriber does not in any manner identify the personality of that subscriber or signify anything concerning his character." P. 141.

60. SCIENCE DOES NOT EXPLAIN EVERYTHING

"Technical analysis does not reveal what a person or a thing can do. For example: Water is used effectively to extinguish fire. That water will put out fire is a fact of everyday experience, but no analysis of water could ever be made to disclose such a property. Analysis determines that water is composed of hydrogen and oxygen; a further study of these elements discloses that oxygen is the real supporter of combustion and that hydrogen will itself freely burn.

"Your religion is becoming real because it is emerging from the slavery of fear and the bondage of superstition. Your philosophy struggles for emancipation from dogma and tradition. Your science is engaged in the agelong contest between truth and error while it fights for deliverance from the bondage of abstraction, the slavery of mathematics, and the relative blindness of mechanistic materialism." P. 141.

61. DEATH STARTS THE ETERNAL VOYAGE OF DISCOVERY

"Love of adventure, curiosity, and dread of monotony—these traits inherent in evolving human nature—were not put there just to aggravate and annoy you during your short sojourn on earth, but rather to suggest to you that death is only the beginning of an endless career of adventure, an everlasting life of anticipation, an eternal voyage of discovery." *P. 159.*

"Curiosity—the spirit of investigation, the urge of discovery, the drive of exploration—is a part of the inborn and divine endowment of evolutionary space creatures. These natural impulses were not given you merely to be frustrated and repressed. True, these ambitious urges must frequently be restrained during your short life on earth, disappointment must be often experienced, but they are to be fully realized and gloriously gratified during the long ages to come." *P. 160.*

62. AUTOCRACY AND DEMOCRACY MEET ON UVERSA

"It is on such worlds as Uversa that the beings representative of the autocracy of perfection and the democracy of evolution meet face to face. The executive branch of the supergovernment originates in the realms of perfection; the legislative branch springs from the flowering of the evolutionary universes." *P. 179.*

63. WE NEVER ESCAPE THE BADGE OF OUR NATIVITY

"Through this personal influence of the Seven Master Spirits every creature of every order of intelligent beings, outside of Paradise and Havona, must bear the characteristic stamp of individuality indicative of the ancestral nature of some one of these Seven Paradise Spirits. As concerns the seven superuniverses, each native creature, man or angel, will forever bear this badge of natal identification." *P. 190.*

64. INNATE RESPONSES OF THE COSMIC MIND

"The cosmic mind unfailingly responds (recognizes response) on three levels of universe reality. These responses are self-evident to clear-reasoning and deep-thinking minds. These levels of reality are:

"1. *Causation*—the reality domain of the physical senses, the scientific realms of logical uniformity, the differentiation of the factual and the nonfactual, reflective conclusions based on cosmic response. This is the mathematical form of the cosmic discrimination.

"2. *Duty*—the reality domain of morals in the philosophic realm, the arena of reason, the recognition of relative right and wrong. This is the judicial form of the cosmic discrimination.

"3. *Worship*—the spiritual domain of the reality of religious experience, the personal realization of divine fellowship, the recognition of spirit values, the assurance of eternal survival, the ascent from the status of servants of God to the joy and liberty of the sons of God. This is the highest insight of the cosmic mind, the reverential and worshipful form of the cosmic discrimination." *P. 192*.

65. PERSONALITY CAN LOOK BEFORE IT LEAPS

"The selective response of an animal is limited to the motor level of behavior. The supposed insight of the higher animals is on a motor level and usually appears only after the experience of motor trial and error. Man is able to exercise scientific, moral, and spiritual insight prior to all exploration or experimentation.

"Only a personality can know what it is doing before it does it; only personalities possess insight in advance of experience. A personality can look before it leaps and can therefore learn from looking as well as from leaping. A nonpersonal animal ordinarily learns only by leaping." *P. 193*.

66. INNATE SCOPE OF THE COSMIC MIND

"The cosmic-mind-endowed, Adjuster-indwelt, personal creature possesses innate recognition-realization of energy reality, mind reality, and spirit reality. The will creature is thus equipped to discern the fact, the law, and the love of God. Aside from these three inalienables of human consciousness, all human experience is really subjective except that intuitive realization of validity attaches to the *unification* of these three universe reality responses of cosmic recognition.

"The God-discerning mortal is able to sense the unification value of these three cosmic qualities in the evolution of the surviving soul, man's supreme undertaking in the physical tabernacle where the moral mind collaborates with the indwelling divine spirit to dualize the immortal soul. From its earliest inception the soul is *real*; it has cosmic survival qualities." *P. 195*.

67. THE CREATION OF MAJESTON

"The creation of Majeston signalized the first supreme creative act of the Supreme Being. This will to action was volitional in the Supreme Being, but the stupendous reaction of the Deity Absolute was not foreknown. Not since the eternity-appearance of Havona had the universe witnessed such a tremendous factualization of such a gigantic and far-flung alignment of power and co-ordination of functional spirit activities. The Deity response to the creative wills of the Supreme Being and his associates was vastly beyond their purposeful intent and greatly in excess of their conceptual forecasts.

"We stand in awe of the possibility of what the future ages, wherein the Supreme and the Ultimate may attain new levels of divinity and ascend to new domains of personality function, may witness in the realms of the deitization of still other unexpected and undreamed of beings who will possess unimagined powers of enhanced universe co-ordination. There would seem to be no limit to the Deity Absolute's potential of response to such unification of relationships between experiential Deity and the existential Paradise Trinity." P. 200.

68. ONLY-BEGOTTEN SONS

"Each Creator Son is the only-begotten and only-begettable offspring of the perfect union of the original concepts of the two infinite and eternal and perfect minds of the ever-existent Creators of the universe of universes. There never can be another such Son because each Creator Son is the unqualified, finished, and final expression and embodiment of all of every phase of every feature of every possibility of every divine reality that could, throughout all eternity, ever be found in, expressed by, or evolved from, those divine creative potentials which united to bring this Michael Son into existence. Each Creator Son is the absolute of the united deity concepts which constitute his divine origin." P. 235. **John 3:16.**

69. REBELLION-TESTED MORTALS — MIGHTY MESSENGERS

"Mighty Messengers belong to the ascendant group of the Trinitized Sons. They are a class of perfected mortals who have been rebellion tested or otherwise equally proved as to their personal loyalty; all have passed through some definite test of universe allegiance. At some time in their Paradise ascent they stood firm and loyal in the face of the disloyalty of their superiors, and some did actively and loyally function in the places of such unfaithful leaders." P. 245.

"Every ascendant mortal of insurrectionary experience who functions loyally in the face of rebellion is eventually destined to become a Mighty Messenger of the superuniverse service. Likewise is any ascendant creature who effectively prevents such upheavals of error, evil, or sin; for action designed to prevent rebellion or to effect higher types of loyalty in a universe crisis is regarded as of even greater value than loyalty in the face of actual rebellion." P. 245.

"I am a Mighty Messenger, and it may interest Urantians to know that the companion and associate of my mortal experience was also triumphant in the great test, and that, though we were many times and for long periods separated in the agelong inward ascent to Havona, we were embraced in the same seven-hundred thousand group, and that we spent our time passing through Vicegerington in close and loving association. We were finally commissioned and together assigned to Uversa of Orvonton, and we are often dispatched in company for the execution of assignments requiring the services of two Messengers." P. 245.

"You mortals who read this message may yourselves ascend to Paradise, attain the Trinity embrace, and in remote future ages be attached to the service of the Ancients of Days in one of the seven superuniverses, and sometime be assigned to enlarge the revelation of truth to some evolving inhabited planet, even as I am now functioning on Urantia." P. 247.

70. PURPOSE OF TRIALS AND TROUBLES

"The confusion and turmoil of Urantia do not signify that the Paradise Rulers lack either interest or ability to manage affairs differently. The Creators are possessed of full power to make Urantia a veritable paradise, but such an Eden would not contribute to the development of those strong, noble, and experienced characters which the Gods are so surely forging out on your world between the anvils of necessity and the hammers of anguish. Your anxieties and sorrows, your trials and disappointments, are just as much a part of the divine plan on your sphere as are the exquisite perfection and infinite adaptation of all things to their supreme purpose on the worlds of the central and perfect universe." P. 258. **John 16:33. Acts 14:22. Rom. 12:12. 2 Cor. 1:4. Rev. 7:14.**

71. HOW A CENSUS DIRECTOR FUNCTIONS

"The Census Directors are concerned with human beings—as with other will creatures—only to the extent of recording the fact of will function. They are not concerned with the records of your life and its doings; they are not in any sense recording personalities. The Census Director of Nebadon, number 81,412 of Orvonton, now stationed on Salvington, is at this very moment personally conscious and aware of your living presence here on Urantia; and he will afford the records confirmation of your death the moment you cease to function as a will creature." P. 267.

72. GRANDFANDA DISCOVERS HAVONA

"The name of this pilgrim discoverer of Havona is *Grandfanda*, and he hailed from planet 341 of system 84 in constellation 62 of local universe 1,131 situated in superuniverse number one. His arrival was the signal for the establishment of the broadcast service of the universe of universes. Theretofore only the broadcasts of the superuniverses and the local universes had been in operation, but the announcement of the arrival of Grandfanda at the portals of Havona signalized the inauguration of the 'space reports of glory,' so named because the initial universe broadcast reported the Havona arrival of the first of the evolutionary beings to attain entrance upon the goal of ascendant existence." P. 270.

73. AFFECTION FOR OUR MORONTIA COMPANIONS

"These Morontia Companions are such friendly associates that, when you finally leave the last phase of the morontia experience, as you prepare to embark upon the superuniverse spirit adventure, you will truly regret that these companionable creatures cannot accompany you, but they serve exclusively in the local universes. At every stage of the ascending career all contactable personalities will be friendly and companionable, but not until you meet the Paradise Companions will you find another group so devoted to friendship and companionship." P. 282.

74. PILGRIM ARRIVALS IN HAVONA

"When, through and by the ministry of all the helper hosts of the universal scheme of survival, you are finally deposited on the receiving world of Havona, you arrive with only one sort of perfection—*perfection of purpose*. Your purpose has been thoroughly proved; your faith has been tested. You are known to be disappointment proof. Not even the failure to discern the Universal Father can shake the faith or seriously disturb the trust of an ascendant mortal who has passed through the experience that all must traverse in order to attain the perfect spheres of Havona. By the time you reach Havona, your sincerity has become sublime. Perfection of purpose and divinity of desire, with steadfastness of faith, have secured your entrance to the settled abodes of eternity; your deliverance from the uncertainties of time is full and complete; and now must you come face to face with the problems of Havona and the immensities of Paradise, to meet which you have so long been in training in the experiential epochs of time on the world schools of space.

"Faith has won for the ascendant pilgrim a perfection of purpose which admits the children of time to the portals of eternity. Now must the pilgrim helpers begin the work of developing that perfection of under standing and that technique of comprehension which are so indispensable to Paradise perfection of personality.

"*Ability to comprehend is the mortal passport to Paradise*. Willingness to believe is the key to Havona. The acceptance of sonship, co-operation with the indwelling Adjuster, is the price of evolutionary survival." P. 290.

Part I: *The Central and Superuniverses*

75. BATTLE CRY OF HAVONA PILGRIMS

"That, then, is the primary or elementary course which confronts the faith tested and much-traveled pilgrims of space. But long before reaching Havona, these ascendant children of time have learned to feast upon uncertainty, to fatten upon disappointment, to enthuse over apparent defeat, to invigorate in the presence of difficulties, to exhibit indomitable courage in the face of immensity, and to exercise unconquerable faith when confronted with the challenge of the inexplicable. Long since, the battle cry of these pilgrims became: 'In *liaison with God, nothing—absolutely nothing—is impossible.*'" P. 291. **Matt. 19:26. Luke 1:37; 18:27. Mark 10:27.**

76. FINDING GOD ON PARADISE

"The attainment of the Universal Father is the passport to eternity, notwithstanding the remaining circuits to be traversed. It is therefore a momentous occasion on the pilot world of circle number three when the transit trio announce that the last venture of time is about to ensue; that another creature of space seeks entry to Paradise through the portals of eternity.

"The test of time is almost over; the race for eternity has been all but run. The days of uncertainty are ending; the temptation to doubt is vanishing; the injunction to be *perfect* has been obeyed. From the very bottom of intelligent existence the creature of time and material personality has ascended the evolutionary spheres of space, thus proving the feasibility of the ascension plan while forever demonstrating the justice and righteousness of the command of the Universal Father to his lowly creatures of the worlds: 'Be you perfect, even as I am perfect.'

"Step by step, life by life, world by world, the ascendant career has been mastered, and the goal of Deity has been attained. Survival is complete in perfection, and perfection is replete in the supremacy of divinity. Time is lost in eternity; space is swallowed up in worshipful identity and harmony with the Universal Father. The broadcasts of Havona flash forth the space reports of glory, the good news that in very truth the conscientious creatures of animal nature and material origin have, through evolutionary ascension, become in reality and eternally the perfected sons of God." Pp. 294, 295. **Matt. 5:48.**

77. GRADUATION FROM HAVONA

"And now, at the culmination of the Havona career, as you mortals go to sleep on the pilot world of the inner circuit, you go to alone to your rest as you did on the worlds of your origin when you closed your eyes in the natural sleep of mortal death, nor as you did when you entered the long transit trance preparatory for the journey to Havona. Now, as you prepare for the attainment rest, there moves over by your side your long-time associate of the first circle, the majestic complement of rest, who prepares to enter the rest as one with you, as the pledge of Havona that your transition is complete, and that you await only the final touches of perfection.

"Your first transition was indeed death, the second an ideal sleep, and now the third metamorphosis is the true rest, the relaxation of the ages." *P. 297*.

78. LAST RESURRECTION ON PARADISE

"You enter the rest on the final Havona circuit and are eternally resurrected on Paradise. And as you there spiritually repersonalize, you will immediately recognize the instigator of rest who welcomes you to the eternal shores as the very primary supernaphim who produced the final sleep on the innermost circuit of Havona; and you will recall the last grand stretch of faith as you once again made ready to commend the keeping of your identity into the hands of the Universal Father.

"The last rest of time has been enjoyed; the last transition sleep has been experienced; now you awake to life everlasting on the shores of the eternal abode. 'And there shall be no more sleep. The presence of God and his Son are before you, and you are eternally his servants; you have seen his face, and his name is your spirit. There shall be no light there; and they need no light of the sun, for the Great Source and Center gives them light; they shall live forever and ever. And God shall wipe away all tears from their eyes; there shall be no more death, neither sorrow nor crying, neither shall there be any more pain, for the former things have passed away.'" *P. 299*. **Rev. 22:4,5**.

79. LEARNING HOW TO WORSHIP

"It is the task of the conductors of worship so to teach the ascendant creatures how to worship that they may be enabled to gain this satisfaction of self expression and at the same time be able to give attention to the essential activities of the Paradise regime. Without improvement in the technique of worship it would require hundreds of years for the average mortal who reaches Paradise to give full and satisfactory expression to his emotions of intelligent appreciation and ascendant gratitude. The conductors of worship open up new and hitherto unknown avenues of expression so that these wonderful children of the womb of space and the travail of time are enabled to gain the full satisfactions of worship in much less time." *P. 304*.

80. THE MERCY TRIAL BALANCE

"The Memory of Mercy is a living trial balance, a current statement of your account with the supernatural forces of the realms. These are the living records of mercy ministration which are read into the testimony of the courts of Uversa when each individual's right to unending life comes up for adjudication, when 'thrones are cast up and the Ancients of Days are seated. The broadcasts of Uversa issue and come forth from before them; thousands upon thousands minister to them, and ten thousand times ten thousand stand before them. The judgment is set, and the books are opened.' And the books which are opened on such a momentous occasion are the living records of the tertiary seconaphim of the superuniverses. The formal records are on file to corroborate the testimony of the Memories of Mercy if they are required." *P. 314*. **Dan. 7:9,10.**

81. THE CELESTIAL VOCATION GUIDES

"On Urantia, you grotesquely essay to read character and to estimate specific abilities, but on Uversa we actually do these things in perfection. These seconaphim weigh trustworthiness in the living scales of unerring character appraisal, and when they have looked at you, we have only to look at them to know the limitations of your ability to discharge responsibility, execute trust, and fulfill missions. Your assets of trustworthiness are clearly set forth alongside your liabilities of possible default or betrayal.

"It is the plan of your superiors to advance you by augmented trusts just as fast as your character is sufficiently developed to gracefully bear these added responsibilities, but to overload the individual only courts disaster and insures disappointment. And the mistake of placing responsibility prematurely upon either man or angel may be avoided by utilizing the ministry of these infallible estimators of the trust capacity of the individuals of time and space. These seconaphim ever accompany Those High in Authority, and never do these executives make assignments until their candidates have been weighed in the secoraphic balances and pronounced 'not wanting.'" *P. 316*.

82. POWER CENTERS NEVER PLAY

"Having no ascendant past to revert to in memory, power centers and physical controllers never play; they are thoroughly businesslike in all their actions. They are always on duty; there is no provision in the universal scheme for the interruption of the physical lines of energy; never for a fraction of a second can these beings relinquish their direct supervision of the energy circuits of time and space." *P. 323.*

83. THE MASTER FORCE ORGANIZERS

"Primary Master Force Organizers are the manipulators of the primordial or basic space forces of the Unqualified Absolute; they are nebulae creators. They are the living instigators of the energy cyclones of space and the early organizers and directionizers of these gigantic manifestations. These force organizers transmute *primordial force* (pre-energy not responsive to direct Paradise gravity) into primary or *puissant* energy, energy transmuting from the exclusive grasp of the Unqualified Absolute to the gravity grasp of the Isle of Paradise. They are thereupon succeeded by the associate force organizers, who continue the process of energy transmutation from the primary through the secondary or *gravity-energy* stage." *P. 329.*

84. DIVERSE FUNCTIONS OF GOD

"God, as a superperson, eventuates; God, as a person, creates; God, as a preperson, fragments; and such an Adjuster fragment of himself evolves the spirit soul upon the material and mortal mind in accordance with the freewill choosing of the personality which has been bestowed upon such a mortal creature by the parental act of God as a Father." *P. 333.*

85. OUR STATUS FROM DEATH TO RESURRECTION

"The passing of time is of no moment to sleeping mortals; they are wholly unconscious and oblivious to the length of their rest. On reassembly of personality at the end of an age, those who have slept five thousand years will react no differently than those who have rested five days. Aside from this time delay these survivors pass on through the ascension regime identically with those who avoid the longer or shorter sleep of death." *P. 341.*

"The physical body of mortal flesh is not a part of the reassembly of the sleeping survivor; the physical body has returned to dust. The seraphim of assignment sponsors the new body, the morontia form, as the new life vehicle for the immortal soul and for the indwelling of the returned Adjuster. The Adjuster is the custodian of the spirit transcript of the mind of the sleeping survivor. The assigned seraphim is the keeper of the surviving identity—

the immortal soul—as far as it has evolved. And when these two, the Adjuster and the seraphim, reunite their personality trusts, the new individual constitutes the resurrection of the old personality, the survival of the evolving morontia identity of the soul. Such a reassociation of soul and Adjuster is quite properly called a resurrection, a reassembly of personality factors; but even this does not entirely explain the reappearance of the surviving *personality*. Though you will probably never understand the fact of such an inexplicable transaction, you will sometime experientially know the truth of it if you do not reject the plan of mortal survival." P. 341.

86. ARRIVING IN HAVONA

"The first act of your Havona career will be to recognize and thank your transport seconaphim for the long and safe journey. Then you are presented to those beings who will sponsor your early Havona activities. Next you go to register your arrival and prepare your message of thanksgiving and adoration for dispatch to the Creator Son of your local universe, the universe Father who made possible your sonship career. This concludes the formalities of the Havona arrival; whereupon you are accorded a long period of leisure for free observation, and this affords opportunity for looking up your friends, fellows, and associates of the long ascension experience. You may also consult the broadcasts to ascertain who of your fellow pilgrims have departed for Havona since the time of your leaving Uversa." P. 343.

87. COMPOSITION OF MORTAL CORPS OF THE FINALITY

"The inhabitants of the central universe are received into the corps in the ratio of one in a thousand—a finaliter company. The corps is organized for temporary service in companies of one thousand, the ascendant creatures numbering 997 to one Havona native and one Gravity Messenger. Finaliters are thus mobilized in companies, but the finality oath is administered individually. It is an oath of sweeping implications and eternal import. The Havona native takes the same oath and becomes forever attached to the corps." P. 346.

88. THE MASTER ARCHITECTS

"These seven groups of Master Architects total 28,011 universe planners. On Paradise there is a tradition that far back in eternity there was attempted the eventuation of the 28,012th Master Architect, but that this being failed to absonitize, experiencing personality seizure by the Universal Absolute. It is possible that the ascending series of the Master Architects attained the limit of absonity in the 28,011th Architect, and that the 28,012th attempt encountered the mathematical level of the presence of the Absolute. In other words, at the 28,012th eventuation level the quality of absonity equivalated to the level of the Universal and attained the value of the Absolute." P. 352.

89. THE MORTAL FINALITY CORPS

"The gathering together of these seven finaliter corps signifies reality mobilization of potentials, personalities, minds, spirits, absonites, and experiential actualities that probably transcend even the future master universe functions of the Supreme Being. These seven finaliter corps probably signify the present activity of the Ultimate Trinity engaged in mustering the forces of the finite and the absonite in preparation for inconceivable developments in the universes of outer space. Nothing like this mobilization has taken place since the near times of eternity when the Paradise Trinity similarly mobilized the then existing personalities of Paradise and Havona and commissioned them as administrators and rulers of the projected seven superuniverses of time and space. The seven finaliter corps represent the divinity response of the grand universe to the future needs of the undeveloped potentials in the outer universes of future- eternal activities." P. 353.

"Evolutionary mortals are born on the planets of space, pass through the morontia worlds, ascend the spirit universes, traverse the Havona spheres, find God, attain Paradise, and are mustered into the primary Corps of the Finality, therein to await the next assignment of universe service. There are six other assembling finality corps, but Grandfanda, the first mortal ascender, presides as Paradise chief of all orders of finaliters. And as we view this sublime spectacle, we all exclaim: What a glorious destiny for the animal-origin children of time, the material sons of space!" P. 354.

Part II

THE LOCAL UNIVERSE

90. EVOLUTIONARY ORIGIN NOT A STIGMA

"The perfection of the creatures of time, when finally achieved, is wholly an acquirement, a bona fide personality possession. While the elements of grace are freely admixed, nevertheless, the creature attainments are the result of individual effort and actual living, personality reaction to the existing environment.

"The fact of animal evolutionary origin does not attach stigma to any personality in the sight of the universe as that is the exclusive method of producing one of the two basic types of finite intelligent will creatures. When the heights of perfection and eternity are attained, all the more honor to those who began at the bottom and joyfully climbed the ladder of life, round by round, and who, when they do reach the heights of glory, will have gained a personal experience which embodies an actual knowledge of every phase of life from the bottom to the top." P. 361.

91. THE FATHER'S MAGNANIMOUS SELF BESTOWAL

"In this universal bestowal of himself we have abundant proof of both the magnitude and the magnanimity of the Father's divine nature. If God has withheld aught of himself from the universal creation, then of that residue he is in lavish generosity bestowing the Thought Adjusters upon the mortals of the realms, the Mystery Monitors of time, who so patiently indwell the mortal candidates for life everlasting.

"The Universal Father has poured out himself, as it were, to make all creation rich in personality possession and potential spiritual attainment. God has given us himself that we may be like him, and he has reserved for himself of power and glory only that which is necessary for the maintenance of those things for the love of which he has thus divested himself of all things else." P. 364.

92. THE FATHER'S ETERNAL PURPOSE

"There is a great and glorious purpose in the march of the universes through space. All of your mortal struggling is not in vain. We are all part of an immense plan, a gigantic enterprise, and it is the vastness of the undertaking that renders it impossible to see very much of it at any one time and during any one life. We are all a part of an eternal project which the Gods are supervising and outworking. The whole marvelous and universal mechanism moves on majestically through space to the music of the meter of the infinite thought and the eternal purpose of the First Great Source and Center.

"The eternal purpose of the eternal God is a high spiritual ideal. The events of time and the struggles of material existence are but the transient scaffolding which bridges over to the other side, to the promised land of spiritual reality and supernal existence. Of course, you mortals find it difficult to grasp the idea of an eternal purpose; you are virtually unable to comprehend the thought of eternity, something never beginning and never ending. Everything familiar to you has an end." *P. 364.* **Eph. 3:11.**

93. THE RACE FOR ETERNITY IS ON

"There is in the mind of God a plan which embraces every creature of all his vast domains, and this plan is an eternal purpose of boundless opportunity, unlimited progress, and endless life. And the infinite treasures of such a matchless career are yours for the striving!

"The goal of eternity is ahead! The adventure of divinity attainment lies before you! The race for perfection is on! whosoever will may enter, and certain victory will crown the efforts of every human being who will run the race of faith and trust, depending every step of the way on the leading of the indwelling Adjuster and on the guidance of that good spirit of the Universe Son, which so freely has been poured out upon all flesh." *P. 365.*

94. MICHAEL IS JUST AS EFFICIENT AS THE ETERNAL SON

"In the person of the Creator Son we have a ruler and divine parent who is just as mighty, efficient, and beneficent as would be the Universal Father and the Eternal Son if both were present on Salvington and engaged in the administration of the affairs of the universe of Nebadon." *P. 367.*

95. THE GIFT OF HIGH SPIRITUAL FORCES

"From the heights of eternal glory the divine Spirit descends, by a long series of steps, to meet you as you are and where you are and then, in the partnership of faith, lovingly to embrace the soul of mortal origin and to embark on the sure and certain retracement of those steps of condescension, never stopping until the evolutionary soul is safely exalted to the very heights of bliss from which the divine Spirit originally sallied forth on this mission of mercy and ministry.

"Spiritual forces unerringly seek and attain their own original levels. Having gone out from the Eternal, they are certain to return thereto, bringing with them all those children of time and space who have espoused the leading and teaching of the indwelling Adjuster, those who have been truly 'born of the Spirit,' the faith sons of God." *P. 380.*

96. THE NEED FOR LIVING TRUTH

"The dead theory of even the highest religious doctrines is powerless to transform human character or to control mortal behavior. What the world of today needs is the truth which your teacher of old declared: 'Not in word only but also in power and in the Holy Spirit.' The seed of theoretical truth is dead, the highest moral concepts without effect, unless and until the divine Spirit breathes upon the forms of truth and quickens the formulas of righteousness." *P. 380*.

97. THE REFRESHING WATER OF LIFE

"It is the presence of the divine Spirit, the water of life, that prevents the consuming thirst of mortal discontent and that indescribable hunger of the unspiritualized human mind. Spirit-motivated beings 'never thirst, for this spiritual water shall be in them a well of satisfaction springing up into life everlasting.' Such divinely watered souls are all but independent of material environment as regards the joys of living and the satisfactions of earthly existence. They are spiritually illuminated and refreshed, morally strengthened and endowed." *P. 381*. **John 4:13,14.**

98. MAN'S DUAL NATURE

"In every mortal there exists a dual nature: the inheritance of animal tendencies and the high urge of spirit endowment. During the short life you live on Urantia, these two diverse and opposing urges can seldom be fully reconciled; they can hardly be harmonized and unified; but throughout your lifetime the combined Spirit ever ministers to assist you in subjecting the flesh more and more to the leading of the Spirit. Even though you must live your material life through, even though you cannot escape the body and its necessities, nonetheless, in purpose and ideals you are empowered increasingly to subject the animal nature to the mastery of the Spirit. There truly exists within you a conspiracy of spiritual forces, a confederation of divine powers, whose exclusive purpose is to effect your final deliverance from material bondage and finite handicaps.

"The purpose of all this ministration is, 'That you may be strengthened with power through His spirit in the inner man.' And all this represents but the preliminary steps to the final attainment of the perfection of faith and service, that experience wherein you shall be 'filled with all the fullness of God,' 'for all those who are led by the spirit of God are the sons of God.'" *P. 381*. **Eph. 3:16,19. Rom. 8:14.**

99. THE SPIRIT LEADS — BUT NEVER DRIVES

"The Spirit never *drives*, only leads. If you are a willing learner, if you want to attain spirit levels and reach divine heights, if you sincerely desire to reach the eternal goal, then the divine Spirit will gently and lovingly lead you along the pathway of sonship and spiritual progress. Every step you take must be one of willingness, intelligent and cheerful cooperation. The domination of the Spirit is never tainted with coercion nor compromised by compulsion.

"And when such a life of spirit guidance is freely and intelligently accepted, there gradually develops within the human mind a positive consciousness of divine contact and assurance of spirit communion; sooner or later 'the Spirit bears witness with your spirit (the Adjuster) that you are a child of God.' Already has your own Thought Adjuster told you of your kinship to God so that the record testifies that the Spirit bears witness '*with* your spirit,' not *to* your spirit." *P. 381*. **Rom. 8:16.**

100. THE FRUITS OF THE SPIRIT

"The consciousness of the spirit domination of a human life is presently attended by an increasing exhibition of the characteristics of the Spirit in the life reactions of such a spirit-led mortal, 'for the fruits of the spirit are love, joy, peace, long-suffering, gentleness, goodness, faith, meekness, and temperance.' Such spirit-guided and divinely illuminated mortals, while they yet tread the lowly paths of toil and in human faithfulness perform the duties of their earthly assignments, have already begun to discern the lights of eternal life as they glimmer on the faraway shores of another world;..." *P. 381*.

101. THE SURE GUIDANCE OF THE SPIRIT

"Having started out on the way of life everlasting, having accepted the assignment and received your orders to advance, do not fear the dangers of human forgetfulness and mortal inconstancy, do not be troubled with doubts of failure or by perplexing confusion, do not falter and question your status and standing, for in every dark hour, at every crossroad in the forward struggle, the Spirit of Truth will always speak, saying, 'This is the way.'" *P. 383*.

102. CONFLICTS OF THE FLESH AND THE SPIRIT

"The progression of eternity does not consist solely in spiritual development. Intellectual acquisition is also a part of universal education. The experience of the mind is broadened equally with the expansion of the spiritual horizon. Mind and spirit are afforded like opportunities for training and advancement. But in all this superb training of mind and spirit you are forever free from the handicaps of mortal flesh. No longer must you constantly referee the conflicting contentions of your divergent spiritual and material natures. At last you are qualified to enjoy the unified urge of a glorified mind long since divested of primitive animalistic trends towards things material." *Pp. 412-13.*

103. THE HAIRS OF OUR HEADS ARE NUMBERED

"The seraphim are so created as to function on both spiritual and literal levels. There are few phases of morontia or spirit activity which are not open to their ministrations. While in personal status angels are not so far removed from human beings, in certain functional performances seraphim far transcend them. They possess many powers far beyond human comprehension. For example: You have been told that the 'very hairs of your head are numbered,' and it is true they are, but a seraphim does not spend her time counting them and keeping the number corrected up to date. Angels possess inherent and automatic (that is, automatic as far as you could perceive) powers of knowing such things; you would truly regard a seraphim as a mathematical prodigy. Therefore, numerous duties which would be tremendous tasks for mortals are performed with exceeding ease by seraphim." *P. 419.* **Luke 12:7.**

104. HOW GOD LIVES WITH US

"God the Father does not, cannot, thus downstep himself to make such near personal contact with the almost limitless number of ascending creatures throughout the universe of universes. But the Father is not deprived of personal contact with his lowly creatures; you are not without the divine presence. Although God the Father cannot be with you by direct personality manifestation, he is in you and of you in the identity of the indwelling Thought Adjusters, the divine Monitors. Thus does the Father, who is the farthest from you in personality and in spirit, draw the nearest to you in the personality circuit and in the spirit touch of inner communion with the very souls of his mortal sons and daughters." *P. 445.*

105. WE ARE REALLY THE SONS OF GOD

"It is a solemn and supernal fact that such lowly and material creatures as Urantia human beings are the sons of God, faith children of the Highest. 'Behold, what manner of love the Father has bestowed upon us that we should be called the sons of God.' 'As many as received him, to them gave he the power to recognize that they are the sons of God.' While 'it does not yet appear what you shall be,' even now 'you are the faith sons of God'; 'for you have not received the spirit of bondage again to fear, but you have received the spirit of sonship, whereby you cry, "our Father."' Spoke the prophet of old in the name of the eternal God: 'Even to them will I give in my house a place and a name better than sons; I will give them an everlasting name, one that shall not be cut off.' 'And because you are sons, God has sent forth the spirit of his Son into your hearts.'" *P. 448*. **1 John 3:1,2. John 1:12. Rom. 8:15. Isa. 56:5. Gal. 4:6.**

106. FIVE REASONS FOR SONSHIP

"All evolutionary worlds of mortal habitation harbor these faith sons of God, sons of grace and mercy, mortal beings belonging to the divine family and accordingly called the sons of God. Urantia mortals are entitled to regard theselves as being the sons of God because:

"1. You are sons of spiritual promise, faith sons; you have accepted the status of sonship. You believe in the reality of your sonship, and thus does your sonship with God become eternally real.

"2. A Creator Son of God became one of you; he is your elder brother in fact; and if in spirit you become truly related brothers of Christ, the victorious Michael, then in spirit must you also be sons of that Father which you have in common—even the Universal Father of all.

"3. You are sons because the spirit of a Son has been poured out upon you, has been freely and certainly bestowed upon all Urantia races. This spirit ever draws you toward the divine Son, who is its source, and toward the Paradise Father, who is the source of that divine Son.

"4. Of his divine free-willness, the Universal Father has given you your creature personalities. You have been endowed with a measure of that divine spontaneity of freewill action which God shares with all who may become his sons.

"5. There dwells within you a fragment of the Universal Father, and you are thus directly related to the divine Father of all the Sons of God." *P. 448*.

107. CALCIUM ESCAPING FROM THE SUN

"As your physicists have suspected, these mutilated remnants of solar calcium literally ride the light beams for varied distances, and thus their widespread dissemination throughout space is tremendously facilitated. The sodium atom, under certain modifications, is also capable of light and energy locomotion. The calcium feat is all the more remarkable since this element has almost twice the mass of sodium. Local space-permeation by calcium is due to the fact that it escapes from the solar photosphere, in modified form, by literally riding the outgoing sunbeams. Of all the solar elements, calcium, notwithstanding its comparative bulk—containing as it does twenty revolving electrons—is the most successful in escaping from the solar interior to the realms of space. This explains why there is a calcium layer, a gaseous stone surface, on the sun six thousand miles thick; and this despite the fact that nineteen lighter elements, and numerous heavier ones, are underneath." P. 462.

"The agility of this acrobatic calcium electron is indicated by the fact that, when tossed by the temperature-X-ray solar forces to the circle of the higher orbit, it only remains in that orbit for about one one-millionth of a second; but before the electric-gravity power of the atomic nucleus pulls it back into its old orbit, it is able to complete one million revolutions about the atomic center." P. 462.

108. ENERGY IS ETERNAL BUT NOT INFINITE

"Energy is eternal but not infinite; it ever responds to the all-embracing grasp of Infinity. Forever force and energy go on; having gone out from Paradise, they must return thereto, even if age upon age be required for the completion of the ordained circuit. That which is of Paradise Deity origin can have only a Paradise destination or a Deity destiny." P. 468.

109. THE ENDLESS ENERGY CHANGES

"We do not fully comprehend the almost endless changes to which physical energy may be subject. In one universe it appears as light, in another as light plus heat, in another as forms of energy unknown on Urantia; in untold millions of years it may reappear as some form of restless, surging electrical energy or megnetic power; and still later on it may again appear in a subsequent universe as some form of variable matter going through a series of metamorphoses, to be followed by its outward physical disappearance in some great cataclysm of the realms. And then, after countless ages and almost endless wandering through numberless universes, again may this same energy re-emerge and many times change its form and potential; and so do these transformations continue through successive ages and throughout countless realms. Thus matter sweeps on, undergoing the transmutations of time but swinging ever true to the circle of eternity; even if long prevented from returning to its source, it is ever responsive thereto, and it ever proceeds in the path ordained by the Infinite Personality who sent it forth." P. 472.

110. SIZE OF THE ELECTRON

"If the mass of matter should be magnified until that of an electron equaled one tenth of an ounce, then were size to be proportionately magnified, the volume of such an electron would become as large of that of the earth. If the volume of a proton—eighteen hundred times as heavy as an electron—should be magnified to the size of the head of a pin, then, in comparison, a pin's head would attain a diameter equal to that of the earth's orbit around the sun." P. 477.

111. ATOMIC INTERNAL SPACE

"Within the atom the electrons revolve about the central proton with about the same comparative room the planets have as they revolve about the sun in the space of the solar system. There is the same relative distance, in comparison with actual size, between the atomic nucleus and the inner electronic circuit as exists between the inner planet, Mercury, and your sun." P. 477.

112. SEVEN GROUPS OF CHEMICAL ELEMENTS

"This sevenfold persistence of creative constitution is exhibited in the chemical domains as a recurrence of similar physical and chemical properties in segregated periods of seven when the basic elements are arranged in the order of their atomic weights. When the Urantia chemical elements are thus arranged in a row, any given quality or property tends to recur by sevens. This periodic change by sevens recurs diminishingly and with variations throughout the entire chemical table, being most markedly observable in the earlier or lighter atomic groupings. Starting from any one element, after noting some one property, such a quality will change for six consecutive elements, but on reaching the eighth, it tends to reappear, that is, the eighth chemically active element resembles the first, the ninth the second, and so on. Such a fact of the physical world unmistakably points to the sevenfold constitution of ancestral energy and is indicative of the fundamental reality of the sevenfold diversity of the creations of time and space. Man should also note that there are seven colors in the natural spectrum." P. 480.

113. RELATION OF MIND, MATTER, AND SPIRIT

"Mind universally dominates matter, even as it is in turn responsive to the ultimate overcontrol of spirit. And with mortal man, only that mind which freely submits itself to the spirit direction can hope to survive the mortal time-space existence as an immortal child of the eternal spirit world of the Supreme, the Ultimate, and the Absolute: the Infinite." P. 484.

114. CONFUSION ABOUT THE MOST HIGHS

"The Psalmist knew that Edentia was ruled by three Constellation Fathers and accordingly spoke of their abode in the plural: 'There is a river, the streams whereof shall make glad the city of God, the most holy place of the tabernacles of the Most Highs.'

"Down through the ages there has been great confusion on Urantia regarding the various universe rulers. Many later teachers confused their vague and indefinite tribal deities with the Most High Fathers. Still later, the Hebrews merged all of these celestial rulers into a composite Deity. One teacher understood that the Most Highs were not the Supreme Rulers, for he said, "He who dwells in the secret place of the Most High shall abide under the shadow of the Almighty.' In the Urantia records it is very difficult at times to know exactly who is referred to by the term 'Most High.' But Daniel fully understood these matters. He said, 'The Most High rules in the kingdom of men and gives it to whomsoever he will.'" *P. 488*. **Ps. 46:4; 91:1. Dan. 4:17; 5:21.**

115. BOTANICAL BEAUTIES OF EDEN

"If you enjoy the flowers, shrubs, and trees of Urantia, then will you feast your eyes upon the botanical beauty and the floral grandeur of the supernal gardens of Edentia. But it is beyond my powers of description to undertake to convey to the mortal mind an adequate concept of these beauties of the heavenly worlds. Truly, eye has not seen such glories as await your arrival on these worlds of the mortal-ascension adventure." *P. 493*.

116. MORONTIA MUSIC

"The best music of Urantia is just a fleeting echo of the magnificent strains heard by the celestial associates of your musicians, who left but snatches of these harmonies of morontia forces on record as the musical melodies of sound harmonics. Spirit-morontia music not infrequently employs all seven modes of expression and reproduction, so that the human mind is tremendously handicapped in any attempt to reduce these melodies of the higher spheres to mere notes of musical sound. Such an effort would be something like endeavoring to reproduce the strains of a great orchestra by means of a single musical instrument.

"While you have assembled some beautiful melodies on Urantia, you have not progressed musically nearly so far as many of your neighboring planets in Satania. If Adam and Eve had only survived, then would you have had music in reality; but the gift of harmony, so large in their natures, has been so diluted by strains of unmusical tendencies that only once in a thousand mortal lives is there any great appreciation of harmonics. But be not discouraged; some day a real musician may appear on Urantia, and whole peoples will be enthralled by the magnificent strains of his melodies. One such human being could forever change the course of a whole nation, even the entire civilized world. It is literally true, 'melody has power a whole world to transform.' Forever, music will remain the universal language of men, angels, and spirits. Harmony is the speech of Havona." P. 500.

117. BEAUTY, RHYTHM, AND HARMONY

"Beauty, rhythm, and harmony are intellectually associated and spiritually akin. Truth, fact, and relationship are intellectually inseparable and associated with the philosophic concepts of beauty. Goodness, righteousness, and justice are philosophically interrelated and spiritually bound up together with living truth and divine beauty." P. 507.

"These divine qualities are perfectly and absolutely unified in God. And every God-knowing man or angel possesses the potential of unlimited selfexpression on ever-progressive levels of unified self-realization by the technique of the never-ending achievement of Godlikeness—the experiential blending in the evolutionary experience of eternal truth, universal beauty, and divine goodness." P. 507.

118. SATANIA PROBATION NURSERY

"This probation nursery of Satania is maintained by certain morontia personalities on the finaliters' world, one half of the planet being devoted to this work of child rearing. Here are received and reassembled certain children of surviving mortals, such as those offspring who perished on the evolutionary worlds before acquiring spiritual status as individuals. The ascension of either of its natural parents insures that such a mortal child of the realms will be accorded repersonalization on the system finaliter planet and there be permitted to demonstrate by subsequent freewill choice whether or not it elects to follow the parental path of mortal ascension. Children here appear as on the nativity world except for the absence of sex differentiation. There is no reproduction of mortal kind after the life experience on the inhabited worlds." P. 516.

119. FIRST MANSION WORLD

"On the first mansion world all survivors must pass the requirements of the parental commission from their planets. The present Urantia commission consists of twelve parental couples, recently arrived, who have had mortal experience in rearing three or more children to the pubescent age. Service on this commission is rotational and is for only ten years as a rule. All who fail to satisfy these commissioners as to their parental experience must further qualify by service in the homes of the Material Sons on Jerusem or in part in the probationary nursery on the finaliters' world.

"But irrespective of parental experience, mansion world parents who have growing children in the probation nursery are given every opportunity to collaborate with the morontia custodians of such children regarding their instruction and training. These parents are permitted to journey there for visits as often as four times a year. And it is one of the most touchingly beautiful scenes of all the ascending career to observe the mansion world parents embrace their material offspring on the occasions of their periodic pilgrimages to the finaliter world. While one or both parents may leave a mansion world ahead of the child, they are quite often contemporary for a season.

"No ascending mortal can escape the experience of rearing children—their ownor others-either on the material worlds or subsequently on the finaliter world or on Jerusem. Fathers must pass through this essential experience just as certainly as mothers. It is an unfortunate and mistaken notion of modern peoples on Urantia that child culture is largely the task of mothers. Children need fathers as well as mothers. and fathers need this parental experience as much as do mothers." P. 531.

120. TAKE UP WHERE WE LEAVE OFF DOWN HERE

"On the mansion worlds the resurrected mortal survivors resume their lives just where they left off when overtaken by death. When you go from Urantia to the first mansion world, you will notice considerable change, but if you had come from a more normal and progressive sphere of time, you would hardly notice the difference except for the fact that you were in possession of a different body; the tabernacle of flesh and blood has been left behind on the world of nativity." P. 52.

121. MANSION WORLD ARRIVALS

"From the resurrection halls you proceed to the Melchizedek sector, where you are assigned permanent residence. Then you enter upon ten days of personal liberty. You are free to explore the immediate vicinity of your new home and to familiarize yourself with the program which lies immediately ahead. You also have time to gratify your desire to consult the registry and call upon your loved ones and other earth friends who may have preceded you to these worlds. At the end of your ten-day period of leisure you begin the second step in the Paradise journey, for the mansion worlds are actual training spheres, not merely detention planets." P. 533.

122. DETAILS OF THE MORONTIA LIFE

"Though you have morontia bodies, you continue, through all seven of these worlds, to eat, drink, and rest. You partake of the morontia order of food, a kingdom of living energy unknown on the material worlds. Both food and water are fully utilized in the morontia body; there is no residual waste. Pause to consider: Mansonia number one is a very material sphere, presenting the early beginnings of the morontia regime. You are still a near human and not far removed from the limited viewpoints of mortal life, but each world discloses definite progress. From sphere to sphere you grow less material, more intellectual, and slightly more spiritual. The spiritual is greatest on the last three of these seven progressive worlds." *P. 535.*

123. ON MANSION WORLD NO. FIVE

"A real birth of cosmic consciousness takes place on mansonia number five. You are becoming universe minded. This is indeed a time of expanding horizons. It is beginning to dawn upon the enlarging minds of the ascending mortals that some stupendous and magnificent, some supernal and divine, destiny awaits all who complete the progressive Paradise ascension, which has been so laboriously but so joyfully and auspiciously begun. At about this point the average mortal ascender begins to manifest bona fide experiential enthusiasm for the Havona ascent. Study is becoming voluntary, unselfish service natural, and worship spontaneous. A real morontia character is budding; a real morontia creature is evolving." *P. 537.*

124. THE TIME OF ADJUSTER FUSION

"This is a brilliant age for ascending mortals and usually witnesses the perfect fusion of the human mind and the divine Adjuster. In potential, this fusion may have occurred previously, but the actual working identity many times is not achieved until the time of the sojourn on the fifth mansion world or even the sixth.

"The union of the evolving immortal soul with the eternal and divine Adjuster is signalized by the seraphic summoning of the supervising superangel for resurrected survivors and of the archangel of record for those going to judgment on the third day; and then, in the presence of such a survivor's morontia associates these messengers of confirmation speak: 'This is a beloved son in whom I am well pleased.' This simple ceremony marks the entrance of an ascending mortal upon the eternal career of Paradise service.

"Immediately upon the confirmation of Adjuster fusion the new morontia being is introduced to his fellows for the first time by his new name and is granted the forty days of spiritual retirement from all routine activities wherein to commune with himself and to choose some one of the optional routes to Havona and to select from the differential techniques of Paradise attainment." *P. 538.* **Luke 3:22. Rev. 2:17.**

125. DEPARTURE FOR JERUSEM

"The personnel of the seventh mansonia assemble on the sea of glass to witness your departure for Jerusem with residential status. Hundreds or thousands of times you may have visited Jerusem, but always as a guest; never before have you proceeded toward the system capital in the company of a group of your fellows who were bidding an eternal farewell to the whole mansonia career as ascending mortals. You will soon be welcomed on the receiving field of the headquarters world as Jerusem citizens." *P. 539.*

126. JOHN HAD A VISION OF THESE EVENTS

"John the Revelator saw a vision of the arrival of a class of advancing mortals from the seventh mansion world to their first heaven, the glories of Jerusem. He recorded: 'And I saw as it were a sea of glass mingled with fire; and those who had gained the victory over the beast that was originally in them and over the image that persisted through the mansion worlds and finally over the last mark and trace, standing on the sea of glass, having the harps of God, and mark and trace, standing on the sea of glass, having the harps of God, and singing the song of deliverance from mortal fear and death.' (Perfected space communication is to be had on all these worlds; and your anywhere reception of such communications is made possible by carrying the 'harp of God,' a morontia contrivance compensating for the inability to directly adjust the immature morontia sensory mechanism to the reception of space communications.)

"Paul also had a view of the ascendant-citizen corps of perfecting mortals on Jerusem, for he wrote: 'But you have come to Mount Zion and to the city of the living God, the heavenly Jerusalem, and to an innumerable company of angels, to the grand assembly of Michael, and to the spirits of just men being made perfect.'" *P. 539.* **Rev. 15:2. Heb. 12:22,23.**

127. THE MORONTIA LIFE

"In the days of the mortal flesh the divine spirit indwells you, almost as a thing apart—in reality an invasion of man by the bestowed spirit of the Universal Father. But in the morontia life the spirit will become a real part of your personality, and as you successively pass through the 570 progressive transformations, you ascend from the material to the spiritual estate of creature life.

"Paul learned of the existence of the morontia worlds and of the reality of morontia materials, for he wrote, 'They have in heaven a better and more enduring substance.' And these morontia materials are real, literal, even as in 'the city which has foundations, whose builder and maker is God.' And each of these marvelous spheres is 'a better country, that is, a heavenly one.'" P. 542. **Heb. 10:34; 11:10.**

128. MORONTIAL RELAXATION

"Joyful mirth and the smile-equivalent are as universal as music. There is a morontial and a spiritual equivalent of mirth and laughter. The ascendant life is about equally divided between work and play—freedom from assignment.

"Celestial relaxation and superhuman humor are quite different from their human analogues, but we all actually indulge in a form of both; and they really accomplish for us, in our state, just about what ideal humor is able to do for you on Urantia. The Morontia Companions are skillful play sponsors, and they are most ably supported by the reversion directors." P. 547.

129. SUPERHUMAN HUMOR

"You would probably best understand the work of the reversion directors if they were likened to the higher types of humorists on Urantia, though that would be an exceedingly crude and somewhat unfortunate way in which to try to convey an idea of the function of these directors of change and relaxation, these ministers of the exalted humor of the morontia and spirit realms.

"In discussing spirit humor, first let me tell you what it is *not*. Spirit jest is never tinged with the accentuation of the misfortunes of the weak and erring. Neither is it ever blasphemous of the righteousness and glory of divinity. Our humor embraces three general levels of appreciation:

"1. *Reminiscent jests*. Quips growing out of the memories of past episodes in one's experience of combat, struggle, and sometimes fearfulness, and ofttimes foolish and childish anxiety. To us, this phase of humor derives from the deep-seated and abiding ability to draw upon the past for memory material with which pleasantly to flavor and otherwise lighten the heavy loads of the present.

"2. *Current humor*. The senselessness of much that so often causes us serious concern, the joy at discovering the unimportance of much of our serious personal anxiety. We are most appreciative of this phase of humor when we are best able to discount the anxieties of the present in favor of the certainties of the future.

"3. *Prophetic joy*. It will perhaps be difficult for mortals to envisage this phase of humor, but we do get a peculiar satisfaction out of the assurance 'that all things work together for good'—for spirits and morontians as well as for mortals. This aspect of celestial humor grows out our faith in the loving overcare of our superiors and in the divine stability of our Supreme Directors." P. 547-8.

130. HUMOR PREVENTS EXALTATION OF EGO

"When we are tempted to magnify our self-importance, if we stop to contemplate the infinity of the greatness and grandeur of out Makers, our own self-glorification becomes sublimely ridiculous, even verging on the humorous. One of the functions of humor is to help all of us take ourselves less seriously. *Humor is the divine antidote for exaltation of ego*.

"The need for the relaxation and diversion of humor is greatest in those orders of ascendant beings who are subjected to sustained stress in their upward struggles. The two extremes of life have little need for humorous diversions. Primitive men have no capacity therefor, and beings of Paradise perfection have no need thereof. The hosts of Havona are naturally a joyous and exhilarating assemblage of supremely happy personalities. On Paradise the quality of worship obviates the necessity for reversion activities. But among those who start their careers far below the goal of Paradise perfection, there is a large place for the ministry of the reversion directors." P. 549.

131. BENEFICIAL INFLUENCE OF HUMOR

"Humor should function as an automatic safety valve to prevent the building up of excessive pressures due to the monotony of sustained and serious selfcontemplation in association with the intense struggle for developmental progress and noble achievement. Humor also functions to lessen the shock of the unexpected impact of fact or of truth, rigid unyielding fact and flexible ever-living truth. The mortal personality, never sure as to which will next be encountered, through humor swiftly grasps—sees the point and achieves insight—the unexpected nature of the situation be it fact or be it truth.

"While the humor of Urantia is exceedingly crude and most inartistic, it does serve a valuable purpose both as a health insurance and as a liberator of emotional pressure, thus preventing injurious nervous tension and overserious selfcontemplation. Humor and play—relaxation—are never reactions of progressive exertion; always are they the echoes of a backward glance, a reminiscence of the past. Even on Urantia and as you now are, you always find it rejuvenating when for a short time you can suspend the exertions of the newer and higher intellectual efforts and revert to the more simple engagements of your ancestors." P. 549-550.

132. THE TWENTY-THIRD PSALM

"Even on Urantia they counsel the human teachers of truth and righteousness to adhere to the preaching of 'the goodness of God, which leads to repentance,' to proclaim 'the love of God, which casts out all fear.' Even so have these truths been declared on your world:

"The Gods are my caretakers; I shall not stray;

"Side by side they lead me in the beautiful paths and glorious refreshing of life everlasting.

"I shall not, in this Divine Presence, want for food nor thirst for water.

"Though I go down into the valley of uncertainty or ascend up into the worlds of doubt,

"Though I move in loneliness or with the fellows of my kind,

"Though I triumph in the choirs of light or falter in the solitary places of the spheres,

"Your good spirit shall minister to me, and your glorious angel will comfort me.

"Though I descend into the depths of darkness and death itself,

"I shall not doubt you nor fear you,

"For I know that in the fullness of time and the glory of your name

"You will raise me up to sit with you on the battlements on high." P. 552.

133. HUMAN PHILOSOPHY CONTRASTED WITH MORONTIA MOTA

"Not long since, while executing an assignment on the first mansion world of Satania, I had occasion to observe this method of teaching; and though I may not undertake to present the mota content of the lesson, I am permitted to record the twenty-eight statements of human philosophy which this morontia instructor was utilizing as illustrative material designed to assist these new mansion world sojourners in their early efforts to grasp the significance and meaning of mota. These illustrations of human philosophy were:

"1. A display of specialized skill does not signify possession of spiritual capacity. Cleverness is not a substitute for true character.

"2. Few persons live up to the faith which they really have. Unreasoned fear is a master intellectual fraud practiced upon the evolving mortal soul.

"3. Inherent capacities cannot be exceeded; a pint can never hold a quart. The spirit concept cannot be mechanically forced into the material memory mold.

"4. Few mortals ever dare to draw anything like the sum of personality credits established by the combined ministries of nature and grace. The majority of impoverished souls are truly rich, but they refuse to believe it.

"5. Difficulties may challenge mediocrity and defeat the fearful, but they only stimulate the true children of the Most Highs.

"6. To enjoy privilege without abuse, to have liberty without license, to possess power and steadfastly refuse to use it for self-aggrandizement-these are the marks of high civilization.

"7. Blind and unforeseen accidents do not occur in the cosmos. Neither do the celestial beings assist the lower being who refuses to act upon his light of truth.

"8. Effort does not always produce joy, but there is no happiness without intelligent effort.

"9. Action achieves strength; moderation eventuates in charm.

"10. Righteousness strikes the harmony chords of truth, and the melody vibrates throughout the cosmos, even to the recognition of the Infinite.

"11. The weak indulge in resolutions, but the strong act. Life is but a day's work—do it well. The act is ours; the consequences God's.

"12. The greatest affliction of the cosmos is never to have been afflicted. Mortals only learn wisdom by experiencing tribulation.

"13. Stars are best discerned from the lonely isolation of experiential depths, not from the illuminated and ecstatic mountain tops.

"14. Whet the appetites of your associates for truth; give advice only when it is asked for.

"15. Affectation is the ridiculous effort of the ignorant to appear wise, the attempt of the barren soul to appear rich.

"16. You cannot perceive spiritual truth until you feelingly experience it, and many truths are not really felt except in adversity.

"17. Ambition is dangerous until it is fully socialized. You have not truly acquired any virtue until your acts make you worthy of it.

"18. Impatience is a spirit poison; anger is like a stone hurled into a hornet's nest.

"19. Anxiety must be abandoned. The disappointments hardest to bear are those which never come.

"20. Only a poet can discern poetry in the commonplace prose of routine existence.

"21. The high mission of any art is, by its illusions, to foreshadow a higher universe reality, to crystallize the emotions of time into the thought of eternity.

"22. The evolving soul is not made divine by what it does, but by what it strives to do.

"23. Death added nothing to the intellectual possession or to the spiritual endowment, but it did add to the experiential status the consciousness of *survival*.

"24. The destiny of eternity is determined moment by moment by the achievements of the day by day living. The acts of today are the destiny of tomorrow.

"25. Greatness lies not so much in possessing strength as in making a wise and divine use of such strength.

"26. Knowledge is possessed only by sharing; it is safeguarded by wisdom and socialized by love.

"27. Progress demands development of individuality; mediocrity seeks perpetuation in standardization.

"28. The argumentative defense of any proposition is inversely proportional to the truth contained.

"Such is the work of the beginners on the first mansion world while the more advanced pupils on the later worlds are mastering the higher levels of cosmic insight and morontia mota." P. 556-7.

134. MAN NOT AN EVOLUTIONARY ACCIDENT

"The early stages of life evolution are not altogether in conformity with your present-day views. *Mortal man is not an evolutionary accident.* There is a precise system, a universal law, which determines the unfolding of the planetary life plan on the spheres of space. Time and the production of large numbers of a species are not the controlling influences. Mice reproduce much more rapidly than elephants, yet elephants evolve more rapidly than mice." P. 560.

135. COMPENSATION FOR URANTIA ISOLATION

"On first thought it might appear that Urantia and its associated isolated worlds are most unfortunate in being deprived of the beneficent presence and influence of such superhuman personalities as a Planetary Prince and a Material Son and Daughter. But isolation of these spheres affords their races a unique opportunity for the exercise of faith and for the development of a peculiar quality of confidence in cosmic reliability which is not dependent on sight or any other material consideration. It may turn out, eventually, that mortal creatures hailing from the worlds quarantined in consequence of rebellion are extremely fortunate. We have discovered that such ascenders are very early intrusted with numerous special assignments to cosmic undertakings where unquestioned faith and sublime confidence are essential to achievement." P. 578.

136. THE AGONDONTERS

"On Jerusem the ascenders from these isolated worlds occupy a residential sector by themselves and are known as the *agondonters*, meaning evolutionary will creatures who can believe without seeing, persevere when isolated, and triumph over insuperable difficulties even when alone. This functional grouping of the agondonters persists throughout the ascension of the local universe and the traversal of the superuniverse; it disappears during the sojourn in Havona but promptly reappears upon the attainment of Paradise and definitely persists in the Corps of the Mortal Finality. Tabamantia is an *agondonter* of finaliter status, having survived from one of the quarantined spheres involved in the first rebellion ever to take place in the universes of time and space." P. 579.

137. RACE IMPROVEMENT

"One of the great achievements of the age of the prince is this restriction of the multiplication of mentally defective and socially unfit individuals. Long before the times of the arrival of the second Sons, the Adams, most worlds seriously address themselves to the tasks of race purification, something which the Urantia peoples have not even yet seriously undertaken.

"This problem of race improvement is not such an extensive undertaking when it is attacked at this early date in human evolution. The preceding period of tribal struggles and rugged competition in race survival has weeded out most of the abnormal and defective strains. An idiot does not have much chance of survival in a primitive and warring tribal social organization. It is the false sentiment of your partially perfected civilizations that fosters, protects, and perpetuates the hopelessly defective strains of evolutionary human stocks.

"It is neither tenderness nor altruism to bestow futile sympathy upon degenerated human beings, unsalvable abnormal and inferior mortals. There exist on even the most normal of the evolutionary worlds sufficient differences between individuals and between numerous social groups to provide for the full exercise of all those noble traits of altruistic sentiment and unselfish mortal ministry without perpetuating the socially unfit and the morally degenerate strains of evolving humanity. There is abundant opportunity for the exercise of tolerance and the function of altruism in behalf of those unfortunate and needy individuals who have not irretrievably lost their moral heritage and forever destroyed their spiritual birthright." P. 592.

138. MIXING GOOD AND BAD STOCKS

"The Adamic progeny never amalgamate with the inferior strains of the evolutionary races. Neither is it the divine plan for the Planetary Adam or Eve to mate, personally, with the evolutionary peoples. This race—improvement project is the task of their progeny. But the offspring of the Material Son and Daughter are mobilized for generations before the racial-amalgamation ministry is inaugurated." P. 593.

139. THE NEW AND LIVING WAY

"On Urantia the establishment of this 'new and living way' was a matter of fact as well as of truth. The isolation of Urantia in the Lucifer rebellion had suspended the procedure whereby mortals can pass, upon death, directly to the shores of the mansion worlds. Before the days of Christ Michael on Urantia all souls slept on until the dispensational or special millennial resurrections.

Even Moses was not permitted to go over to the other side until the occasion of a special resurrection, the fallen Planetary Prince, Calagastia, contesting such a deliverance. But ever since the day of Pentecost, Urantia mortals again may proceed directly to the morontia spheres." *P. 596.* **Heb. 10:20.**

140. HIGH STATUS OF NORMAL WORLDS

"If you could be transplanted from your backward and confused world to some normal planet now in the postbestowal Son age, you would think you had been translated to the heaven of your traditions. You would hardly believe that you were observing the normal evolutionary workings of a mortal sphere of human habitation. These worlds are in the spiritual circuits of their realm, and they enjoy all the advantages of the universe broadcasts and the reflectivity services of the superuniverse." *P. 598.*

141. LIFE ON A PROGRESSIVE WORLD

"The physical administration of a world during this age requires about one hour each day on the part of every adult individual; that is, the equivalent of one Urantia hour. The planet is in close touch with universe affairs, and its people scan the latest broadcasts with the same keen interest you now manifest in the latest editions of your daily newspapers. These races are occupied with a thousand things of interest unknown on your world.

"Increasingly, true planetary allegiance to the Supreme Being grows. Generation after generation, more and more of the race step into line with those who practice justice and live mercy. Slowly but surely the world is being won to the joyous service of the Sons of God. The physical difficulties and material problems have been largely solved; the planet is ripening for advanced life and a more settled existence." *P. 599.*

142. LIFE ON A RENOVATED PLANET

"This is the same renovated earth, the advanced planetary stage, that the olden seer envisioned when he wrote: '"For, as the new heavens and the new earth, which I will make, shall remain before me, so shall you and your children survive; and it shall come to pass that from one new moon to another and from one Sabbath to another all flesh shall come to worship before me,"says the Lord.'" *P. 600.* **Isa. 65:17; 66:22.**

143. MANOTIA IN THE LUCIFER REBELLION

"Not long since, in describing the experiences associated with the onset of the Lucifer rebellion, Manotia said: 'But my most exhilarating moment was the thrilling adventure connected with the Lucifer rebellion when, as second seraphic commander, I refused to participate in the projected insult to Michael; and the powerful rebels sought my destruction by means of the liaison forces they had arranged. There was a tremendous upheaval on Jerusem, but not a single loyal seraphim was harmed.

"'Upon the default of my immediate superior it devolved upon me to assume command of the angelic hosts of Jerusem as the titular director of the confused seraphic affairs of the system. I was morally upheld by the Melchizedeks, ably assisted by a majority of the Material Sons, deserted by a tremendous group of my own order, but magnificently supported by the ascendant mortals on Jerusem.

"'Having been automatically thrown out of the constellation circuits by the secession of Lucifer, we were dependent on the loyalty of our intelligence corps, who forwarded calls for help to Edentia from the near-by system of Rantulia; and we found that the kingdom of order, the intellect of loyalty, and the spirit of truth were inherently triumphant over rebellion, self-assertion, and so-called personal liberty; we were able to carry on until the arrival of the new System Sovereign, the worthy successor of Lucifer. And immediately thereafter I was assigned to the corps of the Melchizedek receivership of Urantia, assuming jurisdiction over the loyal seraphic orders on the world of the traitorous Caligastia, who had proclaimed his sphere a member of the newly projected system of "liberated worlds and emancipated personalities" proposed in the infamous Declaration of Liberty issued by Lucifer in his call to the "liberty-loving, free-thinking, and forward-looking intelligences of the misruled and maladministered worlds of Satania."

"This angel is still in service on Urantia, functioning as associate chief of seraphim." Pp. 606-7.

144. MORTAL CONSTANCY IN THE LUCIFER REBELLION

"It was over two years of system time from the beginning of the 'war in heaven' until the installation of Lucifer's successor. But at last the new Sovereign came, landing on the sea of glass with his staff. I was among the reserves mobilized on Edentia by Gabriel, and I well remember the first message of Lanaforge to the Constellation Father of Norlatiadek. It read: 'Not a single Jerusem citizen was lost. Every ascendant mortal survived the fiery trial and emerged from the crucial test triumphant and altogether victorious.' And on to Salvington, Uversa, and Paradise went this message of assurance that the survival experience of mortal ascension is the greatest security against rebellion and the surest safeguard against sin. This noble Jerusem band of faithful mortals numbered just 187,432,811." P. 608-9.

145. TRUE AND FALSE LIBERTY

"Of all the perplexing problems growing out of the Lucifer rebellion, none has occasioned more difficulty than the failure of immature evolutionary mortals to distinguish between true and false liberty.

"True liberty is the quest of the ages and the reward of evolutionary progress. False liberty is the subtle deception of the error of time and the evil of space. Enduring liberty is predicated on the reality of justice-intelligence, maturity, fraternity, and equity.

"Liberty is a self-destroying technique of cosmic existence when its motivation is unintelligent, unconditioned, and uncontrolled. True liberty is progressively related to reality and is ever regardful of social equity, cosmic fairness, universe fraternity, and divine obligations.

"Liberty is suicidal when divorced from material justice, intellectual fairness, social forbearance, moral duty, and spiritual values. Liberty is nonexistent apart from cosmic reality, and all personality reality is proportional to its divinity relationships.

"Unbridled self-will and unregulated self-expression equal unmitigated selfishness, the acme of ungodliness. Liberty without the associated and ever-increasing conquest of self is a figment of egoistic mortal imagination. Self-motivated liberty is a conceptual illusion, a cruel deception. License masquerading in the garments of liberty is the forerunner of abject bondage." *P. 613.*

146. THE THEFT OF LIBERTY

"Lucifer's folly was the attempt to do the nondoable, to short-circuit time in an experiential universe. Lucifer's crime was the attempted creative disenfranchisement of every personality in Satania, the unrecognized abridgment of the creature's personal participation—freewill participation—in the long evolutionary struggle to attain the status of light and life both individually and collectively. In so doing this onetime Sovereign of your system set the temporal purpose of his own will directly athwart the eternal purpose of God's will as it is revealed in the bestowal of free will upon all personal creatures. The Lucifer rebellion thus threatened the maximum possible infringement of the freewill choice of the ascenders and servers of the system of Satania—a threat forevermore to deprive every one of these beings of the thrilling experience of contributing something personal and unique to the slowly erecting monument to experiential wisdom which will sometime exist as the perfected system of Satania. Thus does the Lucifer manifesto, masquerading in the habiliments of liberty, stand forth in the clear light of reason as a monumetal threat to consummate the theft of personal liberty and to do it on a scale that has been approached only twice in all the history of Nebadon." *P. 614-615.*

147. THE TIME LAG OF JUSTICE

"The moral will creatures of the evolutionary worlds are always bothered with the unthinking question as to why the all-wise Creators permit evil and sin. They fail to comprehend that both are inevitable if the creature is to be truly free. The free will of evolving man or exquisite angel is not a mere philosophic concept, a symbolic ideal. Man's ability to choose good or evil is a universe reality. This liberty to choose for oneself is an endowment of the Supreme Rulers, and they will not permit any being or group of beings to deprive a single personality in the wide universe of this divinely bestowed liberty—not even to satisfy such misguided and ignorant beings in the enjoyment of this misnamed personal liberty.

"Although conscious and wholehearted identification with evil (sin) is the equivalent of nonexistence (annihilation), there must always intervene between the time of such personal identification with sin and the execution of the penalty—the automatic result of such a willful embrace of evil—a period of time of sufficient length to allow for such an adjudication of such an individual's universe status as will prove entirely satisfactory to all related universe personalities, and which will be so fair and just as to win the approval of the sinner himself." *P. 615.*

148. THE MERCY TIME LAG

"Another problem somewhat difficult of explanation in the constellation of Norlatiadek pertains to the reasons for permitting Lucifer, Satan, and the fallen princes to work mischief so long before being apprehended, interned, and adjudicated.

"Parents, those who have borne and reared children, are better able to understand why Michael, a Creator-father, might be slow to condemn and destroy his own Sons. Jesus' story of the prodigal son well illustrates how a loving father can long wait for the repentance of an erring child.

"The very fact that an evil-doing creature can actually choose to do wrong—commit sin—establishes the fact of free—willness and fully justifies any length delay in the execution of justice provided the extended mercy might conduce to repentance and rehabilitation.

"Most of the liberties which Lucifer sought he already had; others he was to receive in the future. All these precious endowments were lost by giving way to impatience and yielding to a desire to possess what one craves now and to possess it in defiance of all obligation to respect the rights and liberties of all other beings composing the universe of universes. Ethical obligations are innate, divine, and universal." *P. 615-6.*

149. TIME DELAY IN PUNISHING LUCIFER

"Time, even in a universe of time, is relative: If a Urantia mortal of average length of life should commit a crime which precipitated world-wide pandemonium, and if he were apprehended, tried, and executed within two or three days of the commission of the crime, would it seem a long time to you? And yet that would be nearer a comparison with the length of Lucifer's life even if his adjudication, now begun, should not be completed for a hundred thousand Urantia years. The relative lapse of time from the viewpoint of Uversa, where the litigation is pending, could be indicated by saying that the crime of Lucifer was being brought to trial within two and a half seconds of its commission. From the Paradise viewpoint the adjudication is simultaneous with the enactment." *P. 618.*

150. OUR SALVATION UNAFFECTED BY ANOTHER'S SIN

"But one thing should be made clear: If you are made to suffer the evil consequences of the sin of some member of your family, some fellow citizen or fellow mortal, even rebellion in the system or elsewhere—no matter what you may have to endure because of the wrongdoing of your associates, fellows, or superiors—you may rest secure in the eternal assurance that such tribulations are transient afflictions. None of these fraternal consequences of misbehavior in the group can ever jeopardize your eternal prospects or in the least degree deprive you of your divine right of Paradise ascension and God attainment." *P. 619.*

151. COMPENSATIONS FOR REBELLION

"And there is compensation for these trials, delays, and disappointments which invariably accompany the sin of rebellion. Of the many valuable repercussions of the Lucifer rebellion which might be named, I will only call attention to the enhanced careers of those mortal ascenders, the Jerusem citizens, who, by withstanding the sophistries of sin, placed themselves in line for becoming future Mighty Messengers, fellows of my own order. Every being who stood the test of that evil episode thereby immediately advanced his administrative status and enhanced his spiritual worth." *P. 619.*

152. NET RESULTS OF THE LUCIFER REBELLION

"At first the Lucifer upheaval appeared to be an unmitigated calamity to the system and to the universe. Gradually benefits began to accrue. With the passing of twenty-five thousand years of system time (twenty thousand years of Urantia time), the Melchizedeks began to teach that the good resulting from Lucifer's folly had come to equal the evil incurred. The sum of evil had by that time become almost stationary, continuing to increase only on certain isolated worlds, while the beneficial repercussions continued to multiply and extend out through the universe and superuniverse, even to Havona. The Melchizedeks now teach that the good resulting from the Satania rebellion is more than a thousand times the sum of all the evil." P. 619.

153. THE MORONTIA TEMPLE

"The presence of a morontia temple at the capital of an inhabited world is the certificate of the admission of such a sphere to the settled ages of light and life. Before the Teacher Sons leave a world at the conclusion of their terminal mission, they inaugurate this final epoch of evolutionary attainment; they preside on that day when the 'holy temple comes down upon earth.' This event, signaling the dawn of the era of light and life, is always honored by the personal presence of the Paradise bestowal Son of that planet, who comes to witness this great day. There in this temple of unparalleled beauty, this bestowal Son of Paradise proclaims the long-time Planetary Prince as the new Planetary Sovereign and invests such a faithful Lanonandek Son with new powers and extended authority over planetary affairs. The System Sovereign is also present and speaks in confirmation of these pronouncements.

"A morontia temple has three parts: Centermost is the sanctuary of the pradise bestowal Son. On the right is the seat of the former Planetary Prince, now Planetary Sovereign; and when present in the temple, this Lanonandek Son is visible to the more spiritual individuals of the realm, on the left is the seat of the acting chief of finaliters attached to the plant." P. 622.

"Such a morontia temple also serves as the place of assembly for witnessing the translation of living mortals to the morontia existence. It is because the translation temple is composed of morontia material that it is not destroyed by the blazing glory of the consuming fire which so completely obliterates the physical bodies of those mortals who therein experience final fusion with their divine Adjusters. On a large world these departure flares are almost continuous, and as the number of translations increases, subsidiary morontia life shrines are provided in different areas of the planet. Not long since I sojourned on a world in the far north whereon twenty-five morontia shrines were functioning.

"On presettled worlds, planets without morontia temples, these fusion flashes many times occur in the planetary atmosphere, where the material body of a translation candidate is elevated by the midway creatures and the physical controllers." *P. 622.*

154. TRANSLATION FROM THE LIVING

"Natural, physical death is not a mortal inevitability. The majority of advanced evolutionary beings, citizens on worlds existing in the final era of light and life, do not die; they are translated directly from the life in the flesh to the morontia existence.

"This experience of translation from the material life to the morontia state—fusion of the immortal soul with the indwelling Adjuster—increases in frequency commensurate with the evolutionary progress of the planet. At first only a few mortals in each age attain translation levels of spiritual progress, but with the onset of the successive ages of the Teacher Sons, more and more Adjuster fusions occur before the termination of the lengthening lives of these progressing mortals; and by the time of the terminal mission of the Teacher Sons, approximately one quarter of these superb mortals are exempt from natural death." *P. 623.*

"When the family, friends, and working group of such a fusion candidate have forgathered in the morontia temple, they are distributed around the central stage whereon the fusion candidates are resting, meantime freely conversing with their assembled friends. A circle of intervening celestial personalities is arranged to protect the material mortals from the action of the energies manifest at the instant of the 'life flash' which delivers the ascension candidate from the bonds of material flesh, thereby doing for such an evolutionary mortal everything that natural death does for those who are thereby delivered from the flesh.

"Many fusion candidates may be assembled in the spacious temple at the same time. And what a beautiful occasion when mortals thus forgather to witness the ascension of their loved ones in spiritual flames, and what a contrast to those earlier ages when mortals must commit their dead to the embrace of the terrestrial elements! The scenes of weeping and wailing characteristic of earlier epochs of human evolution are now replaced by ecstatic joy and the sublimest enthusiasm as these God-knowing mortals bid their loved ones a transient farewell as they are removed from their material associations by the spiritual fires of consuming grandeur and ascending glory. On worlds settled in light and life, 'funerals' are occasions of supreme joy, profound satisfaction, and inexpressible hope." *P. 623.* **Rev. 21:2-4.**

155. WORLD STATUS IN LIGHT AND LIFE

"As worlds advance in the settled status of light and life, society becomes increasingly peaceful. The individual, while no less independent and devoted to his family, has become more altruistic and fraternal.

"On Urantia, and as you are, you can have little appreciation of the advanced status and progressive nature of the enlightened races of these perfected worlds. These people are the flowering of the evolutionary races. But such beings are still mortal; they continue to breathe, eat, sleep, and drink. This great evolution is not heaven, but it is a sublime foreshadowing of the divine worlds of the Pardise ascent.

"On a normal world the biologic fitness of the mortal race was long since brought up to a high level during the post-Adamic epochs; and now, from age to age throughout the settled eras the physical evolution of man continues. Both vision and hearing are extended. By now the population has become stationary in numbers. Reproduction is regulated in accordance with planetary requirements and innate hereditary endowments: The mortals on a planet during this age are divided into from five to ten groups, and the lower groups are permitted to produce only one half as many children as the higher. The continued improvement of such a magnificent race throughout the era of light and life is largely a matter of the selective reproduction of those racial strains which exhibit superior qualities of a social, philosophic, cosmic, and spiritual nature." *P. 630*.

156. THE EVOLUTIONARY GOAL

"This is the story of the magnificent goal of mortal striving on the evolutionary worlds; and it all takes place even before human beings enter upon their morontia careers; all of this splendid development is attainable by material mortals on the inhabited worlds, the very first stage of that endless and incomprehensible career of Paradise ascension and divinity attainment.

"But can you possibly imagine what sort of evolutionary mortals are now coming up from worlds long existing in the seventh epoch of settled light and life? It is such as these who go on to the morontia worlds of the local universe capital to begin their ascension careers.

"If the mortals of distraught Urantia could only view one of these more advanced worlds long settled in light and life, they would nevermore question the wisdom of the evolutionary scheme of creation. Were there no future of eternal creature progression, still the superb evolutionary attainments of the mortal races on such settled worlds of perfected achievement would amply justify man's creation on the worlds of time and space." *P. 631*.

157. GRAND UNIVERSE SETTLED IN LIGHT AND LIFE

"None of us entertain a satisfactory concept of what will happen when the grand universe (the seven superuniverses as dependent on Havona) becomes entirely settled in light and life. That event will undoubtedly be the most profound occurrence in the annals of eternity since the appearance of the central universe. There are those who hold that the Supreme Being himself will emerge from the Havona mystery enshrouding his spirit person and will become residential on the headquarters of the seventh superuniverse as the almighty and experiential sovereign of the perfected creations of time and space. But we really do not know." P. 636.

158. UNIVERSAL UNITY

"God is unity. Deity is universally co-ordinated. The universe of universes is one vast integrated mechanism which is absolutely controlled by one infinite mind. The physical, intellectual, and spiritual domains of universal creation are divinely correlated. The perfect and imperfect are truly interrelated, and therefore may the finite evolutionary creature ascend to Paradise in obedience to the Universal Father's mandate: 'Be you perfect, even as I am perfect.'" P. 637. **Matt. 5:48.**

159. THE CEASELESS MARCH OF CREATIVE FORCE

"The ceaseless and expanding march of the Paradise creative forces through space seems to presage the ever-extending domain of the gravity grasp of the Universal Father and the never-ending multiplication of varied types of intelligent creatures who are able to love God and be loved by him, and who, by thus becoming God-knowing, may choose to be like him, may elect to attain Paradise and find God." P. 645.

160. PURSUIT OF TRUTH, BEAUTY, AND GOODNESS

"Throughout this glorious age the chief pursuit of the ever-advancing mortals is the quest for a better understanding and a fuller realization of the comprehensible elements of Deity—truth, beauty, and goodness. This represents man's effort to discern God in mind, matter, and spirit. And as the mortal pursues this quest, he finds himself increasingly absorbed in the experiential study of philosophy, cosmology, and divinity.

"Philosophy you somewhat grasp, and divinity you comprehend in worship, social service, and personal spiritual experience, but the pursuit of beauty-cosmology—you all too often limit to the study of man's crude artistic endeavors. Beauty, art, is largely a matter of the unification of contrasts. Variety is essential to the concept of beauty. The supreme beauty, the height of finite art, is the drama of the unification of the vastness of the cosmic extremes of Creator and creature. Man finding God and God finding man—the creature becoming perfect as is the Creator—that is the supernal achievement of the supremely beautiful, the attainment of the apex of cosmic art.

"Hence materialism, atheism, is the maximation of ugliness, the climax of the finite antithesis of the beautiful. Highest beauty consists in the panorama of the unification of the variations which have been born of pre-existent harmonious reality." *P. 646*.

161. SCOPE OF TRUTH, BEAUTY, AND GOODNESS

"Truth is the basis of science and philosophy, presenting the intellectual foundation of religion. Beauty sponsors art, music, and the meaningful rhythms of all human experience. Goodness embraces the sense of ethics, morality, and religion—experiential perfection-hunger." *P. 647*.

"Even truth, beauty, and goodness—man's intellectual approach to the universe of mind, matter, and spirit—must be combined into one unified concept of a divine and supreme *ideal*. As mortal personality unifies the human experience with matter, mind, and spirit, so does this divine and supreme ideal become power-unified in Supremacy and then personalized as a God of fatherly love." *P. 647*.

Part III
THE HISTORY OF URANTIA

162. FIRST ANDRONOVER SUN

"500,000,000,000 years ago the first Andronover sun was born. This blazing streak broke away from the mother gravity grasp and tore out into space on an independent adventure in the cosmos of creation. Its orbit was determined by its path of escape. Such young suns quickly become spherical and start out on their long and eventful careers as the stars of space. Excepting terminal nebular nucleuses, the vast majority of Orvonton suns have had an analogous birth. These escaping suns pass through varied periods of evolution and subsequent universe service." P. 653.

163. BIRTH OF OUR SUN

"6,000,000,000 years ago marks the end of the terminal breakup and the birth of your sun, the fifty-sixth from the last of the Andronover second solar family. This final eruption of the nebular nucleus gave birth to 136,702 suns, most of them solitary orbs. The total number of suns and sun systems having origin in the Andronover nebula was 1,013,628. The number of the solar system sun is 1,013,572.

"And now the great Andronover nebula is no more, but it lives on in the many suns and their planetary families which originated in this mother cloud of space. The final nuclear remnant of this magnificent nebula still burns with a reddish glow and continues to give forth moderate light and heat to its remnant planetary family of one hundred and sixty-five worlds, which now revolve about this venerable mother of two mighty generations of the monarchs of light." P. 655.

164. SUNSPOT CYCLES

"Today, your sun has achieved relative stability, but its eleven and one-half year sunspot cycles betray that it was a variable star in its youth. In the early days of your sun the continued contraction and consequent gradual increase of temperature initiated tremendous convulsions on its surface. These titanic heaves required three and one-half days to complete a cycle of varying brightness. This variable state, this periodic pulsation, rendered your sun highly responsive to certain outside influences which were to be shortly encountered." P. 655.

165. CHEMICAL TYPE OF URANTIA LIFE

"The Satania Life Carriers had projected a sodium chloride pattern of life; therefore no steps could be taken toward planting it until the ocean waters had become sufficiently briny. The Urantia type of protoplasm can function only in a suitable salt solution. All ancestral life—vegetable and animal—evolved in a salt-solution habitat. And even the more highly organized land animals could not continue to live did not this same essential salt solution circulate throughout their bodies in the blood stream which freely bathes, literally submerses, every tiny living cell in this 'briny deep.'

"Your primitive ancestors freely circulated about in the salty ocean; today, this same oceanlike salty solution freely circulates about in your bodies, bathing each individual cell with a chemical liquid in all essentials comparable to the salt water which stimulated the first protoplasmic reactions of the first living cells to function on the planet." P. 664.

166. LIFE IS NOT AN ACCIDENT

"And yet some of the less imaginative of your mortal mechanists insist on viewing material creation and human evolution as an accident. The Urantia midwayers have assembled over fifty thousand facts of physics and chemistry which they deem to be incompatible with the laws of accidental chance, and which they contend unmistakably demonstrate the presence of intelligent purpose in the material creation. And all of this takes no account of their catalogue of more than one hundred thousand findings outside the domain of physics and chemistry which they maintain prove the presence of mind in the planning, creation, and maintenance of the material cosmos." P. 665.

167. TRANSITION FROM VEGETABLE TO ANIMAL LIFE

"450,000,000 years ago the *transition from vegetable to animal life* occurred. This metamorphosis took place in the shallow waters of the sheltered tropic bays and lagoons of the extensive shore lines of the separating continents. And this development, all of which was inherent in the original life patterns, came about gradually. There were many transitional stages between the early primitive vegetable forms of life and the later well-defined animal organisms. Even today the transition slime molds persist, and they can hardly be classified either as plants or as animals.

"Although the evolution of vegetable life can be traced into animal life, and though there have been found graduated series of plants and animals which progressively lead up from the most simple to the most complex and advanced organisms, you will not be able to find such connecting links between the great divisions of the animal kingdom nor between the highest of the prehuman animal types and the dawn men of the human races. These so-called 'missing links' will forever remain missing, for the simple reason that they never existed." P. 669.

Part III: *The History of Urantia*

168. THE GEOLOGIC STONE RECORD BOOK

"All of this story is graphically told within the fossil pages of the vast 'stone book' of world record. And the pages of this gigantic biogeologic record unfailingly tell the truth if you but acquire skill in their interpretation. Many of these ancient sea beds are now elevated high upon land, and their deposits of age upon age tell the story of the life struggles of those early days. It is literally true, as your poet has said, 'The dust we tread upon was once alive.'" *P. 671*.

169. TIME OF BIOLOGIC TRIBULATION

"This age was one of great life impoverishment. Thousands of marine species perished, and life was hardly yet established on land. This was a time of biologic tribulation, the age when life nearly vanished from the face of the earth and from the depths of the oceans. Toward the close of the long marine-life era there were more than one hundred thousand species of living things on earth. At the close of this period of transition less than five hundred had survived." *P. 682*.

170. THE ORIGIN OF MAMMALS

"50,000,000 years ago the land areas of the world were very generally above water or only slightly submerged. The formations and deposits of this period are both land and marine, but chiefly land. For a considerable time the land gradually rose but was simultaneously washed down to the lower levels and toward the seas.

"Early in this period and in North America the placental type of mammals *suddenly* appeared, and they constituted the most important evolutionary development up to this time. Previous orders of nonplacental mammals had existed, but this new type sprang directly and *suddenly* from the pre-existent reptilian ancestor whose descendants had persisted on down through the times of dinosaur decline. The father of the placental mammals was a small, highly active, carnivorous, springing type of dinosaur.

"Basic mammalian instincts began to be manifested in these primitive mammalian types. Mammals possess an immense survival advantage over all other forms of animal life in that they can:

"1. Bring forth relatively mature and well-developed offspring.

"2. Nourish, nurture, and protect their offspring with affectionate regard.

"3. Employ their superior brain power in self-perpetuation.

"4. Utilize increased agility in escaping from enemies.

"5. Apply superior intelligence to environmental adjustment and adaptation." *P. 693*.

171. THE DAWN MAMMALS

"A little more than one million years ago the Mesopotamian dawn mammals, the direct descendants of the North American lemur type of placental mammal, *suddenly* appeared. They were active little creatures, almost three feet tall; and while they did not habitually walk on their hind legs, they could easily stand erect. They were hairy and agile and chattered in monkeylike fashion, but unlike the simian tribes, they were flesh eaters. They had a primitive opposable thumb as well as a highly useful grasping big toe. From this point onward the prehuman species successively developed the opposable thumb while they progressively lost the grasping power of the great toe. The later ape tribes retained the grasping big toe but never developed the human type of thumb." *Pp. 703-4.*

172. THE MID-MAMMALS

"These mid-mammals were the first to exhibit a definite construction propensity, as shown in their rivalry in the building of both treetop homes and their many-tunneled subterranean retreats; they were the first species of mammals ever to provide for safety in both arboreal and underground shelters. They largely forsook the trees as places of abode, living on the ground during the day and sleeping in the treetops at night." *P. 705.*

173. THE PRIMATES

"As time passed, the natural increase in numbers eventually resulted in serious food competition and sex rivalry, all of which culminated in a series of internecine battles that nearly destroyed the entire species. These struggles continued until only one group of less than one hundred individuals was left alive. But peace once more prevailed, and this lone surviving tribe built anew its tree-top bedrooms and once again resumed a normal and semipeaceful existence.

"You can hardly realize by what narrow margins your prehuman ancestors missed extinction from time to time. Had the ancestral frog of all humanity jumped two inches less on a certain occasion, the whole course of evolution would have been markedly changed. The immediate lemurlike mother of the dawn-mammal species escaped death no less than five times by mere hairbreadth margins before she gave birth to the father of the new and higher mammalian order. But the closest call of all was when lightning struck the tree in which the prospective mother of the Primates twins was sleeping. Both of these mid-mammal parents were severely shocked and badly burned; three of their seven children were killed by this bolt from the skies. These evolving animals were almost superstitious. This couple whose treetop home had been struck were really the leaders of the more progressive group of the mid-mammal species; and following their example, more than half the tribe, embracing the more intelligent families, moved about two miles away from this locality and began the construction of new treetop abodes and new ground shelters—their transient retreats in time of sudden danger.

"Soon after the completion of their home, this couple, veterans of so many struggles, found themselves the proud parents of twins, the most interesting and important animals ever to have been born into the world up to that time, for they were the first of the new species of *Primates* constituting the next vital step in prehuman evolution." *Pp. 705-6.*

174. THE FIRST HUMAN BEINGS

"From the year A.D. 1934 back to the birth of the first two human beings is just 993,419 years.

"These two remarkable creatures were true human beings. They possessed perfect human thumbs, as had many of their ancestors, while they had just as perfect feet as the present-day human races. They were walkers and runners, not climbers; the grasping function of the big toe was absent, completely absent. When danger drove them to the treetops, they climbed just like the humans of today would. They would climb up the trunk of a tree like a bear and not as would a chimpanzee or a gorilla, swinging up by the branches.

"These first human beings (and their descendants) reached full maturity at twelve years of age and possessed a potential life span of about seventy-five years.

"Many new emotions early appeared in these human twins. They experienced admiration for both objects and other beings and exhibited considerable vanity. But the most remarkable advance in emotional development was the sudden appearance of a new group of really human feelings, the worshipful group, embracing awe, reverence, humility, and even a primitive form of gratitude. Fear, joined with ignorance of natural phenomena, is about to give birth to primitive religion.

"Not only were such human feelings manifested in these primitive humans, but many more highly evolved sentiments were also present in rudimentary form. They were mildly cognizant of pity, shame, and reproach and were acutely conscious of love, hate, and revenge, being also susceptible to marked feelings of jealousy.

"These first two humans—the twins—were a great trial to their Primates parents. They were so curious and adventurous that they nearly lost their lives on numerous occasions before they were eight years old. As it was, they were rather well scarred up by the time they were twelve.

"Very early they learned to engage in verbal communication; by the age of ten they had worked out an improved sign and word language of almost half a hundred ideas and had greatly improved and expanded the crude communicative technique of their ancestors. But try as hard as they might, they were able to teach only a few of their new signs and symbols to their parents.

"When about nine years of age, they journeyed off down the river one bright day and held a momentous conference. Every celestial intelligence stationed on Urantia, including myself, was present as an observer of the transactions of this noontide tryst. On this eventful day they arrived at an understanding to live with and for each other, and this was the first of a series of such agreements which finally culminated in the decision to flee from their inferior animal associates and to journey northward, little knowing that they were thus to found the human race.

"While we were all greatly concerned with what these two little savages were planning, we were powerless to control the working of their minds; we did not- could not—arbitrarily influence their decisions. But within the permissible limits of planetary function, we, the Life Carriers, together with our associates, all conspired to lead the human twins northward and far from their hairy and partially tree-dwelling people. And so, by reason of their own intelligent choice, the twins did *migrate*, and because of our supervision they migrated *northward* to a secluded region where they escaped the possibility of biologic degradation through admixture with their inferior relatives of the Primates tribes.

"Shortly before their departure from the home forests they lost their mother in a gibbon raid. While she did not possess their intelligence, she did have a worthy mammalian affection of a high order for her offspring, and she fearlessly gave her life in the attempt to save the wonderful pair. Nor was her sacrifice in vain, for she held off the enemy until the father arrived with reinforcements and put the invaders to rout." P. 707-8.

PART III: *THE HISTORY OF URANTIA*

175. SPIRIT OF WORSHIP

"Imagine our joy one day—the twins were about ten years old—when the *spirit of worship* made its first contact with the mind of the female twin and shortly thereafter with the male. We knew that something closely akin to human mind was approaching culmination; and when, about a year later, they finally resolved, as a result of meditative thought and purposeful decision, to flee from home and journey north, then did the *spirit of wisdom* begin to function on Urantia and in these two now recognized human minds." P. 709.

176. URANTIA AN INHABITED WORLD

"We did not have to wait long. At noon, the day after the runaway of the twins, there occurred the initial test flash of the universe circuit signals at the planetary reception-focus of Urantia. We were, of course, all astir with the realization that a great event was impending; but since this world was a life-experiment station, we had not the slightest idea of just how we would be apprised of the recognition of intelligent life on the planet. But we were not long in suspense. On the third day after the elopement of the twins, and before the Life Carrier corps departed, there arrived the Nebadon archangel of initial planetary circuit establishment.

"It was an eventful day on Urantia when our small group gathered about the planetary pole of space communication and received the first message from Salvington over the newly established mind circuit of the planet. And this first message, dictated by the chief of the archangel corps, said:

"'To the Life Carriers on Urantia—Greetings! We transmit assurance of great pleasure on Salvington, Edentia, and Jerusem in honor of the registration on the headquarters of Nebadon of the signal of the existence on Urantia of mind of will dignity. The purposeful decision of the twins to flee northward and segregate their offspring from their inferior ancestors has been noted. This is the first decision of mind—the human type of mind—on Urantia and automatically establishes the circuit of communication over which this initial message of acknowledgment is transmitting.'" P. 709-10.

177. ANDON AND FONTA

"In many respects, Andon and Fonta were the most remarkable pair of human beings that have ever lived on the face of the earth. This wonderful pair, the actual parents of all mankind, were in every way superior to many of their immediate descendants, and they were radically different from all of their ancestors, both immediate and remote." P. 711.

"The decision of Andon and Fonta to flee from the Primates tribes implies a quality of mind far above the baser intelligence which characterized so many of their later descendants who stooped to mate with their retarded cousins of the simian tribes. But their vague feeling of being something more than mere animals was due to the possession of personality and was augmented by the indwelling presence of the Thought Adjusters." P. 711.

"After Andon and Fonta had decided to flee northward, they succumbed to their fears for a time, especially the fear of displeasing their father and immediate family. They envisaged being set upon by hostile relatives and thus recognized the possibility of meeting death at the hands of their already jealous tribesmen. As youngsters, the twins had spent most of their time in each other's company and for this reason had never been overly popular with their animal cousins of the Primates tribe. Nor had they improved their standing in the tribe by building a separate, and a very superior, tree home.

"And it was in this new home among the treetops, one night after they had been awakened by a violent storm, and as they held each other in fearful and fond embrace, that they finally and fully made up their minds to flee from the tribal habitat and the home treetops.

"They had already prepared a crude treetop retreat some half-day's journey to the north. This was their secret and safe hiding place for the first day away from the home forests. Notwithstanding that the twins shared the Primates' deathly fear of being on the ground at nighttime, they sallied forth shortly before nightfall on their northern trek. While it required unusual courage for them to undertake this night journey, even with a full moon, they correctly concluded that they were less likely to be missed and pursued by their tribesmen and relatives. And they safely made their previously prepared rendezvous shortly after midnight.

"On their northward journey they discovered an exposed flint deposit and, finding many stones suitably shaped for various uses, gathered up a supply for the future. In attempting to chip these flints so that they would be better adapted for certain purposes, Andon discovered their sparking quality and conceived the idea of building fire. But the notion did not take firm hold of him at the time as the climate was still salubrious and there was little need of fire." P. 712.

"Andon and Fonta labored incessantly for the nurture and uplift of the clan. They lived to the age of forty-two, when both were killed at the time of an earthquake by the falling of an overhanging rock. Five of their children and eleven grandchildren perished with them, and almost a score of their descendants suffered serious injuries." P. 713.

"They were a wonderful tribe. The males would fight heroically for the safety of their mates and their offspring; the females were affectionately devoted to their children. But their patriotism was wholly limited to the immediate clan. They were very loyal to their families; they would die without question in defense of their children, but they were not able to grasp the idea of trying to make the world a better place for their grandchildren. Altruism was as yet unborn in the human heart, notwithstanding that all of the emotions essential to the birth of religion were already present in these Urantia aborigines." P. 714.

178. SURVIVAL OF ANDON AND FONTA

"Andon and Fonta, the splendid founders of the human race, received recognition at the time of the adjudication of Urantia upon the arrival of the Planetary Prince, and in due time they emerged from the regime of the mansion worlds with citizenship status on Jerusem. Although they have never been permitted to return to Urantia, they are cognizant of the history of the race they founded. They grieved over the Caligastia betrayal, sorrowed because of the Adamic failure, but rejoiced exceedingly when announcement was received that Michael had selected their world as the theater for his final bestowal.

"On Jerusem both Andon and Fonta were fused with their Thought Adjusters, as also were several of their children, including Sontad, but the majority of even their immediate descendants only achieved Spirit fusion.

"Andon and Fonta, shortly after their arrival on Jerusem, received permission from the System Sovereign to return to the first mansion world to serve with the morontia personalities who welcome the pilgrims of time from Urantia to the heavenly spheres. And they have been assigned indefinitely to this service. They sought to send greetings to Urantia in connection with these revelations, but this request was wisely denied them.

"And this is the recital of the most heroic and fascinating chapter in all the history of Urantia, the story of the evolution, life struggles, death, and eternal survival of the unique parents of all mankind." P. 717.

179. HEROIC STRUGGLES OF PRIMITIVE MEN

"The struggles of these early ages were characterized by courage, bravery, and even heroism. And we all regret that so many of those sterling and rugged traits of your early ancestors have been lost to the later-day races. While we appreciate the value of many of the refinements of advancing civilization, we miss the magnificent persistency and superb devotion of your early ancestors, which often- times bordered on grandeur and sublimity." P. 729.

180. MAN'S ASCENT FROM SEAWEED TO LORDSHIP

"The story of man's ascent from seaweed to the lordship of earthly creation is indeed a romance of biologic struggle and mind survival. Man's primordial ancestors were literally the slime and ooze of the ocean bed in the sluggish and warm-water bays and lagoons of the vast shore lines of the ancient inland seas, those very waters in which the Life Carriers established the three independent life implantations on Urantia." P. 731.

181. THE ANCESTRAL FROG

"You have been informed that Urantia mortals evolved by way of primitive frog development, and that this ascending strain, carried in potential in a single frog, narrowly escaped extinction on a certain occasion. But it should not be inferred that the evolution of mankind would have been terminated by an accident at this juncture. At that very moment we were observing and fostering no less than one thousand different and remotely situated mutating strains of life which could have been directed into various different patterns of prehuman development. This particular ancestral frog represented our third selection, the two prior life strains having perished in spite of all our efforts toward their conservation." P. 733-4.

182. SCIENTIFIC SELECTION VS. NATURAL SELECTION

"Mankind on Urantia must solve its problems of mortal development with the human stocks it has—no more races will evolve from prehuman sources throughout all future time. But this fact does not preclude the possibility of the attainment of vastly higher levels of human development through the intelligent fostering of the evolutionary potentials still resident in the mortal races. That which we, the Life Carriers, do toward fostering and conserving the life strains before the appearance of human will, man must do for himself after such an event and subsequent to our retirement from active participation in evolution. In a general way, man's evolutionary destiny is in his own hands, and scientific intelligence must sooner or later supersede the random functioning of uncontrolled natural selection and chance survival." P. 734.

Part III: *The History of Urantia*

183. URANTIA A LIFE-EXPERIMENT WORLD

"Do not overlook the fact that Urantia was assigned to us as a life-experiment world. On this planet we made our sixtieth attempt to modify and, if possible, improve the Satania adaptation of the Nebadon life designs, and it is of record that we achieved numerous beneficial modifications of the standard life patterns. To be specific, on Urantia we worked out and have satisfactorily demonstrated not less than twenty-eight features of life modification which will be of service to all Nebadon through out all future time.

"But the establishment of life on no world is ever experimental in the sense that something untried and unknown is attempted. The evolution of life is a technique ever progressive, differential, and variable, but never haphazard, uncontrolled, nor wholly experimental, in the accidental sense.

"Many features of human life afford abundant evidence that the phenomenon of mortal existence was intelligently planned, that organic evolution is not a mere cosmic accident. When a living cell is injured, it possesses the ability to elaborate certain chemical substances which are empowered so to stimulate and activate the neighboring normal cells that they immediately begin the secretion of certain substances which facilitate healing processes in the wound; and at the same time these normal and uninjured cells begin to proliferate-they actually start to work creating new cells to replace any fellow cells which may have been destroyed by the accident.

"This chemical action and reaction concerned in wound healing and cell reproduction represents the choice of the Life Carriers of a formula embracing over one hundred thousand phases and features of possible chemical reactions and biologic repercussions. More than half a million specific experiments were made by the Life Carriers in their laboratories before they finally settled upon this formula for the Urantia life experiment.

"When Urantia scientists know more of these healing chemicals, they will become more efficient in the treatment of injuries, and indirectly they will know more about controlling certain serious diseases.

"Since life was established on Urantia, the Life Carriers have improved this healing technique as it has been introduced on another Satania world, in that it affords more pain relief and exercises better control over the proliferation capacity of the associated normal cells.

"There were many unique features of the Urantia life experiment, but the two outstanding episodes were the appearance of the Andonic race prior to the evolution of the six colored peoples and the later simultaneous appearance of the Sangik mutants in a single family. Urantia is the first world in

Satania where the six colored races sprang from the same human family. They ordinarily arise in diversified strains from independent mutations within the prehuman animal stock and usually appear on earth one at a time and successively over long periods of time, beginning with the red man and passing on down through the colors to indigo.

"Another outstanding variation of procedure was the late arrival of the Planetary Prince. As a rule, the prince appears on a planet about the time of will development; and if such a plan had been followed, Caligastia might have come to Urantia even during the lifetimes of Andon and Fonta instead of almost five hundred thousand years later, simultaneously with the appearance of the six Sangik races." *P. 734-5*.

184. PHYSICS AND CHEMISTRY CAN'T EXPLAIN EVOLUTION

"Physics and chemistry alone cannot explain how a human being evolved out of the primeval protoplasm of the early seas. The ability to learn, memory and differential response to environment, is the endowment of mind. The laws of physics are not responsive to training; they are immutable and unchanging. The reactions of chemistry are not modified by education; they are uniform and dependable. Aside from the presence of the Unqualified Absolute, electrical and chemical reactions are predictable. But mind can profit from experience, can learn from reactive habits of behavior in response to repetition of stimuli." *P. 738*.

185. LENGTH OF LIFE THE YARDSTICK OF TIME

"The individual's yardstick for time measurement is the length of his life. All creatures are thus time conditioned, and therefore do they regard evolution as being a long-drawn-out process. To those of us whose life span is not limited by a temporal existence, evolution does not seem to be such a protracted transaction. On Paradise, where time is nonexistent, these things are all *present* in the mind of Infinity and the acts of Eternity." *P. 739*.

186. SUDDEN MENTAL AND SPIRITUAL TRANSFORMATIONS

"When physical conditions are ripe, *sudden* mental evolutions may take place; when mind status is propitious, *sudden* spiritual transformations may occur; when spiritual values receive proper recognition, then cosmic meanings become discernible, and increasingly the personality is released from the handicaps of time and delivered from the limitations of space." *P. 740*.

187. FREE-WILL SUPREMACY

"The doctrine of a personal devil on Urantia, though it had some foundation in the planetary presence of the traitorous and iniquitous Caligastia, was nevertheless wholly fictitious in its teachings that such a 'devil' could influence the normal human mind against its free and natural choosing. Even before Michael's bestowal on Urantia, neither Caligastia nor Daligastia was ever able to oppress mortals or to coerce any normal individual into doing anything against the human will. The free will of man is supreme in moral affairs; even the indwelling Thought Adjuster refuses to compel man to think a single thought or to perform a single act against the choosing of man's own will." P. 753.

188. THE FORTITUDE OF VAN

"Throughout the seven crucial years of the Caligastia rebellion, Van was wholly devoted to the work of ministry to his loyal army of men, midwayers, and angels. The spiritual insight and moral steadfastness which enabled Van to maintain such an unshakable attitude of loyalty to the universe government was the product of clear thinking, wise reasoning, logical, judgment, sincere motivation, unselfish purpose, intelligent loyalty, experiential memory, disciplined character, and the unquestioning dedication of his personality to the doing of the will of the Father in Paradise." P. 756.

189. AMADON WAS THE HERO OF REBELLION

"Amadon is the outstanding human hero of the Lucifer rebellion. This male descendant of Andon and Fonta was one of the one hundred who contributed life plasm to the Prince's staff, and ever since that event he had been attached to Van as his associate and human assistant. Amadon elected to stand with his chief throughout the long and trying struggle. And it was an inspiring sight to behold this child of the evolutionary races standing unmoved by the sophistries of Daligastia while throughout the seven-year struggle he and his loyal associates resisted with unyielding fortitude all of the deceptive teachings of the brilliant Caligastia." P. 757.

190. WE DO NOT SPIRITUALLY SUFFER FROM ANOTHER'S SIN

"Caligastia rebelled, Adam and Eve did default, but no mortal subsequently born on Urantia has suffered in his personal spiritual experience because of these blunders. Every mortal born on Urantia since Caligastia's rebellion has been in some manner time-penalized, but the future welfare of such souls has never been in the least eternity-jeopardized. No person is ever made to suffer vital spiritual deprivation because of the sin of another. sin is wholly personal as to moral guilt or spiritual consequences, notwithstanding its far-flung repercussions in administrative, intellectual, and social domains." P. 761.

191. THE STEADFAST AMADON

"From Edentia up through Salvington and even on to Uversa, for seven long years the first inquiry of all subordinate celestial life regarding the Satania rebellion, ever and always, was: 'What of Amadon of Urantia, does he still stand unmoved?'

"If the Lucifer rebellion has handicapped the local system and its fallen worlds, if the loss of this Son and his misled associates has temporarily hampered the progress of the constellation of Norlatiadek, then weigh the effect of the far-flung presentation of the inspiring performance of this one child of nature and his determined band of 143 comrades in standing steadfast for the higher concepts of universe management and administration in the face of such tremendous and adverse pressure exerted by his disloyal superiors.

And let me assure you, this has already done more good in the universe of Nebadon and the superuniverse of Orvonton than can ever be outweighed by the sum total of all the evil and sorrow of the Lucifer rebellion.

"And all this is a beautifully touching and superbly magnificent illumination of the wisdom of the Father's universal plan for mobilizing the Corps of Mortal Finality on Paradise and for recruiting this vast group of mysterious servants of the future largely from the common clay of the mortals of ascending progression just such mortals as the impregnable Amadon." P. 762.

192. CULTURE IS NOT HEREDITARY

"Civilization is a racial acquirement; it is not biologically inherent; hence must all children be reared in an environment of culture, while each succeeding generation of youth must receive anew its education. The superior qualities of civilization—scientific, philosophic, and religious—are not transmitted from one generation to another by direct inheritance. These cultural achievements are preserved only by the enlightened conservation of social inheritance." P. 763.

Part III: *The History of Urantia*

193. THE DELUSION OF "BACK TO NATURE"

"The modern phrase, 'back to nature,' is a delusion of ignorance, a belief in the reality of the onetime fictitious 'golden age.' The only basis for the legend of the golden age is the historic fact of Dalamatia and Eden. But these improved societies were far from the realization of utopian dreams." P. 764.

194. DANGERS OF VANITY AND PLEASURE-SEEKING

"Vanity contributed mightily to the birth of society; but at the time of these revelations the devious strivings of a vainglorious generation threaten to swamp and submerge the whole complicated structure of a highly specialized civilization. Pleasure-want has long since superseded hunger-want; the legitimate social aims of self-maintenance are rapidly translating themselves into base and threatening forms of self-gratification. Self-maintenance builds society; unbridled self-gratification unfailingly destroys civilization." P. 766.

195. SAFEGUARDS OF SOCIETY

"Hunger and love drove men together; vanity and ghost fear held them together. But these emotions alone, without the influence of peace-promoting revelations, are unable to endure the strain of the suspicions and irritations of human interassociations. Without help from superhuman sources the strain of society breaks down upon reaching certain limits, and these very influences of social mobilization—hunger, love, vanity, and fear—conspire to plunge mankind into war and bloodshed.

"The peace tendency of the human race is not a natural endowment; it is derived from the teachings of revealed religion, from the accumulated experience of the progressive races, but more especially from the teachings of Jesus, the Prince of Peace." P. 766.

196. BASIC HUMAN INSTITUTIONS

"All human institutions minister to some social need, past or present, notwithstanding that their overdevelopment unfailingly detracts from the worthwhileness of the individual in that personality is overshadowed and initiative is diminished. Man should control his institutions rather than permit himself to be dominated by these creations of advancing civilization.

"Human institutions are of three general classes:

"1. *The institutions of self-maintenance.* These institutions embrace those practices growing out of food hunger and its associated instincts of self-preservation. They include industry, property, war for gain, and all the regulative machinery of society. Sooner or later the fear instinct fosters the establishment of these institutions of survival by means of taboo, convention, and religious sanction. But fear, ignorance, and superstitution have played a prominent part in the early origin and subsequent development of all human institutions.

"2. *The institutions of self-perpetuation.* These are the establishments of society growing out of sex hunger, maternal instinct, and the higher tender emotions of the races. They embrace the social safeguards of the home and the school, of family life, education, ethics, and religion. They include marriage customs, war for defense, and home building.

"3. *The institutions of self-gratification.* These are the practices growing out of vanity proclivities and pride emotions; and they embrace customs in dress and personal adornment, social usages, war for glory, dancing, amusement, games, and other phases of sensual gratification. But civilization has never evolved distinctive institutions of self-gratification." P. 772.

197. CAPITAL AND MODERN SOCIETY

"Though capital has tended to liberate man, it has greatly complicated his social and industrial organization. The abuse of capital by unfair capitalists does not destroy the fact that it is the basis of modern industrial society. Through capital and invention the present generation enjoys a higher degree of freedom than any that ever preceded it on earth. This is placed on record as a fact and not in justification of the many misuses of capital by thoughtless and selfish custodians." P. 777.

198. CARE ABOUT SOCIAL CHANGES

"The present social order is not necessarily right—not divine or sacred—but mankind will do well to move slowly in making changes. That which you have is vastly better than any system known to your ancestors. Make certain that when you change the social order you change for the better. Do not be persuaded to experiment with the discarded formulas of your forefathers. Go forward, not backward! *Let evolution proceed!* Do not take a backward step." P.782.

199. NATURAL RIGHTS

"Nature confers no rights on man, only life and a world in which to live it. Nature does not even confer the right to live, as might be deduced by considering what would likely happen if an unarmed man met a hungry tiger face to face in the primitive forest. Society's prime gift to man is security." P. 793.

200. GOVERNMENTAL RESPONSIBILITIES

"Urantia mortals are entitled to liberty; they should create their systems of government; they should adopt their constitutions or other charters of civil authority and administrative procedure. And having done this, they should select their most competent and worthy fellows as chief executives. For representatives in the legislative branch they should elect only those who are qualified intellectually and morally to fulfill such sacred responsibilities. As judges of their high and supreme tribunals only those who are endowed with natural ability and who have been made wise by replete experience should be chosen." *P. 798.*

201. "GOLDEN RULERS" MUST PROTECT THEMSELVES

"*The appearance of genuine brotherhood* signifies that a social order has arrived in which all men delight in bearing one another's burdens; they actually desire to practice the golden rule. But such an ideal society cannot be realized when either the weak or the wicked lie in wait to take unfair and unholy advantage of those who are chiefly actuated by devotion to the service of truth, beauty, and goodness. In such a situation only one course is practical: The 'golden rulers' may establish a progressive society in which they live according to their ideals while maintaining an adequate defense against their benighted fellows who might seek either to exploit their pacific predilections or to destroy their advancing civilization." *P. 804.*

202. THE IDEAL STATE

"The ideal state undertakes to regulate social conduct only enough to take violence out of individual competition and to prevent unfairness in personal initiative. Here is a great problem in statehood: How can you guarantee peace and quiet in industry, pay the taxes to support state power, and at the same time prevent taxation from handicapping industry and keep the state from becoming parasitical or tyrannical?" *P. 805.*

203. THE PROFIT MOTIVE

"Present-day profit-motivated economics is doomed unless profit motives can be augmented by service motives. Ruthless competition based on narrow-minded self interest is ultimately destructive of even those things which it seeks to maintain. Exclusive and self-serving profit motivation is incompatible with Christian ideals—much more incompatible with the teachings of Jesus.

"In economics, profit motivation is to service motivation what fear is to love in religion. But the profit motive must not be suddenly destroyed or removed;

it keeps many otherwise slothful mortals hard at work. It is not necessary, however, that this social energy arouser be forever selfish in its objectives." *P. 805.*

204. ARRIVAL OF ADAM AND EVE

"And on that day there was great excitement and joy throughout Eden as the runners went in great haste to the rendezvous of the carrier pigeons assembled from near and far, shouting: 'Let loose the birds; let them carry the word that the promised Son has come.' Hundreds of believer settlements had faithfully, year after year, kept up the supply of these home-reared pigeons for just such an occasion.

"As the news of Adam's arrival spread abroad, thousands of the near-by tribesmen accepted the teachings of Van and Amadon, while for months and months pilgrims continued to pour into Eden to welcome Adam and Eve and to do homage to their unseen Father." *P. 829.* **Gen. 1:26,27.**

205. HANDICAPS OF ADAM AND EVE

"Probably no Material Sons of Nebadon were ever faced with such a difficult and seemingly hopeless task as confronted Adam and Eve in the sorry plight of Urantia. But they would have sometime met with success had they been more farseeing and *patient*. Both of them, especially Eve, were altogether too impatient; they were not willing to settle down to the long, long endurance test. They wanted to see some immediate results, and they did, but the results thus secured proved most disastrous both to themselves and to their world." *P. 840.*

206. DEFAULT OF ADAM AND EVE

"It should again be emphasized that Serapatatia was altogether honest and wholly sincere in all that he proposed. He never once suspected that he was playing into the hands of Caligastia and Daligastia. Serapatatia was entirely loyal to the plan of building up a strong reserve of the violet race before attempting the world-wide up stepping of the confused peoples of Urantia. But this would require hundreds of years to consummate, and he was impatient; he wanted to see some immediate results—something in his own lifetime. He made it clear to Eve that Adam was oftentimes discouraged by the little that had been accomplished toward uplifting the world.

"For more than five years these plans were secretly matured. At last they had developed to the point where Eve consented to have a secret conference with Cano, the most brilliant mind and active leader of the near-by colony of friendly Nodites. Cano was very sympathetic with the Adamic regime; in fact, he was the sincere spiritual leader of those neighboring Nodites who favored friendly relations with the Garden.

"The fateful meeting occurred during the twilight hours of the autumn evening, not far from the home of Adam. Eve had never before met the beautiful and enthusiastic Cano—and he was a magnificent specimen of the survival of the superior physique and outstanding intellect of his remote progenitors of the Prince's staff. And Cano also thoroughly believed in the righteousness of the Serapatatia project. (Outside of the Garden, multiple mating was a common practice.)

"Influenced by flattery, enthusiasm, and great personal persuasion, Eve then and there consented to embark upon the much-discussed enterprise, to add her own little scheme of world saving to the larger and more far-reaching divine plan. Before she quite realized what was transpiring, the fatal step had been taken. It was done.

"The celestial life of the planet was astir. Adam recognized that something was wrong, and he asked Eve to come aside with him in the Garden. And now, for the first time, Adam heard the entire story of the long-nourished plan for accelerating world improvement by operating simultaneously in two directions: the prosecution of the divine plan concomitantly with the execution of the Serapatatia enterprise.

"And as the Material Son and Daughter thus communed in the moonlit Garden, 'the voice in the Garden' reproved them for disobedience. And that voice was none other than my own announcement to the Edenic pair that they had transgressed the Garden covenant; that they had disobeyed the instructions of the Melchizedeks; that they had defaulted in the execution of their oaths of trust to the sovereign of the universe.

"Eve had consented to participate in the practice of good and evil. Good is the carrying out of the divine plans; sin is a deliberate transgression of the divine will; evil is the misadaptation of plans and the maladjustment of techniques resulting in universe disharmony and planetary confusion." *P. 841-2.* **Gen. 3:1-13.**

207. DISILLUSIONMENT OF EVE

"Eve's disillusionment was truly pathetic. Adam discerned the whole predicament and, while heartbroken and dejected, entertained only pity and sympathy for his erring mate.

"It was in the despair of the realization of failure that Adam, the day after Eve's misstep, sought out Laotta, the brilliant Nodite woman who was head of the western schools of the Garden, and with premeditation committed the folly of Eve. But do not misunderstand; Adam was not beguiled; he knew exactly what he was about; he deliberately chose to share the fate of Eve. He loved his mate with a supermortal affection, and the thought of the possibility of a lonely vigil on Urantia without her was more than he could endure." *P. 843.*

208. ADAM AND EVE LOSE SOME OF THEIR CHILDREN

"The Edenic caravan was halted on the third day out from the Garden by the arrival of the seraphic transports from Jerusem. And for the first time Adam and Eve were informed of what was to become of their children. While the transports stood by, those children who had arrived at the age of choice (twenty years) were given the option of remaining on Urantia with their parents or of becoming wards of the Most Highs of Norlatiadek. Two thirds chose to go to Edentia; about one third elected to remain with their parents. All children of prechoice age were taken to Edentia. No one could have beheld the sorrowful parting of this Material Son and Daughter and their children without realizing that the way of the transgressor is hard. These offspring of Adam and Eve are now on Edentia; we do not know what disposition is to be made of them.

"It was a sad, sad caravan that prepared to journey on. Could anything have been more tragic! To have come to a world in such high hopes, to have been so auspiciously received, and then to go forth in disgrace from Eden, only to lose more than three fourths of their children even before finding a new abiding place!" *P. 844.*

209. HUMANITY PROFITED MUCH FROM ADAM AND EVE

"Adam and Eve did fall from their high estate of material sonship down to the lowly status of mortal man. But that was not the fall of man. The human race has been uplifted despite the immediate consequences of the Adamic default. Although the divine plan of giving the violet race to the Urantia peoples miscarried, the mortal races have profited enormously from the limited contribution which Adam and his descendants made to the Urantia races." *P. 845.*

210. THE FOLLY OF IMPATIENCE

"Never, in all your ascent to Paradise, will you gain anything by impatiently attempting to circumvent the established and divine plan by short cuts, personal inventions, or other devices for improving on the way of perfection, to perfection, and for eternal perfection." *P. 846.*

211. ADAM'S BODY CELLS RESISTANT TO DISEASE

"The body cells of the Material Sons and their progeny are far more resistant to disease than are those of the evolutionary beings indigenous to the planet. The body cells of the native races are akin to the living disease-producing microscopic and ultramicroscopic organisms of the realm. These facts explain why the Urantia peoples must do so much by way of scientific effort to withstand so many physical disorders. You would be far more disease resistant if your races carried more of the Adamic life." *P. 851*.

212. MISFORTUNES AND COMPENSATIONS OF URANTIA

"Misfortune has not, however, been the sole lot of Urantia; this planet has also been the most fortunate in the local universe of Nebadon. Urantians should count it all gain if the blunders of their ancestors and the mistakes of their early world rulers so plunged the planet into such a hopeless state of confusion, all the more confounded by evil and sin, that this very background of darkness should so appeal to Michael of Nebadon that he selected this world as the arena wherein to reveal the loving personality of the Father in heaven. It is not that Urantia needed a Creator Son to set its tangled affairs in order; it is rather that the evil and sin on Urantia afforded the Creator Son a more striking background against which to reveal the matchless love, mercy, and patience of the Paradise Father." *P. 853*.

213. SURVIVAL OF ADAM AND EVE

"They did not long rest in the oblivion of the unconscious sleep of the mortals of the realm. On the third day after Adam's death, the second following his reverent burial, the orders of Lanaforge, sustained by the acting Most High of Edentia and concurred in by the Union of Days on Salvington, acting for Michael, were placed in Gabriel's hands, directing the special roll call of the distinguished survivors of the Adamic default on Urantia. And in accordance with this mandate of special resurrection, number twentysix of the Urantia series, Adam and Eve were repersonalized and reassembled in the resurrection halls of the mansion worlds of Satania together with 1,316 of their associates in the experience of the first garden. Many other loyal souls had already been translated at the time of Adam's arrival, which was attended by a dispensational adjudication of both the sleeping survivors and of the living qualified ascenders." *P. 853*.

214. CONTRIBUTION OF ADAM AND EVE

"And thus ends the story of the Planetary Adam and Eve of Urantia, a story of trial, tragedy, and triumph, at least personal triumph for your well-meaning but deluded Material Son and Daughter and undoubtedly, in the end, a story of ultimate triumph for their world and its rebellion-tossed and evil-harassed inhabitants. When all is summed up, Adam and Eve made a mighty contribution to the speedy civilization and accelerated biologic progress of the human race. They left a great culture on earth, but it was not possible for such an advanced civilization to survive in the face of the early dilution and the eventual submergence of the Adamic inheritance. It is the people who make a civilization; civilization does not make the people." *P. 854*.

215. ADAMSON AND RATTA

"Adamson was among that group of the children of Adam and Eve who elected to remain on earth with their father and mother. Now this eldest son of Adam had often heard from Van and Amadon the story of their highland home in the north, and sometime after the establishment of the second garden he determined to go in search of this land of his youthful dreams." *P. 861*.

"A company of twenty-seven followed Adamson northward in quest of these people of his childhood fantasies. In a little over three years Adamson's party actually found the object of their adventure, and among these people he discovered a wonderful and beautiful woman, twenty years old, who claimed to be the last pure-line descendant of the Prince's staff. This woman, Ratta, said that her ancestors were all descendants of two of the fallen staff of the Prince. She was the last of her race, having no living brothers or sisters. She had about decided not to mate, had about made up her mind to die without issue, but she lost her heart to the majestic Adamson. And when she heard the story of Eden, how the predictions of Van and Amadon had really come to pass, and as she listened to the recital of the Garden default, she was encompassed with but a single thought—to marry this son and heir of Adam. And quickly the idea grew upon Adamson. In a little more than three months they were married.

"Adamson and Ratta had a family of sixty-seven children. They gave origin to a great line of the world's leadership, but they did something more. It should be remembered that both of these beings were really superhuman. Every fourth child born to them was of a unique order. It was often invisible. Never in the world's history had such a thing occurred. Ratta was greatly perturbed—even superstitious—but Adamson well knew of the existence of the primary midwayers, and he concluded that something similar was transpiring before his eyes. When the second strangely behaving offspring arrived, he decided to mate them, since one was male and the other female, and this is the origin of the secondary order of midwayers. Within one hundred years, before this phenomenon ceased, almost two thousand were brought into being." *P. 861*. **Gen. 6:4**.

216. VALUE OF RACIAL MIXTURES

"Race mixture is always advantageous in that it favors versatility of culture and makes of a progressive civilization, but if the inferior elements of racial stocks predominate, such achievements will be short-lived. A polyglot culture can be preserved only if the superior stocks reproduce themselves in a safe margin over the inferior. Unrestrained multiplication of inferiors, with decreasing reproduction of superiors, is unfailingly suicidal of cultural civilization.

"Had the Andite conquerors been in numbers three times what they were, or had they driven out or destroyed the least desirable third of the mixed orange-green-indigo inhabitants, then would India have become one of the world's leading centers of cultural civilization and undoubtedly would have attracted more of the later waves of Mesopotamians that flowed into Turkestan and thence northward to Europe." *P. 880.*

217. THE TOOLS OF CIVILIZATION

"You who now live amid latter-day scenes of budding culture and beginning progress in social affairs, who actually have some little spare time in which to *think* about society and civilization, must not overlook the fact that your early ancestors had little or no leisure which could be devoted to thoughtful reflection and social thinking.

"The first four great advances in human civilization were:

"1. The taming of fire.

"2. The domestication of animals.

"3. The enslavement of captives.

"4. Private property." *P. 901.*

218. FAMILY, THE MASTER CIVILIZER

"While religious, social, and educational institutions are all essential to the survival of cultural civilization, *the family is the master civilizer*. A child learns most of the essentials of life from his family and the neighbors.

"The humans of olden times did not possess a very rich social civilization, but such as they had they faithfully and effectively passed on to the next generation. And you should recognize that most of these civilizations of the past continued to evolve with a bare minimum of other institutional influences because the home was effectively functioning. Today the human races possess a rich social and cultural heritage, and it should be wisely and effectively passed on to succeeding generations. The family as an educational institution must be maintained." *P. 913.*

219. SUPREME VALUE OF MARRIAGE

"While the sexes never can hope fully to understand each other, they are effectively complementary, and though co-operation is often more or less personally antagonistic, it is capable of maintaining and reproducing society. Marriage is an institution designed to compose sex differences, meanwhile effecting the continuation of civilization and insuring the reproduction of the race.

"Marriage is the mother of all human institutions, for it leads directly to home founding and home maintenance, which is the structural basis of society. The family is vitally linked to the mechanism of self-maintenance; it is the sole hope of race perpetuation under the mores of civilization, while at the same time it most effectively provides certain highly satisfactory forms of self-gratification. The family is man's greatest purely human achievement, combining as it does the evolution of the biologic relations of male and female with the social relations of husband and wife." P. 939.

220. DANGERS OF SELF-GRATIFICATION

"The great threat against family life is the menacing rising tide of self-gratification, the modern pleasure mania. The prime incentive to marriage used to be economic; sex attraction was secondary. Marriage, founded on self-maintenance, led to self-perpetuation and concomitantly provided one of the most desirable forms of self-gratification. It is the only institution of human society which embraces all three of the great incentives for living." P. 942.

"There is real danger in the combination of restlessness, curiosity, adventure, and pleasure-abandon characteristic of the post-Andite races. The hunger of the soul cannot be satisfied with physical pleasures; the love of home and children is not augmented by the unwise pursuit of pleasure. Though you exhaust the resources of art, color, sound, rhythm, music, and adornment of person, you cannot hope thereby to elevate the soul or to nourish the spirit. Vanity and fashion cannot minister to home building and child culture; pride and rivalry are powerless to enhance the survival qualities of succeeding generations." P. 942.

221. ENJOYING WHOLESOME PLEASURES

"Let man enjoy himself; let the human race find pleasure in a thousand and one ways; let evolutionary mankind explore all forms of legitimate self-gratification, the fruits of the long upward biologic struggle. Man has well earned some of his present-day joys and pleasures. But look you well to the goal of destiny! Pleasures are indeed suicidal if they succeed in destroying property, which has become the institution of self-maintenance; and self-gratifications have indeed cost a fatal price if they bring about the collapse of marriage, the decadence of family life, and the destruction of the home—man's supreme evolutionary acquirement and civilization's only hope of survival." P. 943.

222. MISSION OF PRIMITIVE RELIGION

"Primitive religion prepared the soil of the human mind, by the powerful and awesome force of false fear, for the bestowal of a bona fide spiritual force of supernatural origin, the Thought Adjuster. And the divine Adjusters have ever since labored to transmute God-fear into God-love. Evolution may be slow, but it is unerringly effective." P. 957.

223. MAGIC, THE COCOON OF SCIENCE

"Ancient magic was the cocoon of modern science, indispensable in its time but now no longer useful. And so the phantasms of ignorant superstition agitated the primitive minds of men until the concepts of science could be born. Today, Urantia is in the twilight zone of this intellectual evolution. One half the world is grasping eagerly for the light of truth and the facts of scientific discovery, while the other half languishes in the arms of ancient superstition and but thinly disguised magic." P. 973.

224. SIN REDEFINED

"*Sin must be redefined as deliberate disloyalty to Deity.* There are degrees of disloyalty: the partial loyalty of indecision; the divided loyalty of confliction; the dying loyalty of indifference; and the death of loyalty exhibited in devotion to godless ideals.

"The sense or feeling of guilt is the consciousness of the violation of the mores; it is not necessarily sin. There is no real sin in the absence of conscious disloyalty to Deity." P. 984. **1 John 3:4.**

225. FORGIVENESS OF SIN

"The forgiveness of sin by Deity is the renewal of loyalty relations following a period of the human consciousness of the lapse of such relations as the consequence of conscious rebellion. The forgiveness does not have to be sought, only received as the consciousness of re-establishment of loyalty relations between the creature and the Creator. And all the loyal sons of God are happy, service-loving, and ever-progressive in the Paradise ascent." *P. 985*.

226. EVOLUTION ACHIEVES ITS END

"Evolution unerringly achieves its end: It imbues man with that superstitious fear of the unknown and dread of the unseen which is the scaffolding for the God concept. And having witnessed the birth of an advanced comprehension of Deity, through the co-ordinate action of revelation, this same technique of evolution then unerringly sets in motion those forces of thought which will inexorably obliterate the scaffolding, which has served its purpose." *P. 990*.

227. PRAYER AND THE ALTER EGO

"Enlightened prayer must recognize not only an external and personal God but also an internal and impersonal Divinity, the indwelling Adjuster. It is altogether fitting that man, when he prays, should strive to grasp the concept of the Universal Father on Paradise; but the more effective technique for most practical purposes will be to revert to the concept of a near-by alter ego, just as the primitive mind was wont to do, and then to recognize that the idea of this alter ego has evolved from a mere fiction to the truth of God's indwelling mortal man in the factual presence of the Adjuster so that man can talk face to face, as it were, with a real and genuine and divine alter ego that indwells him and is the very presence and essence of the living God, the Universal Father." *P. 997*.

228. PRAYER DOES NOT CHANGE GOD

"Remember, even if prayer does not change God, it very often effects great and lasting changes in the one who prays in faith and confident expectation. Prayer has been the ancestor of much peace of mind, cheerfulness, calmness, courage, self-mastery, and fair-mindedness in the men and women of the evolving races." *P. 998*.

229. PRAYER AND CIVILIZATION

"Do not be so slothful as to ask God to solve your difficulties, but never hesitate to ask him for wisdom and spiritual strength to guide and sustain you while you yourself resolutely and courageously attack the problems at hand.

"Prayer has been an indispensable factor in the progress and preservation of religious civilization, and it still has mighty contributions to make to the further enhancement and spiritualization of society if those who pray will only do so in the light of scientific facts, philosophic wisdom, intellectual sincerity, and spiritual faith. Pray as Jesus taught his disciples—honestly, unselfishly, with fairness, and without doubting." *P. 999.*

230. THOUGHTS ABOUT PRAYING

"But real praying does attain reality. Even when the air currents are ascending, no bird can soar except by outstretched wings. Prayer elevates man because it is a technique of progressing by the utilization of the ascending spiritual currents of the universe.

"Genuine prayer adds to spiritual growth, modifies attitudes, and yields that satisfaction which comes from communion with divinity. It is a spontaneous outburst of God-consciousness.

"God answers man's prayer by giving him an increased revelation of truth, an enhanced appreciation of beauty, and an augmented concept of goodness. Prayer is a subjective gesture, but it contacts with mighty objective realities on the spiritual levels of human experience; it is a meaningful reach by the human for superhuman values. It is the most potent spiritual-growth stimulus.

"Words are irrelevant to prayer; they are merely the intellectual channel in which the river of spiritual supplication may chance to flow. The word value of a prayer is purely autosuggestive in private devotions and sociosuggestive in group devotions. God answers the soul's attitude, not the words.

"Prayer is not a technique of escape from conflict but rather a stimulus to growth in the very face of conflict. Pray only for values, not things; for growth, not for gratification." *P. 1002.*

231. CONDITIONS OF EFFECTIVE PRAYER

"If you would engage in effective praying, you should bear in mind the laws of prevailing petitions:

"1. You must qualify as a potent prayer by sincerely and courageously facing the problems of universe reality. You must possess cosmic stamina.

"2. You must have honestly exhausted the human capacity for human adjustment. You must have been industrious.

"3. You must surrender every wish of mind and every craving of soul to the transforming embrace of spiritual growth. You must have experienced an enhancement of meanings and an elevation of values.

"4. You must make a wholehearted choice of the divine will. You must obliterate the dead center of indecision.

"5. You not only recognize the Father's will and choose to do it, but you have effected an unqualified consecration, and a dynamic dedication, to the actual doing of the Father's will.

"6. Your prayer will be directed exclusively for divine wisdom to solve the specific human problems encountered in the Paradise ascension—the attainment of divine perfection.

"7. And you must have faith—living faith." *P. 1002*.

232. PRIMITIVE RELIGION AND CIVILIZATION

"Religion facilitated the accumulation of capital; it fostered work of certain kinds; the leisure of the priests promoted art and knowledge; the race, in the end, gained much as a result of all these early errors in ethical technique. The shamans, honest and dishonest, were terribly expensive, but they were worth all they cost. The learned professions and science itself emerged from the parasitical priesthoods. Religion fostered civilization and provided societal continuity; it has been the moral police force of all time. Religion provided that human discipline and self-control which made *wisdom* possible. Religion is the efficient scourge of evolution which ruthlessly drives indolent and suffering humanity from its natural state of intellectual inertia forward and upward to the higher levels of reason and wisdom." *P. 1006*.

233. THE URANTIA REVELATION

"...The papers, of which this is one, constitute the most recent presentation of truth to the mortals of Urantia. These papers differ from all previous revelations, for they are not the work of a single universe personality but a composite presentation by many beings. But no revelation short of the attainment of the Universal Father can ever be complete. All other celestial ministrations are no more than partial, transient, and practically adapted to local conditions in time and space. While such admissions as this may possibly detract from the immediate force and authority of all revelations, the time has arrived on Urantia when it is advisable to make such frank statements, even at the risk of weakening the future influence and authority of this, the most recent of the revelations of truth to the mortal races of Urantia." *P. 1008*.

234. THE SAGE OF SALEM

"It was 1,973 years before the birth of Jesus that Machiventa was bestowed upon the human races of Urantia. His coming was unspectacular; his materialization was not witnessed by human eyes. He was first observed by mortal man on that eventful day when he entered the tent of Amdon, a Chaldean herder of Sumerian extraction. And the proclamation of his mission was embodied in the simple statement which he made to this shepherd, 'I am Melchizedek, priest of El Elyon, the Most High, the one and only God.'" *P. 1015.*

"In personal appearance, Melchizedek resembled the then blended Nodite and Sumerian peoples, being almost six feet in height and possessing a commanding presence. He spoke Chaldean and a half dozen other languages. He dressed much as did the Canaanite priests except that on his breast he wore an emblem of three concentric circles, the Satania symbol of the Paradise Trinity. In the course of his ministry this insignia of three concentric circles became regarded as so sacred by his followers that they never dared to use it, and it was soon forgotten with the passing of a few generations." *P. 1015.*

"This incarnated Melchizedek received a Thought Adjuster, who indwelt his superhuman personality as the monitor of time and the mentor of the flesh, thus gaining that experience and practical introduction to Urantian problems and to the technique of indwelling an incarnated Son which enabled this spirit of the Father to function so valiantly in the human mind of the later Son of God, Michael, when he appeared on earth in the likeness of mortal flesh. And this is the only Thought Adjuster who ever functioned in two minds on Urantia, but both minds were divine as well as human." *P. 1016.*

235. THE SALEM RELIGION

"Melchizedek taught that at some future time another Son of God would come in the flesh as he had come, but that he would be born of a woman; and that is why numerous later teachers held that Jesus was a priest, or minister, 'forever after the order of Melchizedek.'

"And thus did Melchizedek prepare the way and set the monotheistic stage of world tendency for the bestowal of an actual Paradise Son of the one God, whom he so vividly portrayed as the Father of all, and whom he represented to Abraham as a God who would accept man on the simple terms of personal faith. And Michael, when he appeared on earth, confirmed all that Melchizedek had taught concerning the Paradise Father.

"The ceremonies of the Salem worship were very simple. Every person who signed or marked the clay-tablet rolls of the Melchizedek church committed to memory, and subscribed to, the following belief:

"1. I believe in El Elyon, the Most High God, the only Universal Father and Creator of all things.

"2. I accept the Melchizedek covenant with the Most High, which bestows the favor of God on my faith, not on sacrifices and burnt offerings.

"3. I promise to obey the seven commandments of Melchizedek and to tell the good news of this covenant with the Most High to all men.

"And that was the whole of the creed of the Salem colony. But even such a short and simple declaration of faith was altogether too much and too advanced for the men of those days. They simply could not grasp the idea of getting divine favor for nothing—by faith. They were too deeply confirmed in the belief that man was born under forfeit to the gods. Too long and too earnestly had they sacrificed and made gifts to the priests to be able to comprehend the good news that salvation, divine favor, was a free gift to all who would believe in the Melchizedek covenant. But Abraham did believe halfheartedly, and even that was 'counted for righteousness.'

"The seven commandments promulgated by Melchizedek were patterned along the lines of the ancient Dalamatian supreme law and very much resembled the seven commands taught in the first and second Edens. These commands of the Salem religion were:

"1. You shall not serve any God but the Most High Creator of heaven and earth.

"2. You shall not doubt that faith is the only requirement for eternal salvation.

"3. You shall not bear false witness.

"4. You shall not kill.

"5. You shall not steal.

"6. You shall not commit adultery.

"7. You shall not show disrespect for your parents and elders." *Pp. 1017-8*.

236. MELCHIZEDEK AND ABRAHAM

"And Melchizedek made a formal covenant with Abraham at Salem. Said he to Abraham: "Look now up to the heavens and number the stars if you are able; so numerous shall your seed be.' And Abraham believed Melchizedek, 'and it was counted to him for righteousness.' And then Melchizedek told Abraham the story of the future occupation of Canaan by his offspring after their sojourn in Egypt.

"This covenant of Melchizedek with Abraham represents the great Urantian agreement between divinity and humanity whereby God agrees to do *everything*; man only agrees to *believe* God's promises and follow his instructions. Heretofore it had been believed that salvation could be secured only by

PART III: *The History of Urantia*

works—sacrifices and offerings; now, Melchizedek again brought to Urantia the good news that salvation, favor with God, is to be had by *faith*. But this gospel of simple faith in God was too advanced; the Semitic tribesmen subsequently preferred to go back to the older sacrifices and atonement for sin by the shedding of blood." *Pp. 1020-21*. **Gen. 22:16-18; 26:4,5.**

237. URANTIA IS WAITING FOR MICHAEL'S MESSAGE

"All Urantia is waiting for the proclamation of the ennobling message of Michael, unencumbered by the accumulated doctrines and dogmas of nineteen centuries of contact with the religions of evolutionary origin. The hour is striking for presenting to Buddhism, to Christianity, to Hinduism, even to the peoples of all faiths, not the gospel about Jesus, but the living, spiritual reality of the gospel of Jesus." *P. 1041.*

238. MISTAKES OF MELCHIZEDEK MISSIONARIES

"Melchizedek had warned his followers to teach about the one God, the Father and Maker of all, and to preach only the gospel of divine favor through faith alone. But it has often been the error of the teachers of new truth to attempt too much, to attempt to supplant slow evolution by sudden revolution. The Melchizedek missionaries in Mesopotamia raised a moral standard too high for the people; they attempted too much, and their noble cause went down in defeat. They had been commissioned to preach a definite gospel, to proclaim the truth of the reality of the Universal Father, but they became entangled in the apparently worthy cause of reforming the mores, and thus was their great mission sidetracked and virtually lost in frustration and oblivion." *P. 1043.*

239. MOSES AND IKHNATON

"Moses, the greatest character between Melchizedek and Jesus, was the joint gift to the world of the Hebrew race and the Egyptian royal family; and had Ikhnaton possessed the versatility and ability of Moses, had he manifested a political genius to match his surprising religious leadership, then would Egypt have become the great monotheistic nation of that age; and if this had happened, it is barely possible that Jesus might have lived the greater portion of his mortal life in Egypt.

"Never in all history did any king so methodically proceed to swing a whole nation from polytheism to monotheism as did this extraordinary Ikhnaton. With the most amazing determination this young ruler broke with the past, changed his name, abandoned his capital, built an entirely new city, and created a new art and literature for a whole people. But he went too fast; he built too much, more than could stand when he had gone. Again, he failed to provide for the material stability and prosperity of his people, all of which reacted unfavorably against his religious teachings when the subsequent floods of adversity and oppression swept over the Egyptians." *P. 1047.*

240. THE MATCHLESS MOSES

"The beginning of the evolution of the Hebraic concepts and ideals of a Supreme Creator dates from the departure of the Semites from Egypt under that great leader, teacher, and organizer, Moses. His mother was of the royal family of Egypt; his father was a Semitic liaison officer between the government and the Bedouin captives. Moses thus possessed qualities derived from superior racial sources; his ancestry was so highly blended that it is impossible to classify him in any one racial group. Had he not been of this mixed type, he would never have displayed that unusual versatility and adaptability which enabled him to manage the diversified horde which eventually became associated with those Bedouin Semites who fled from Egypt to the Arabian desert under his leadership.

"Despite the enticements of the culture of the Nile kingdom, Moses elected to cast his lot with the people of his father. At the time this great organizer was formulating his plans for the eventual freeing of his father's people, the Bedouin captives hardly had a religion worthy of the name; they were virtually without a true concept of God and without hope in the world.

"No leader ever undertook to reform and uplift a more forlorn, downcast, dejected, and ignorant group of human beings. But these slaves carried latent possibilities of development in their hereditary strains, and there were a sufficient number of educated leaders who had been coached by Moses in preparation for the day of revolt and the strike for liberty to constitute a corps of efficient organizers. These superior men had been employed as native overseers of their people; they had received some education because of Moses' influence with the Egyptian rulers." *P. 1055.*

"Under the teachings of Moses this tribal nature god, Yahweh, became the Lord God of Israel, who followed them through the wilderness and even into exile, where he presently was conceived of as the God of all peoples. The later captivity that enslaved the Jews in Babylon finally liberated the evolving concept of Yahweh to assume the monotheistic role of the God of all nations. "The most unique and amazing feature of the religious history of the Hebrews concerns this continuous evolution of the concept of Deity from the primitive god of Mount Horeb up through the teachings of their successive spiritual leaders to the high level of development depicted in the Deity doctrines of the Isaiahs, who proclaimed that magnificent concept of the loving and merciful Creator Father.

"Moses was an extraordinary combination of military leader, social organizer, and religious teacher. He was the most important individual world teacher and leader between the times of Machiventa and Jesus. Moses attempted to introduce many reforms in Israel of which there is no record. In the space of one man's life he led the polyglot horde of so-called Hebrews out of slavery and uncivilized roaming while he laid the foundation for the subsequent birth of a nation and the perpetuation of a race." P. 1057.

241. THE BOOK OF PSALMS

"The Psalms are the work of a score or more of authors; many were written by Egyptian and Mesopotamian teachers. During these times when the Levant worshiped nature gods, there were still a goodly number who believed in the supremacy of El Elyon, the Most High.

"No collection of religious writings gives expression to such a wealth of devotion and inspirational ideas of God as the Book of Psalms. And it would be very helpful if, in the perusal of this wonderful collection of worshipful literature, consideration could be given to the source and chronology of each separate hymn of praise and adoration, bearing in mind that no other single collection covers such a great range of time. This Book of Psalms is the record of the varying concepts of God entertained by the believers of the Salem religion throughout the Levant and embraces the entire period from Amenemope to Isaiah. In the Psalms God is depicted in all phases of conception, from the crude idea of a tribal deity to the vastly expanded ideal of the later Hebrews, wherein Yahweh is pictured as a loving ruler and merciful Father.

"And when thus regarded, this group of Psalms constitutes the most valuable and helpful assortment of devotional sentiments ever assembled by man up to the times of the twentieth century. The worshipful spirit of this collection of hymns transcends that of all other sacred books of the world." P. 1060.

242. THE PROPHET SAMUEL

"Samuel was a rough-and-ready type of man, a practical reformer who could go out in one day with his associates and overthrow a score of Baal sites. The progress he made was by sheer force of compulsion; he did little preaching, less teaching, but he did act. One day he was mocking the priest of Baal; the next, chopping in pieces a captive king. He devotedly believed in the one God, and he had a clear concept of that one God as creator of heaven and earth: 'The pillars of the earth are the Lord's, and he has set the world upon them.'" P. 1062.

"And he preached anew the story of God's sincerity, his convenant-keeping reliability. Said Samuel: 'The Lord will not forsake his people.' 'He has made with us an everlasting covenant, ordered in all things and sure.' And so, throughout all Palestine there sounded the call back to the worship of the supreme Yahweh. Ever this energetic teacher proclaimed, 'You are great, O Lord God, for there is none like you, neither is there any God beside you.'" P. 1063. **1 Sam. 2:8; 12:22. 2 Sam. 23:5; 7:22.**

243. AMOS AND HOSEA

"Amos proclaimed Yahweh the 'God of all nations' and warned the Israelites that ritual must not take the place of righteousness. And before this courageous teacher was stoned to death, he had spread enough leaven of truth to save the doctrine of the supreme Yahweh; he had insured the further evolution of the Melchizedek revelation.

"Hosea followed Amos and his doctrine of a universal God of justice by the resurrection of the Mosaic concept of a God of love. Hosea preached forgiveness through repentance, not by sacrifice. He proclaimed a gospel of loving-kindness and divine mercy, saying: 'I will betroth you to me forever; yes, I will betroth you to me in righteousness and judgment and in loving-kindness and in mercies. I will even betroth you to me in faithfulness.' 'I will love them freely, for my anger is turned away.'" P. 1066. **Hos. 2:19,20; 14:4.**

244. ISAIAH THE SECOND

"No prophet or religious teacher from Machiventa to the time of Jesus attained the high concept of God that Isaiah the second proclaimed during these days of the captivity. It was no small, anthropomorphic, man-made God that this spiritual leader proclaimed. 'Behold he takes up the isles as a very little thing.' 'And as the heavens are higher than the earth, so are my ways higher than your ways and my thoughts higher than your thoughts.'" P. 1068.

"This Isaiah conducted a far-flung propaganda of the gospel of the enlarging concept of a supreme Yahweh. He vied with Moses in the eloquence with which he portrayed the Lord God of Israel as the Universal Creator. He was poetic in his portrayal of the infinite attributes of the Universal Father. No more beautiful pronouncements about the heavenly Father have ever been made. Like the Psalms, the writings of Isaiah are among the most sublime and true presentations of the spiritual concept of God ever to greet the ears of mortal man prior to the arrival of Michael on Urantia. Listen to his portrayal of Deity: 'I am the high and lofty one who inhabits eternity.' 'I am the first and the last, and beside me there is no other God.' 'And the Lord's hand is not shortened that it cannot save, neither his ear heavy that it cannot hear.' And it was a new doctrine in Jewry when this benign but commanding prophet persisted in the preachment of divine constancy, God's faithfulness. He declared that 'God would not forget, would not forsake.'" P. 1069. **Isa, 40:15; 55:9; 57:15; 44:6; 50:2; 49:15.**

245. PURPOSE OF CHRIST'S BESTOWAL

"A Creator Son did not incarnate in the likeness of mortal flesh and bestow himself upon the humanity of Urantia to reconcile an angry God but rather to win all mankind to the recognition of the Father's love and to the realization of their sonship with God. After all, even the great advocate of the atonement doctrine realized something of this truth, for he declared that 'God was in Christ reconciling the world to himself.'" *P. 1083.* **2 Cor. 5:19.**

246. RELIGION AND SOCIAL RECONSTRUCTION

"But religion should not be directly concerned either with the creation of new social orders or with the preservation of old ones. True religion does oppose violence as a technique of social evolution, but it does not oppose the intelligent efforts of society to adapt its usages and adjust its institutions to new economic conditions and cultural requirements." *P. 1086.*

"Religion must become a forceful influence for moral stability and spiritual progression functioning dynamically in the midst of these ever-changing conditions and never-ending economic adjustments.

"Urantia society can never hope to settle down as in past ages. The social ship has steamed out of the sheltered bays of established tradition and has begun its cruise upon the high seas of evolutionary destiny; and the soul of man, as never before in the world's history, needs carefully to scrutinize its charts of morality and painstakingly to observe the compass of religious guidance. The paramount mission of religion as a social influence is to stabilize the ideals of mankind during these dangerous times of transition from one phase of civilization to another, from one level of culture to another." *P. 1086.*

247. INSTITUTIONAL RELIGION

"Institutional religion is now caught in the stalemate of a vicious circle. It cannot reconstruct society without first reconstructing itself; and being so much an integral part of the established order, it cannot reconstruct itself until society has been radically reconstructed.

"Religionists must function in society, in industry, and in politics as *individuals*, not as groups, parties, or institutions. A religious group which presumes to function as such, apart from religious activities, immediately becomes a political party, an economic organization, or a social institution. Religious collectivism must confine its efforts to the furtherance of religious causes." *P. 1087.*

"Modern religion finds it difficult to adjust its attitude toward the rapidly shifting social changes only because it has permitted itself to become so thoroughly traditionalized, dogmatized, and institutionalized. The religion of living experience finds no difficulty in keeping ahead of all these social developments and economic upheavals, amid which it ever functions as a moral stabilizer, social guide, and spiritual pilot. True religion carries over from one age to another the worthwhile culture and that wisdom which is born of the experience of *knowing God and striving to be like him.*" P. 1088.

248. RELIGION AND THE RELIGIONIST

"Early Christianity was entirely free from all civil entanglements, social commitments, and economic alliances. Only did later institutionalized Christianity become an organic part of the political and social structure of Occidental civilization.

"The kingdom of heaven is neither a social nor economic order; it is an exclusively spiritual brotherhood of God-knowing individuals. True, such a brotherhood is in itself a new and amazing social phenomenon attended by astounding political and economic repercussions." P. 1088.

"Religionists, as a group, must never concern themselves with anything but *religion*, albeit any one such religionist, as an individual citizen, may become the outstanding leader of some social, economic, or political reconstruction movement.

"It is the business of religion to create, sustain, and inspire such a cosmic loyalty in the individual citizen as will direct him to the achievement of success in the advancement of all these difficult but desirable social services." P. 1089.

"Genuine religion renders the religionist socially fragrant and creates insights into human fellowship. But the formalization of religious groups many times destroys the very values for the promotion of which the group was organized. Human friendship and divine religion are mutually helpful and significantly illuminating if the growth in each is equalized and harmonized. Religion puts new meaning into all group associations—families, schools, and clubs. It imparts new values to play and exalts all true humor.

"Social leadership is transformed by spiritual insight; religion prevents all collective movements from losing sight of their true objectives. Together with children, religion is the great unifier of family life, provided it is a living and growing faith. Family life cannot be had without children; it can be lived without religion, but such a handicap enormously multiplies the difficulties of this intimate human association. During the early decades of the twentieth century, family life, next to personal religious experience, suffers most from the decadence consequent upon the transition from old religious loyalties to the emerging new meanings and values.

"True religion is a meaningful way of living dynamically face to face with the commonplace realties of everyday life. But if religion is to stimulate individual development of character and augment integration of personality, it must not be standardized. If it is to stimulate evaluation of experience and serve as a value-lure, it must not be stereotyped. If religion is to promote supreme loyalties, it must not be formalized.

"No matter what upheavals may attend the social and economic growth of civilization, religion is genuine and worth while if it fosters in the individual an experience in which the sovereignty of truth, beauty, and goodness prevails, for such is the true spiritual concept of supreme reality. And through love and worship this becomes meaningful as fellowship with man and sonship with God." *P. 1089.*

249. SECTARIANISM

"Sectarianism is a disease of institutional religion, and dogmatism is an enslavement of the spiritual nature. It is far better to have a religion without a church than a church without religion. The religious turmoil of the twentieth century does not, in and of itself, betoken spiritual decadence. Confusion goes before growth as well as before destruction." *P. 1092.*

"But as religion becomes institutionalized, its power for good is curtailed, while the possibilities for evil are greatly multiplied. The dangers of formalized religion are: fixation of beliefs and crystallization of sentiments; accumulation of vested interests with increase of secularization; tendency to standardize and fossilize truth; diversion of religion from the service of God to the service of the church; inclination of leaders to become administrators instead of ministers; tendency to form sects and competitive divisions; establishment of oppressive ecclesiastical authority; creation of the aristocratic 'chosen-people' attitude; fostering of false and exaggerated ideas of sacredness; the routinizing of religion and the petrification of worship; tendency to venerate the past while ignoring present demands; failure to make up-to-date interpretations of religion; entanglement with functions of secular institutions; it creates the evil discrimination of religious castes; it becomes an intolerant judge of orthodoxy; it fails to hold the interest of adventurous youth and gradually loses the saving message of the gospel of eternal salvation." *P. 1092.*

250. RELIGIOUS GROWTH

"The experience of dynamic religious living transforms the mediocre individual into a personality of idealistic power. Religion ministers to the progress of all through fostering the progress of each individual, and the progress of each is augmented through the achievement of all.

"Spiritual growth is mutually stimulated by intimate association with other religionists. Love supplies the soil for religious growth—an objective lure in the place of subjective gratification—yet it yields the supreme subjective satisfaction. And religion ennobles the commonplace drudgery of daily living." *P. 1094.*

"Give every developing child a chance to grow his own religious experience; do not force a ready-made adult experience upon him. Remember, year-by-year progress through an established educational regime does not necessarily mean intellectual progress, much less spiritual growth. Enlargement of vocabulary does not signify development of character. Growth is not truly indicated by mere products but rather by progress. Real educational growth is indicated by enhancement of ideals, increased appreciation of values, new meanings of values, and augmented loyalty to supreme values." *P. 1094.*

"Spiritual growth is first an awakening to needs, next a discernment of meanings, and then a discovery of values. The evidence of true spiritual development consists in the exhibition of a human personality motivated by love, activated by unselfish ministry, and dominated by the wholehearted worship of the perfection ideals of divinity. And this entire experience constitutes the reality of religion as contrasted with mere theological beliefs." *P. 1095.*

251. THE BELIEVER'S SURETY

"Jesus portrayed the profound surety of the God-knowing mortal when he said: 'To a God-knowing kingdom believer, what does it matter if all things earthly crash?' Temporal securities are vulnerable, but spiritual sureties are impregnable. When the flood tides of human adversity, selfishness, cruelty, hate, malice, and jealousy beat about the mortal soul, you may rest in the assurance that there is one inner bastion, the citadel of the spirit, which is absolutely unassailable; at least this is true of every human being who has dedicated the keeping of his soul to the indwelling spirit of the eternal God.

"After such spiritual attainment, whether secured by gradual growth or specific crisis, there occurs a new orientation of personality as well as the development of a new standard of values. Such spirit-born individuals are so remotivated in life that they can calmly stand by while their fondest ambitions perish and their keenest hopes crash; they positively know that such catastrophes are but the redirecting cataclysms which wreck one's temporal creations preliminary to the rearing of the more noble and enduring realities of a new and more sublime level of universe attainment." P. 1096.

252. PROBLEMS OF SPIRITUAL GROWTH

"Man cannot cause growth, but he can supply favorable conditions. Growth is always unconscious, be it physical, intellectual, or spiritual. Love thus grows; it cannot be created, manufactured, or purchased; it must grow. Evolution is a cosmic technique of growth. Social growth cannot be secured by legislation, and moral growth is not had by improved administration. Man may manufacture a machine, but its real value must be derived from human culture and personal appreciation. Man's sole contribution to growth is the mobilization of the total powers of his personality—living faith.

"Religious living is devoted living, and devoted living is creative living, original and spontaneous. New religious insights arise out of conflicts which initiate the choosing of new and better reaction habits in the place of older and inferior reaction patterns. New meanings only emerge amid conflict; and conflict persists only in the face of refusal to espouse the higher values connoted in superior meanings.

"Religious perplexities are inevitable; there can be no growth without psychic conflict and spiritual agitation. The organization of a philosophic standard of living entails considerable commotion in the philosophic realms of the mind. Loyalties are not exercised in behalf of the great, the good, the true, and the noble without a struggle. Effort is attendant upon clarification of spiritual vision and enhancement of cosmic insight. And the human intellect protests against being weaned from subsisting upon the nonspiritual energies of temporal existence. The slothful animal mind rebels at the effort required to wrestle with cosmic problem solving.

"But the great problem of religious living consists in the task of unifying the soul powers of the personality by the dominance of LOVE. Health, mental efficiency, and happiness arise from the unification of physical systems, mind systems, and spirit systems. Of health and sanity man understands much, but of happiness he has truly realized very little. The highest happiness is indissolubly linked with spiritual progress. Spiritual growth yields lasting joy, peace which passes all understanding." P. 1097-8.

253. MARKS OF RELIGIOUS LIVING

"The marks of human response to the religious impulse embrace the qualities of nobility and grandeur. The sincere religionist is conscious of universe citizenship and is aware of making contact with sources of superhuman power. He is thrilled and energized with the assurance of belonging to a superior and ennobled fellowship of the sons of God. The consciousness of self-worth has become augmented by the stimulus of the quest for the highest universe objectives—supreme goals.

"The self has surrendered to the intriguing drive of an all-encompassing motivation which imposes heightened self-discipline, lessens emotional conflict, and makes mortal life truly worth living. The morbid recognition of human limitations is changed to the natural consciousness of mortal shortcomings, associated with moral determination and spiritual aspiration to attain the highest universe and superuniverse goals. And this intense striving for the attainment of supermortal ideals is always characterized by increasing patience, forbearance, fortitude, and tolerance.

"But true religion is a living love, a life of service. The religionist's detachment from much that is purely temporal and trivial never leads to social isolation, and it should not destroy the sense of humor. Genuine religion takes nothing away from human existence, but it does add new meanings to all of life; it generates new types of enthusiasm, zeal, and courage. It may even engender the spirit of the crusader, which is more than dangerous if not controlled by spiritual insight and loyal devotion to the common place social obligations of human loyalties.

"One of the most amazing earmarks of religious living is that dynamic and sublime peace, that peace which passes all human understanding, that cosmic poise which betokens the absence of all doubt and turmoil. Such levels of spiritual stability are immune to disappointment. Such religionists are like the Apostle Paul, who said: 'I am persuaded that neither death, nor life, nor angels, nor principalities, nor powers, nor things present, nor things to come, nor height, nor depth, nor anything else shall be able to separate us from the love of God.'

"There is a sense of security, associated with the realization of triumphing glory, resident in the consciousness of the religionist who has grasped the reality of the Supreme, and who pursues the goal of the Ultimate." *P. 1100-1.*

254. JESUS' RELIGIOUS EXPERIENCE

"Of Jesus it was truly said, 'He trusted God.' As a man among men he most sublimely trusted the Father in heaven. He trusted his Father as a little child trusts his earthly parent. His faith was perfect but never presumptuous. No matter how cruel nature might appear to be or how indifferent to man's welfare on earth, Jesus never faltered in his faith. He was immune to disappointment and impervious to persecution. He was untouched by apparent failure.

"He loved men as brothers, at the same time recognizing how they differed in innate endowments and acquired qualities. 'He went about doing good.'

"Jesus was an unusually cheerful person, but he was not a blind and unreasoning optimist. His constant word of exhortation was, 'Be of good cheer.' He could maintain this confident attitude because of his unswerving trust in God and his unshakable confidence in man. He was always touchingly considerate of all men because he loved them and believed in them. Still he was always true to his convictions and magnificently firm in his devotion to the doing of his Father's will.

"The Master was always generous. He never grew weary of saying, 'It is more blessed to give than to receive.' Said he, 'Freely you have received, freely give.' And yet, with all of his unbounded generosity, he was never wasteful or extravagant. He taught that you must believe to receive salvation. 'For every one who seeks shall receive.'

"He was candid, but always kind. Said he, 'If it were not so, I would have told you.' He was frank, but always friendly. He was outspoken in his love for the sinner and in his hatred for sin. But throughout all this amazing frankness he was unerringly *fair*.

"Jesus was consistently cheerful, notwithstanding he sometimes drank deeply of the cup of human sorrow. He fearlessly faced the realities of existence, yet was he filled with enthusiasm for the gospel of the kingdom. But he controlled his enthusiasm; it never controlled him. He was unreservedly dedicated to 'the Father's business.' This divine enthusiasm led his unspiritual brethren to think he was beside himself, but the onlooking universe appraised him as the model of sanity and the pattern of supreme mortal devotion to the high standards of spiritual living. And his controlled enthusiasm was contagious; his associates were constrained to share his divine optimism.

"This man of Galilee was not a man of sorrows; he was a soul of gladness. Always was he saying, 'Rejoice and be exceedingly glad.' But when duty required, he was willing to walk courageously through the 'valley of the shadow of death.' He was gladsome but at the same time humble.

"His courage was equaled only by his patience. When pressed to act prematurely, he would only reply, 'My hour has not yet come.' He was never in a hurry; his composure was sublime. But he was often indignant at evil, intolerant of sin. He was often mightily moved to resist that which was inimical to the welfare of his children on earth. But his indignation against sin never led to anger at the sinner.

"His courage was magnificent, but he was never foolhardy. His watchword was, '*Fear not*.' His bravery was lofty and his courage often heroic. But his courage was linked with discretion and controlled by reason. It was courage born of faith, not the recklessness of blind presumption. He was truly brave but never audacious.

"The Master was a pattern of reverence. The prayer of even his youth began, 'Our Father who is in heaven, hallowed be your name.' He was even respectful of the faulty worship of his fellows. But this did not deter him from making attacks on religious traditions or assaulting errors of human belief. He was reverential of true holiness, and yet he could justly appeal to his fellows, saying, 'Who among you convicts me of sin?'

"Jesus was great because he was good, and yet he fraternized with the little children. He was gentle and unassuming in his personal life, and yet he was the perfected man of a universe. His associates called him Master unbidden.

"Jesus was the perfectly unified human personality. And today, as in Galilee, he continues to unify mortal experience and to co-ordinate human endeavors. He unifies life, ennobles character, and simplifies experience. He enters the human mind to elevate, transform, and transfigure it. It is literally true: 'If any man has Christ Jesus within him, he is a new creature; old things are passing away; behold, all things are becoming new.'" *Pp. 1102-3.* **Act. 20:35; Matt. 10:8; John 14:2; Luke 11:10; Luke 2:49; Matt. 5:12; Ps. 23:4; John 2:4; Luke 12:7,32; Luke 11:2; John 8:46; 2 Cor. 5:17.**

255. THINKING VS. FEELING

"The divine spirit makes contact with mortal man, not by feelings or emotions, but in the realm of the highest and most spiritualized thinking. It is your *thoughts*, not your feelings, that lead you Godward. *The divine nature may be perceived only with the eyes of the mind.* But the mind that really discerns God, hears the indwelling Adjuster, is the pure mind. 'Without holiness no man may see the Lord.' All such inner and spiritual communion is termed spiritual insight. Such religious experiences result from the impress made upon the mind of man by the combined operations of the Adjuster and the Spirit of Truth as they function amid and upon the ideas, ideals, insights, and spirit strivings of the evolving sons of God.

"Religion lives and prospers, then, not by sight and feeling, but rather by faith and insight. It consists not in the discovery of new facts or in the finding of a unique experience, but rather in the discovery of new and spiritual *meanings* in facts already well known to mankind. The highest religious experience is not dependent on prior acts of belief, tradition, and authority; neither is religion the offspring of sublime feelings and purely mystical emotions. It is, rather, a profoundly deep and actual experience of spiritual communion with the spirit influences resident within the human mind, and as far as such an experience is definable in terms of psychology, it is simply the experience of experiencing the reality of believing in God as the reality of such a purely personal experience." *P. 1104-5*.

256. THE MARKS OF FAITH

"Through religious faith the soul of man reveals itself and demonstrates the potential divinity of its emerging nature by the characteristic manner in which it induces the mortal personality to react to certain trying intellectual and testing social situations. Genuine spiritual faith (true moral consciousness) is revealed in that it:

"1. Causes ethics and morals to progress despite inherent and adverse animalistic tendencies.

"2. Produces a sublime trust in the goodness of God even in the face of bitter disappointment and crushing defeat.

"3. Generates profound courage and confidence despite natural adversity and physical calamity.

"4. Exhibits inexplicable poise and sustaining tranquillity notwithstanding baffling diseases and even acute physical suffering.

"5. Maintains a mysterious poise and composure of personality in the face of maltreatment and the rankest injustice.

"6. Maintains a divine trust in ultimate victory in spite of the cruelties of seemingly blind fate and the apparent utter indifference of natural forces to human welfare.

"7. Persists in the unswerving belief in God despite all contrary demonstrations of logic and successfully withstands all other intellectual sophistries.

"8. Continues to exhibit undaunted faith in the soul's survival regardless of the deceptive teachings of false science and the persuasive delusions of unsound philosophy.

"9. Lives and triumphs irrespective of the crushing overload of the complex and partial civilizations of modern times.

"10. Contributes to the continued survival of altruism in spite of human selfishness, social antagonisms, industrial greeds, and political maladjustments.

"11. Steadfastly adheres to a sublime belief in universe unity and divine guidance regardless of the perplexing presence of evil and sin.

"12. Goes right on worshiping God in spite of anything and everything. Dares to declare, 'Even though he slay me, yet will I serve him.'" *P. 1108.*

257. FAITH VS. BELIEF

"Belief is always limiting and binding; faith is expanding and releasing. Belief fixates, faith liberates. But living religious faith is more than the association of noble beliefs; it is more than an exalted system of philosophy; it is a living experience concerned with spiritual meanings, divine ideals, and supreme values; it is God-knowing and man-serving. Beliefs may become group possessions, but faith must be personal. Theologic beliefs can be suggested to a group, but faith can rise up only in the heart of the individual religionist." *P. 1114.*

"Faith does not shackle the creative imagination, neither does it maintain an unreasoning prejudice toward the discoveries of scientific investigation. Faith vitalizes religion and constrains the religionist heroically to live the golden rule. The zeal of faith is according to knowledge, and its strivings are the preludes to sublime peace." *P. 1115.*

258. FROM DARKNESS TO LIGHT

"To the unbelieving materialist, man is simply an evolutionary accident. His hopes of survival are strung on a figment of mortal imagination; his fears, loves, longings, and beliefs are but the reaction of the incidental juxtaposition of certain lifeless atoms of matter. No display of energy nor expression of trust can carry him beyond the grave. The devotional labors and inspirational genius of the best of men are doomed to be extinguished by death, the long and lonely night of eternal oblivion and soul extinction. Nameless despair is man's only reward for living and toiling under the temporal sun of mortal existence. Each day of life slowly and surely tightens the grasp of a pitiless doom which a hostile and relentless universe of matter has decreed shall be the crowning insult to everything in human desire which is beautiful, noble, lofty, and good.

"But such is not man's end and eternal destiny; such a vision is but the cry of despair uttered by some wandering soul who has become lost in spiritual darkness, and who bravely struggles on in the face of the mechanistic sophistries of a material philosophy, blinded by the confusion and distortion of a complex learning. And all this doom of darkness and all this destiny of despair are forever dispelled by one brave stretch of faith on the part of the most humble and unlearned of God's children on earth.

"This saving faith has its birth in the human heart when the moral consciousness of man realizes that human values may be translated in mortal experience from the material to the spiritual, from the human to the divine, from time to eternity." *P. 1118.*

259. IN THE PRESENCE OF THE ETERNAL

"It is difficult to identify and analyze the factors of a religious experience, but it is not difficult to observe that such religious practitioners live and carry on as if already in the presence of the Eternal. Believers react to this temporal life as if immortality already were within their grasp. In the lives of such mortals there is a valid originality and a spontaneity of expression that forever segregate them from those of their fellows who have imbibed only the wisdom of the world. Religionists seem to live in effective emancipation from harrying haste and the painful stress of the vicissitudes inherent in the temporal currents of time; they exhibit a stabilization of personality and a tranquillity of character not explained by the laws of physiology, psychology, and sociology." *Pp. 1119-20.*

260. THE DISCOVERY OF GOD

"Religious desire is the hunger quest for divine reality. Religious experience is the realization of the consciousness of having found God. And when a human being does find God, there is experienced within the soul of that being such an indescribable restlessness of triumph in discovery that he is impelled to seek loving service-contact with his less illuminated fellows, not to disclose that he has found God, but rather to allow the overflow of the welling-up of eternal goodness within his own soul to refresh and ennoble his fellows. Real religion leads to increased social service." *P. 1121.*

261. KNOWING A GOD OF SALVATION

"The religionist of philosophic attainment has faith in a personal God of personal salvation, something more than a reality, a value, a level of achievement, an exalted process, a transmutation, the ultimate of time-space, an idealization, the personalization of energy, the entity of gravity, a human projection, the idealization of self, nature's upthrust, the inclination to goodness, the forward impulse of evolution, or a sublime hypothesis. The religionist has faith in a God of love. Love is the essence of religion and the wellspring of superior civilization.

"Faith transforms the philosophic God of probability into the saving God of certainty in the personal religious experience. Skepticism may challenge the theories of theology, but confidence in the dependability of personal experience affirms the truth of that belief which has grown into faith.

"Convictions about God may be arrived at through wise reasoning, but the individual becomes God-knowing only by faith, through personal experience. In much that pertains to life, probability must be reckoned with, but when contacting with cosmic reality, certainty may be experienced when such meanings and values are approached by living faith. The God-knowing soul dares to say, 'I know,' even when this knowledge of God is questioned by the unbeliever who denies such certitude because it is not wholly supported by intellectual logic. To every such doubter the believer only replies, 'How do you know that I do not know?'" *Pp. 1124-5*.

262. DIVERSE VIEWS OF GOD

"To science God is a possibility, to psychology a desirability, to philosophy a probability, to religion a certainty, an actuality of religious experience. Reason demands that a philosophy which cannot find the God of probability should be very respectful of that religious faith which can and does find the God of certitude. Neither should science discount religious experience on grounds of credulity, not so long as it persists in the assumption that man's intellectual and philosophic endowments emerged from increasingly lesser intelligences the further back they go, finally taking origin in primitive life which was utterly devoid of all thinking and feeling." *P. 1125*.

263. GONE ARE GUILT AND ISOLATION

"*Jesus swept away all of the ceremonials of* sacrifice and atonement. He destroyed the basis of all this fictitious guilt and sense of isolation in the universe by declaring that man is a child of God; the creature-Creator relationship was placed on a child-parent basis. God becomes a loving Father to his mortal sons and daughters. All ceremonials not a legitimate part of such an intimate family relationship are forever abrogated." *P. 1133*.

264. HOW WE GET OUR IDEALISM

"It is fatal to man's idealism when he is taught that all of his altruistic impulses are merely the development of his natural herd instincts. But he is ennobled and mightily energized when he learns that these higher urges of his soul emanate *from the spiritual forces that indwell his mortal mind*.

"It lifts man out of himself and beyond himself when he once fully realizes that there lives and strives within him something which is eternal and divine. And so it is that a living faith in the superhuman origin of our ideals validates our belief that we are the sons of God and makes real our altruistic convictions, the feelings of the brotherhood of man." *P. 1134*.

265. REASON AND FAITH

"*Reason* is the act of recognizing the conclusions of consciousness with regard to the experience in and with the physical world of energy and matter. *Faith* is the act of recognizing the validity of spiritual consciousness— something which is incapable of other mortal proof. *Logic* is the synthetic truth-seeking progression of the unity of faith and reason and is founded on the constitutive mind endowments of mortal beings, the innate recognition of things, meanings, and values." P. 1139.

"Although both science and philosophy may assume the probability of God by their reason and logic, only the personal religious experience of a spiritled man can affirm the certainty of such a supreme and personal Deity. By the technique of such an incarnation of living truth the philosophic hypothesis of the probability of God becomes a religious reality." P. 1140.

"Faith most willingly carries reason along as far as reason can go and then goes on with wisdom to the full philosophic limit; and then it dares to launch out upon the limitless and never-ending universe journey in the sole company of TRUTH." *P. 1141*.

266. THE TRANSCENDENCE OF RELIGIOUS EXPERIENCE

"There is a reality in religious experience that is proportional to the spiritual content, and such a reality is transcendent to reason, science, philosophy, wisdom, and all other human achievements. The convictions of such an experience are unassailable; the logic of religious living is incontrovertible; the certainty of such knowledge is superhuman; the satisfactions are superbly divine, the courage indomitable, the devotions unquestioning, the loyalties supreme, and the destinies final—eternal, ultimate, and universal." *P. 1142*.

267. HOW GOD LIVES WITHIN US

"Although the Universal Father is personally resident on Paradise, at the very center of the universes, he is also actually present on the worlds of space in the minds of his countless children of time, for he indwells them as the Mystery Monitors. The eternal Father is at one and the same time farthest removed from, and most intimately associated with, his planetary mortal sons.

"The Adjusters are the actuality of the Father's love incarnate in the souls of men; they are the veritable promise of man's eternal career imprisoned within the mortal mind; they are the essence of man's perfected finaliter personality, which he can foretaste in time as he progressively masters the divine technique of achieving the living of the Father's will, step by step, through the ascension of universe upon universe until he actually attains the divine presence of his Paradise Father." *P. 1176*.

268. THE DIVINE "PILOT LIGHT"

"There is a characteristic light, a spirit luminosity, which accompanies this divine presence, and which has become generally associated with Thought Adjusters. In the universe of Nebadon this Paradise luminosity is widespreadly known as the 'pilot light'; on Uversa it is called the 'light of life.' On Urantia this phenomenon has sometimes been referred to as that 'true light which lights every man who comes into the world.'" *P. 1181.* **John 1:9.**

269. THOUGHT ADJUSTERS AND HUMAN WILL

"Why then, if Thought Adjusters possess volition, are they subservient to the mortal will? We believe it is because Adjuster volition, though absolute in nature, is prepersonal in manifestation. Human will functions on the personality level of universe reality, and throughout the cosmos the impersonal—the nonpersonal, the subpersonal, and the prepersonal—is ever responsive to the will and acts of existent personality." *P. 1183.*

270. MISSION OF THOUGHT ADJUSTERS

"The mission of the Thought Adjusters to the human races is to represent, to be, the Universal Father to the mortal creatures of time and space; that is the fundamental work of the divine gifts. Their mission is also that of elevating the mortal minds and of translating the immortal souls of men up to the divine heights and spiritual levels of Paradise perfection. And in the experience of thus transforming the human nature of the temporal creature into the divine nature of the eternal finaliter, the Adjusters bring into existence a unique type of being, a being consisting in the eternal union of the perfect Adjuster and the perfected creature which it would be impossible to duplicate by any other universe technique." *P. 1185.*

271. TIME OF ADJUSTER TRANSIT

"When once the Adjusters are actually dispatched from Divinington, practically no time intervenes between that moment and the hour of their appearance in *the minds of their chosen subjects*. The average transit time of an Adjuster from Divinington to Urantia is 117 hours, 42 minutes, and 7 seconds. Virtually all of this time is occupied with registration on Uversa." *P. 1186.*

272. AGE AT THE ADJUSTER'S ARRIVAL

"Adjusters reach their human subjects on Urantia, on the average, just prior to the sixth birthday. In the present generation it is running five years, ten months, and four days; that is, on the 2,134th day of terrestrial life." *Pp. 1186-7.*

273. ADJUSTERS CONSERVE ALL TRUE VALUES

"What the Thought Adjuster cannot utilize in your present life, those truths which he cannot successfully transmit to the man of his betrothal, he will faithfully preserve for use in the next stage of existence, just as he now carries over from circle to circle those items which he fails to register in the experience of the human subject, owing to the creature's inability, or failure, to give a sufficient degree of co-operation.

"One thing you can depend upon: The Adjusters will never lose anything committed to their care; never have we known these spirit helpers to default. Angels and other high types of spirit beings, not excepting the local universe type of Sons, may occasionally embrace evil, may sometimes depart from the divine way, but Adjusters never falter. They are absolutely dependable, and this is equally true of all seven groups.

"Your Adjuster is the potential of your new and next order of existence, the advance bestowal of your eternal sonship with God. By and with the consent of your will, the Adjuster has the power to subject the creature trends of the material mind to the transforming actions of the motivations and purposes of the emerging morontial soul." *P. 1191*.

274. HOW THE ADJUSTERS HELP US

"The Mystery Monitors are not thought helpers; they are thought adjusters. They labor with the material mind for the purpose of constructing, by adjustment and spiritualization, a new mind for the new worlds and the new name of your future career. Their mission chiefly concerns the future life, not this life. They are called heavenly helpers, not earthly helpers. They are not interested in making the mortal career easy; rather are they concerned in making your life reasonably difficult and rugged, so that decisions will be stimulated and multiplied. The presence of a great Thought Adjuster does not bestow ease of living and freedom from strenuous thinking, *but such a divine gift should confer a sublime peace of mind* and a superb tranquillity of spirit.

"Your transient and ever-changing emotions of joy and sorrow are in the main purely human and material reactions to your internal psychic climate and to your external material environment. Do not, therefore, look to the Adjuster for selfish consolation and mortal comfort. It is the business of the Adjuster to *prepare you for the eternal adventure, to assure your survival*. It is not the mission of the Mystery Monitor to smooth your ruffled feelings or to minister to your injured pride; it is the preparation of your soul for the long ascending career that engages the attention and occupies the time of the Adjuster." *P. 1191-2*.

275. ADJUSTERS LIKE TO TALK WITH US

"The Adjusters are the eternal ancestors, the divine originals, of your evolving immortal souls; they are the unceasing urge that leads man to attempt the mastery of the material and present existence in the light of the spiritual and future career. The Monitors are the prisoners of undying hope, the founts of everlasting progression. And how they do enjoy communicating with their subjects in more or less direct channels! How they rejoice when they can dispense with symbols and other methods of indirection and flash their messages straight to the intellects of their human partners!" P. 1193.

276. TRIUMPHANT FAITH

"You humans have begun an endless unfolding of an almost infinite panorama, a limitless expanding of never-ending, ever-widening spheres of opportunity for exhilarating service, matchless adventure, sublime uncertainty, and boundless attainment. When the clouds gather overhead, your faith should accept the fact of the presence of the indwelling Adjuster, and thus you should be able to look beyond the mists of mortal uncertainty into the clear shining of the sun of eternal righteousness on the beckoning heights of the mansion worlds of Satania." P. 1194.

277. POSSIBILITY OF HEARING THE ADJUSTER

"It is sometimes possible to have the mind illuminated, to hear the divine voice that continually speaks within you, so that you may become partially conscious of the wisdom, truth, goodness, and beauty of the potential personality constantly indwelling you." P. 1199.

278. PERSONALIZED ADJUSTERS

"Personalized Adjusters are the all-wise and powerful executives of the Architects of the Master Universe. They are the personal agents of the full ministry of the Universal Father—personal, prepersonal, and superpersonal. They are the personal ministers of the extraordinary, the unusual, and the unexpected throughout all the realms of the transcendental absonite spheres of the domain of God the Ultimate, even to the levels of God the Absolute." P. 1201.

279. HOW THE ADJUSTERS WORK WITHIN US

"Adjusters should not be thought of as living in the material brains of human beings. They are not organic parts of the physical creatures of the realms. The Thought Adjuster may more properly be envisaged as indwelling the mortal mind of man rather than as existing within the confines of a single physical organ. And indirectly and unrecognized the Adjuster is constantly communicating with the human subject, especially during those sublime experiences of the worshipful contact of mind with spirit in the superconsciousness.

"I wish it were possible for me to help evolving mortals to achieve a better understanding and attain a fuller appreciation of the unselfish and superb work of the Adjusters living within them, who are so devoutly faithful to the task of fostering man's spiritual welfare. These Monitors are efficient ministers to the higher phases of men's minds; they are wise and experienced manipulators of the spiritual potential of the human intellect. These heavenly helpers are dedicated to the stupendous task of guiding you safely inward and upward to the celestial haven of happiness. These tireless toilers are consecrated to the future personification of the triumph of divine truth in your life everlasting. They are the watchful workers who pilot the God-conscious human mind away from the shoals of evil while expertly guiding the evolving soul of man toward the divine harbors of perfection on far-distant and eternal shores. The Adjusters are loving leaders, your safe and sure guides through the dark and uncertain mazes of your short earthly career; they are the patient teachers who so constantly urge their subjects forward in the paths of progressive perfection. They are the careful custodians of the sublime values of creature character. I wish you could love them more, co-operate with them more fully, and cherish them more affectionately." *P. 1203*.

280. CARE OF THE ADJUSTER'S EARTHLY TABERNACLE

"The Adjuster remains with you in all disaster and through every sickness which does not wholly destroy the mentality. But how unkind knowingly to defile or otherwise deliberately to pollute the physical body, which must serve as the earthly tabernacle of this marvelous gift from God. All physical poisons greatly retard the efforts of the Adjuster to exalt the material mind, while the mental poisons of fear, anger, envy, jealousy, suspicion, and intolerance likewise tremendously interfere with the spiritual progress of the evolving soul." *P. 1204*. **1 Cor. 3:17**.

281. THE SUPERB GAME OF THE AGES

"Adjusters are playing the sacred and superb game of the ages; they are engaged in one of the supreme adventures of time in space. And how happy they are when your co-operation permits them to lend assistance in your short struggles of time as they continue to prosecute their larger tasks of eternity. But usually, when your Adjuster attempts to communicate with you, the message is lost in the material currents of the energy streams of human mind; only occasionally do you catch an echo, a faint and distant echo, of the divine voice." *P. 1205*.

282. TOO MUCH THOUGHT ON THE TRIFLES OF LIVING

"I cannot but observe that so many of you spend so much time and thought on mere trifles of living, while you almost wholly overlook the more essential realities of everlasting import, those very accomplishments which are concerned with the development of a more harmonious working agreement between you and your Adjusters. *The great goal of human existence is to attune to the divinity of the indwelling Adjuster;* the great achievement of mortal life is the attainment of a true and understanding consecration to the eternal aims of the divine spirit who waits and works within your mind. But a devoted and determined effort to realize eternal destiny is wholly compatible with a light-hearted and joyous life and with a successful and honorable career on earth. Co-operation with the Thought Adjuster does not entail self-torture, mock piety, or hypocritical and ostentatious self-abasement; the ideal life is one of loving service rather than an existence of fearful apprehension." P. 1206.

283. HOW ADJUSTERS WORK WITH THE MIND

"The Thought Adjuster is engaged in a constant effort so to spiritualize your mind as to evolve your morontia soul; but you yourself are mostly unconscious of this inner ministry. You are quite incapable of distinguishing the product of your own material intellect from that of the conjoint activities of your soul and the Adjuster.

"Certain abrupt presentations of thoughts, conclusions, and other pictures of mind are sometimes the direct or indirect work of the Adjuster; but far more often they are the sudden emergence into consciousness of ideas which have been grouping themselves together in the submerged mental levels, natural and everyday occurrences of normal and ordinary psychic function inherent in the circuits of the evolving animal mind. (In contrast with these subconscious emanations, the revelations of the Adjuster appear through the realms of the superconscious.)

"Trust all matters of mind beyond the dead level of consciousness to the custody of the Adjusters. In due time, if not in this world then on the mansion worlds, they will give good account of their stewardship, and eventually will they bring forth those meanings and values intrusted to their care and keeping. They will resurrect every worthy treasure of the mortal mind if you survive." P. 1207.

284. RELATION OF ADJUSTER TO CONSCIENCE

"Do not confuse and confound the mission and influence of the Adjuster with what is commonly called conscience; they are not directly related. Conscience is a human and purely psychic reaction. It is not to be despised, but it is hardly the voice of God to the soul, which indeed the Adjuster's would be if such a voice could be heard. Conscience, rightly, admonishes you to do right; but the Adjuster, in addition, endeavors to tell you what truly is right; that is, when and as you are able to perceive the Monitor's leading." *Pp. 1207-8*.

285. INTELLECTUAL AND SPIRITUAL DEVELOPMENT

"When the development of the intellectual nature proceeds faster than that of the spiritual, such a situation renders communication with the Thought Adjuster both difficult and dangerous. Likewise, overspiritual development tends to produce a fanatical and perverted interpretation of the spirit leadings of the divine indweller. Lack of spiritual capacity makes it very difficult to transmit to such a material intellect the spiritual truths resident in the higher superconsciousness. It is to the mind of perfect poise, housed in a body of clean habits, stabilized neural energies, and balanced chemical function—when the physical, mental, and spiritual powers are in triune harmony of development—that a maximum of light and truth can be imparted with a minimum of temporal danger or risk to the real welfare of such a being. By such a balanced growth does man ascend the circles of planetary progression one by one, from the seventh to the first." *P. 1209*.

286. GREAT DAYS FOR THE ADJUSTER

"The great days in the individual careers of Adjusters are: first, when the human subject breaks through into the third psychic circle, thus insuring the Monitor's self-activity and increased range of function (provided the indweller was not already self-acting); then, when the human partner attains the first psychic circle, and they are thereby enabled to intercommunicate, at least to some degree; and last, when they are finally and eternally fused.

"The achievement of the seven cosmic circles does not equal Adjuster fusion. There are many mortals living on Urantia who have attained their circles; but fusion depends on yet other greater and more sublime spiritual achievements, upon the attainment of a final and complete attunement of the mortal will with the will of God as it is resident in the Thought Adjuster." *P. 1212*.

287. ADJUSTER SOUL PARTNERSHIP

"When the evolving soul and the divine Adjuster are finally and eternally fused, each gains all of the experiencible qualities of the other. This coordinate personality possesses all of the experiential memory of survival once held by the ancestral mortal mind and then resident in the morontia soul, and in addition thereto this potential finaliter embraces all the experiential memory of the Adjuster throughout the mortal indwellings of all time." *Pp. 1212-13.*

288. MESSAGE OF ADJUSTER TO ITS SOUL

"During the making and breaking of a contact between the mortal mind of a destiny reservist and the planetary supervisors, sometimes the indwelling Adjuster is so situated that it becomes possible to transmit a message to the mortal partner. Not long since, on Urantia, such a message was transmitted by a self-acting Adjuster to the human associate, a member of the reserve corps of destiny. This message was introduced by these words: 'And now, without injury or jeopardy to the subject of my solicitous devotion and without intent to overchastise or discourage, for me, make record of this my plea to him.' Then followed a beautifully touching and appealing admonition. Among other things, the Adjuster pleaded 'that he more faithfully give me his sincere co-operation, more cheerfully endure the tasks of my emplacement, more faithfully carry out the program of my arrangement, more patiently go through the trials of my selection, more persistently and cheerfully tread the path of my choosing, more humbly receive credit that may accrue as a result of my ceaseless endeavors—thus transmit my admonition to the man of my indwelling. Upon him I bestow the supreme devotion and affection of a divine spirit. And say further to my beloved subject that I will function with wisdom and power until the very end, until the last earth struggle is over; I will be true to my personality trust. And I exhort him to survival, not to disappoint me, not to deprive me of the reward of my patient and intense struggle. On the human will our achievement of personality depends. Circle by circle I have patiently ascended this human mind, and I have testimony that I am meeting the approval of the chief of my kind. Circle by circle I am passing on to judgment. I await with pleasure and without apprehension the roll call of destiny; I am prepared to submit all to the tribunals of the Ancients of Days.'" *Pp. 1213-14.*

PART III: *The History of Urantia*

289. THE MYSTERY OF THE EVOLVING SOUL

"The presence of the divine Adjuster in the human mind makes it forever impossible for either science or philosophy to attain a satisfactory comprehension of the evolving soul of the human personality. The morontia soul is the child of the universe and may be really known only through cosmic insight and spiritual discovery." P. 1215.

290. SCOPE OF THE MATERIAL MIND

"Material mind is the arena in which human personalities live, are selfconscious, make decisions, choose God or forsake him, eternalize or destroy themselves." P. 1216.

"Mind is the cosmic instrument on which the human will can play the discords of destruction, or upon which this same human will can bring forth the exquisite melodies of God identification and consequent eternal survival. The Adjuster bestowed upon man is, in the last analysis, impervious to evil and incapable of sin, but mortal mind can actually be twisted, distorted, and rendered evil and ugly by the sinful machinations of a perverse and self-seeking human will. Likewise can this mind be made noble, beautiful, true, and good—actually great—in accordance with the spirit-illuminated will of a God-knowing human being." P. 1217.

291. THE ADJUSTER IS OUR SHIP'S PILOT

"Mind is your ship, the Adjuster is your pilot, the human will is captain. The master of the mortal vessel should have the wisdom to trust the divine pilot to guide the ascending soul into the morontia harbors of eternal survival. Only by selfishness, slothfulness, and sinfulness can the will of man reject the guidance of such a loving pilot and eventually wreck the mortal career upon the evil shoals of rejected mercy and upon the rocks of embraced sin. With your consent, this faithful pilot will safely carry you across the barriers of time and the handicaps of space to the very source of the divine mind and on beyond, even to the Paradise Father of Adjusters." P. 1217.

292. VALUES OF THE INNER AND OUTER WORLDS

"The inner and the outer worlds have a different set of values. Any civilization is in jeopardy when three quarters of its youth enter materialistic professions and devote themselves to the pursuit of the sensory activities of the outer world. Civilization is in danger when youth neglect to interest themselves in ethics, sociology, eugenics, philosophy, the fine arts, religion, and cosmology.

"Only in the higher levels of the superconscious mind as it impinges upon the spirit realm of human experience can you find those higher concepts in association with effective master patterns which will contribute to the building of a better and more enduring civilization. Personality is inherently creative, but it thus functions only in the inner life of the individual.

"Snow crystals are always hexagonal in form, but no two are ever alike. Children conform to types, but no two are exactly alike, even in the case of twins. Personality follows types but is always unique.

"Happiness and joy take origin in the inner life. You cannot experience real joy all by yourself. A solitary life is fatal to happiness. Even families and nations will enjoy life more if they share it with others." P. 1220.

293. THE CONSECRATION OF WILL

"Such a creature choice is not a surrender of will. It is a consecration of will, an expansion of will, a glorification of will, a perfecting of will; and such choosing raises the creature will from the level of temporal significance to that higher estate wherein the personality of the creature son communes with the personality of the spirit Father." P. 1221.

294. CO-OPERATION WITH THE ADJUSTER

"May I admonish you to heed the distant echo of the Adjuster's faithful call to your soul? The indwelling Adjuster cannot stop or even materially alter your career struggle of time; the Adjuster cannot lessen the hardships of life as you journey on through this world of toil. The divine indweller can only patiently forbear while you fight the battle of life as it is lived on your planet; but you could, if you only would—as you work and worry, as you fight and toil—permit the valiant Adjuster to fight with you and for you. You could be so comforted and inspired, so enthralled and intrigued, if you would only allow the Adjuster constantly to bring forth the pictures of the real motive, the final aim, and the eternal purpose of all this difficult, uphill struggle with the commonplace problems of your present material world.

"Why do you not aid the Adjuster in the task of showing you the spiritual counterpart of all these strenuous material efforts? Why do you not allow the Adjuster to strengthen you with the spiritual truths of cosmic power while you wrestle with the temporal difficulties of creature existence? Why do you not encourage the heavenly helper to cheer you with the clear vision of the eternal outlook of universal life as you gaze in perplexity at the problems of the passing hour? Why do you refuse to be enlightened and inspired by the universe viewpoint while you toil amidst the handicaps of time and flounder in the maze of uncertainties which beset your mortal life journey? Why not allow the Adjuster to spiritualize your thinking, even though your feet must tread the material paths of earthly endeavor?" *P. 1223*.

295. ADJUSTER HANDICAPS

"The higher human races of Urantia are complexly admixed; they are a blend of many races and stocks of different origin. This composite nature renders it exceedingly difficult for the Monitors to work efficiently during life and adds definitely to the problems of both the Adjuster and the guardian seraphim after death. Not long since I was present on Salvington and heard a guardian of destiny present a formal statement in extenuation of the difficulties of ministering to her mortal subject. This seraphim said:

"'Much of my difficulty was due to the unending conflict between the two natures of my subject: the urge of ambition opposed by animal indolence; the ideals of a superior people crossed by the instincts of an inferior race; the high purposes of a great mind antagonized by the urge of a primitive inheritance; the long-distance view of a far-seeing Monitor counteracted by the nearsightedness of a creature of time; the progressive plans of an ascending being modified by the desires and longings of a material nature; the flashes of universe intelligence cancelled by the chemical-energy mandates of the evolving race; the urge of angels opposed by the emotions of an animal; the training of an intellect annulled by the tendencies of instinct; the experience of the individual opposed by the accumulated propensities of the race; the aims of the best overshadowed by the drift of the worst; the flight of genius neutralized by the gravity of mediocrity; the progress of the good retarded by the inertia of the bad; the art of the beautiful besmirched by the presence of evil; the buoyancy of health neutralized by the debility of disease; the fountain of faith polluted by the poisons of fear; the spring of joy embittered by the waters of sorrow; the gladness of anticipation disillusioned by the bitterness of realization; the joys of living ever threatened by the sorrows of death. Such a life on such a planet! And yet, because of the ever-present help and urge of the Thought Adjuster, this soul did achieve a fair degree of happiness and success and has even now ascended to the judgment halls of mansonia.'" *Pp. 1223-4*.

296. HOW ADJUSTER GAINS PERSONALITY

"And it is this very power of choice, the universe insignia of free-will creaturehood, that constitutes man's greatest opportunity and his supreme cosmic responsibility. Upon the integrity of the human volition depends the eternal destiny of the future finaliter; upon the sincerity of the mortal free will the divine Adjuster depends for eternal personality; upon the faithfulness of mortal choice the Universal Father depends for the realization of a new ascending son; upon the steadfastness and wisdom of decision-actions the Supreme Being depends for the actuality of experiential evolution." *P. 1233*.

297. IS THERE PROBATION AFTER DEATH?

"If ever there is doubt as to the advisability of advancing a human identity to the mansion worlds, the universe governments invariably rule in the personal interests of that individual; they unhesitatingly advance such a soul to the status of a transitional being, while they continue their observations of the emerging morontia intent and spiritual purpose. Thus divine justice is certain of achievement, and divine mercy is accorded further opportunity for extending its ministry.

"The governments of Orvonton and Nebadon do not claim absolute perfection for the detail working of the universal plan of mortal repersonalization, but they do claim to, and actually do, manifest patience, tolerance, understanding, and merciful sympathy. We had rather assume the risk of a system rebellion than to court the hazard of depriving one struggling mortal from any evolutionary world of the eternal joy of pursuing the ascending career.

"This does not mean that human beings are to enjoy a second opportunity in the face of the rejection of a first, not at all. But it does signify that all will creatures are to experience one true opportunity to make one undoubted, self-conscious, and final choice. The sovereign Judges of the universes will not deprive any being of personality status who has not finally and fully made the eternal choice; the soul of man must and will be given full and ample opportunity to reveal its true intent and real purpose." *P. 1233.*

298. THE GREAT MORONTIA CHANGE

"And when you thus awaken on the mansion worlds of Jerusem, you will be so changed, the spiritual transformation will be so great that, were it not for your Thought Adjuster and the destiny guardian, who so fully connect up your new life in the new worlds with your old life in the first world, you would at first have difficulty in connecting the new morontia consciousness with the reviving memory of your previous identity. Notwithstanding the continuity of personal selfhood, much of the mortal life would at first seem to be a vague and hazy dream. But time will clarify many mortal associations." *P. 1235.*

299. ADJUSTER FUSION

"Thought Adjuster fusion imparts eternal actualities to personality which were previously only potential. Among these new endowments may be mentioned: fixation of divinity quality, past-eternity experience and memory, immortality, and a phase of qualified potential absoluteness.

"When your earthly course in temporary form has been run, you are to awaken on the shores of a better world, and eventually you will be united with your faithful Adjuster in an eternal embrace. And this fusion constitutes the mystery of making God and man one, the mystery of finite creature evolution, but it is eternally true. Fusion is the secret of the sacred sphere of Ascendington, and no creature, save those who have experienced fusion with the spirit of Deity, can comprehend the true meaning of the actual values which are conjoined when the identity of a creature of time becomes eternally one with the spirit of Paradise Deity." P. 1237.

300. GRANDEUR OF MORTAL DESTINY

"We believe that the mortals of Adjuster fusion, together with their finaliter associates, are destined to function in some manner in the administration of the universes of the first outer space level. We have not the slightest doubt that in due time these enormous galaxies will become inhabited universes. And we are equally convinced that among the administrators thereof will be found the Paradise finaliters whose natures are the cosmic consequence of the blending of creature and Creator." P. 1239.

"True it is, you mortals are of earthly, animal origin; your frame is indeed dust. But if you actually will, if you really desire, surely the heritage of the ages is yours, and you shall someday serve throughout the universes in your true characters—children of the Supreme God of experience and divine sons of the Paradise Father of all personalities." P. 1240.

301. GUARDIAN ANGELS NOT A MYTH

"The teaching about guardian angels is not a myth; certain groups of human beings do actually have personal angels. It was in recognition of this that Jesus, in speaking of the children of the heavenly kingdom, said: 'Take heed that you despise not one of these little ones, for I say to you, their angels do always behold the presence of the spirit of my Father.'" P. 1241.

"The ministering personality of the guardian seraphim, the God presence of the indwelling Adjuster, the encircuited action of the Holy Spirit, and the Son-consciousness of the Spirit of Truth are all divinely correlated into a meaningful unity of spiritual ministry in and to a mortal personality. Though hailing from different sources and different levels, these celestial influences are all integrated in the enveloping and evolving presence of the Supreme Being." P. 1245. **Matt. 18:10.**

302. THE RESERVE CORPS OF DESTINY

"The reserve corps of destiny consists of living men and women who have been admitted to the special service of the superhuman administration of world affairs. This corps is made up of the men and women of each generation who are chosen by the spirit directors of the realm to assist in the conduct of the ministry of mercy and wisdom to the children of time on the evolutionary worlds. It is the general practice in the conduct of the affairs of the ascension plans to begin this liaison utilization of mortal will creatures immediately they are competent and trustworthy to assume such responsibilities. Accordingly, as soon as men and women appear on the stage of temporal action with sufficient mental capacity, adequate moral status, and requisite spirituality, they are quickly assigned to the appropriate celestial group of planetary personalities as human liaisons, mortal assistants.

"When human beings are chosen as protectors of planetary destiny, when they become pivotal individuals in the plans which the world administrators are prosecuting, at that time the planetary chief of seraphim confirms their temporal attachment to the seraphic corps and appoints personal destiny guardians to serve with these mortal reservists. All reservists have self-conscious Adjusters, and most of them function in the higher cosmic circles of intellectual achievement and spiritual attainment." P. 1257.

"(The cosmic reserve corps of universe-conscious citizens on Urantia now numbers over one thousand mortals whose insight of cosmic citizenship far transcends the sphere of their terrestrial abode, but I am forbidden to reveal the real nature of the function of this unique group of living human beings.)" P. 1258.

303. URANTIA NOT A COSMIC ORPHAN

"Your isolated world is not forgotten in the counsels of the universe. Urantia is not a cosmic orphan stigmatized by sin and shut away from divine watchcare by rebellion. From Uversa to Salvington and on down to Jerusem, even in Havona and on Paradise, they all know we are here; and you mortals now dwelling on Urantia are just as lovingly cherished and just as faithfully watched over as if the sphere had never been betrayed by a faithless Planetary Prince, even more so. It is eternally true, 'the Father himself loves you.'" P. 1259.

304. FINITE AND EVOLUTIONARY DEITY

"If man recognized that his Creators—his immediate supervisors—while being divine were also finite, and that the God of time and space was an evolving and nonabsolute Deity, then would the inconsistencies of temporal inequalities cease to be profound religious paradoxes. No longer would religious faith be prostituted to the promotion of social smugness in the fortunate while serving only to encourage stoical resignation in the unfortunate victims of social deprivation.

"When viewing the exquisitely perfect spheres of Havona, it is both reasonable and logical to believe they were made by a perfect, infinite, and absolute Creator. But that same reason and logic would compel any honest being, when viewing the turmoil, imperfections, and inequities of Urantia, to conclude that your world had been made by, and was being managed by, Creators who were subabsolute, preinfinite, and other than perfect." P. 1268.

"But the local universes are the real laboratories in which are worked out the mind experiments, galactic adventures, divinity unfoldings, and personality progressions which, when cosmically totaled, constitute the actual foundation upon which the Supreme is achieving deity evolution in and by experience." P. 1272.

305. SPRIT DOMINANCE

"In the evolutionary superuniverses energy-matter is dominant except in personality, where spirit through the mediation of mind is struggling for the mastery. The goal of the evolutionary universes is the subjugation of energy-matter by mind, the co-ordination of mind with spirit, and all of this by virtue of the creative and unifying presence of personality. Thus, in relation to personality, do physical systems become subordinate; mind systems, co-ordinate; and spirit systems, directive." P. 1275.

306. GRAND UNIVERSE A LIVING ORGANISM

"The grand universe is not only a material creation of physical grandeur, spirit sublimity, and intellectual magnitude, it is also a magnificent and responsive living organism. There is actual life pulsating throughout the mechanism of the vast creation of the vibrant cosmos. The physical reality of the universes is symbolic of the perceivable reality of the Almighty Supreme; and this material and living organism is penetrated by intelligence circuits, even as the human body is traversed by a network of neural sensation paths. *This physical universe is permeated by* energy lanes which effectively activate material creation, even as the human body is nourished and energized by the circulatory distribution of the assimilable energy products of nourishment. The vast universe is not without those co-ordinating centers of magnificent overcontrol which might be compared to the delicate chemical control system of the human mechanism. But if you only knew something about the physique of a power center, we could, by analogy, tell you so much more about the physical universe." P. 1276.

307. GOD THE SUPREME

"If all grand universers should ever relatively achieve the full living of the will of God, then would the time-space creations be settled in light and life, and then would the Almighty, the deity potential of Supremacy, become factual in the emergence of the divine personality of God the Supreme." *P. 1278*.

"The Supreme is the beauty of physical harmony, the truth of intellectual meaning, and the goodness of spiritual value. He is the sweetness of true success and the joy of everlasting achievement. He is the oversoul of the grand universe, the consciousness of the finite cosmos, the completion of finite reality, and the personification of Creator-creature experience. Throughout all future eternity God the Supreme will voice the reality of volitional experience in the trinity relationships of Deity." *P. 1278*.

"The Supreme is God-in-time; his is the secret of creature growth in time; his also is the conquest of the incomplete present and the consummation of the perfecting future. And the final fruits of all finite growth are: power controlled through mind by spirit by virtue of the unifying and creative presence of personality. The culminating consequence of all this growth is the Supreme Being." *P. 1280*.

308. OUR RELATION TO THE SUPREME BEING

"One of the most intriguing question in finite philosophy is this: Does the Supreme Being actualize in response to the evolution of the grand universe, or does this finite cosmos progressively evolve in response to the gradual actualization of the Supreme? Or is it possible that they are mutually interdependent for their development? that they are evolutionary reciprocals, each initiating the growth of the other? Of this we are certain: Creatures and universes, high and low, are evolving within the Supreme, and as they evolve, there is appearing the unified summation of the entire finite activity of this universe age. And this is the appearance of the Supreme Being, to all personalities the evolution of the almighty power of God the Supreme." *P. 1281*.

"The Supreme is the divine channel through which flows the creative infinity of the triodities that crystallizes into the galactic panorama of space, against which takes place the magnificent personality drama of time: the spirit conquest of energy-matter through the mediation of mind.

"Said Jesus: 'I am the living way,' and so he is the living way from the material level of self-consciousness to the spiritual level of God-consciousness. And even as he is this living way of ascension from the self to God, so is the Supreme the living way from finite consciousness to transcendence of consciousness, even to the insight of absonity." *P. 1281*.

309. THE FINITE GOD

"As we view the ceaseless struggles of the creature creation for perfection of status and divinity of being, we cannot but believe that these unending efforts bespeak the unceasing struggle of the Supreme for divine self-realization. God the Supreme is the finite Deity, and he must cope with the problems of the finite in the total sense of that word. Our struggles with the vicissitudes of time in the evolutions of space are reflections of his efforts to achieve reality of self and completion of sovereignty within the sphere of action which his evolving nature is expanding to the outermost limits of possibility.

"Throughout the grand universe the Supreme struggles for expression. His divine evolution is in measure predicated on the wisdom-action of every personality in existence. When a human being chooses eternal survival, he is co-creating destiny; and in the life of this ascending mortal the finite God finds an increased measure of personality self-realization and an enlargement of experiential sovereignty. But if a creature rejects the eternal career, that part of the Supreme which was dependent on this creature's choice experiences inescapable delay, a deprivation which must be compensated by substitutional or collateral experience; as for the personality of the nonsurvivor, it is absorbed into the oversoul of creation, becoming a part of the Deity of the Supreme." *P. 1283.*

310. WE ARE A PART OF THE SUPREME

"And so the decision awaits each of you as it once awaited each of us: Will you fail the God of time, who is so dependent upon the decisions of the finite mind? will you fail the Supreme personality of the universes by the slothfulness of animalistic retrogression? will you fail the great brother of all creatures, who is so dependent on each creature? can you allow yourself to pass into the realm of the unrealized when before you lies the enchanting vista of the universe career—the divine discovery of the Paradise Father and the divine participation in the search for, and the evolution of, the God of Supremacy?" *P. 1285.*

311. THE OVERSOUL OF CREATION

"The great Supreme is the cosmic oversoul of the grand universe. In him the qualities and quantities of the cosmos do find their deity reflection; his deity nature is the mosaic composite of the total vastness of all creature-Creator nature throughout the evolving universes. And the Supreme is also an actualizing Deity embodying a creative will which embraces an evolving universe purpose." *P. 1285.*

312. FINALITER TRANSCENDATION

"The evolving immortal soul of man, the joint creation of the material mind and the Adjuster, ascends as such to Paradise and subsequently, when mustered into the Corps of the Finality, becomes allied in some new way with the spirit gravity circuit of the Eternal Son by a technique of experience known as *finaliter transcendation*. Such finaliters thus become acceptable candidates for experiential recognition as personalities of God the Supreme. And when these mortal intellects in the unrevealed future assignments of the Corps of the Finality attain the seventh stage of spirit existence, such dual minds will become triune. These two attuned minds, the human and the divine, will become glorified in union with the experiential mind of the then actualized Supreme Being." P. 1286.

313. GOD THE SUPREME OUR EVOLUTIONARY MOTHER

"All soul-evolving humans are literally the evolutionary sons of God the Father and God the Mother, the Supreme Being. But until such time as mortal man becomes soul-conscious of his divine heritage, this assurance of Deity kinship must be faith realized. Human life experience is the cosmic cocoon in which the universe endowments of the Supreme Being and the universe presence of the Universal Father (none of which are personalities) are evolving the morontia soul of time and the human-divine finaliter character of universe destiny and eternal service." P. 1289.

314. OUR RELATION TO THE SUPREME

"The Supreme is not infinite, but he probably embraces all of infinity that a finite creature can ever really comprehend. To understand more than the Supreme is to be more than finite!" P. 1290.

"Man can discover the Father in his heart, but he will have to search for the Supreme in the hearts of all other men; and when all creatures perfectly reveal the love of the Supreme, then will he become a universe actuality to all creatures. And that is just another way of saying that the universes will be settled in light and life." P. 1290.

"But no God-knowing mortal can ever be lonely in his journey through the cosmos, for he knows that the Father walks beside him each step of the way, while the very way that he is traversing is the presence of the Supreme." P. 1291.

315. GOD THE SUPREME, THEN GOD THE ULTIMATE

"The perfected grand universe of those future days will be vastly different from what it is at present. Gone will be the thrilling adventures of the organization of the galaxies of space, the planting of life on the uncertain worlds of time, and the evolving of harmony out of chaos, beauty out of potentials, truth out of meanings, and goodness out of values. The time universes will have achieved the fulfillment of finite destiny! And perhaps for a space there will be rest, relaxation from the agelong struggle for evolutionary perfection. But not for long! Certainly, surely, and inexorably the enigma of the emerging Deity of God the Ultimate will challenge these perfected citizens of the settled universes just as their struggling evolutionary forebears were once challenged by the quest for God the Supreme. The curtain of cosmic destiny will draw back to reveal the transcendent grandeur of the alluring absonite quest for the attainment of the Universal Father on those new and higher levels revealed in the ultimate of creature experience." P. 1293.

316. TRUTH IS TIMELESS

"Things are time conditioned, but truth is timeless. The more truth you know, the more truth you *are*, the more of the past you can understand and of the future you can comprehend.

"Truth is inconcussible—forever exempt from all transient vicissitudes, albeit never dead and formal, always vibrant and adaptable—radiantly alive. But when truth becomes linked with fact, then both time and space condition its meanings and correlate its values. Such realities of truth wedded to fact become concepts and are accordingly relegated to the domain of relative cosmic realities.

"The linking of the absolute and eternal truth of the Creator with the factual experience of the finite and temporal creature eventuates a new and emerging value of the Supreme. The concept of the Supreme is essential to the coordination of the divine and unchanging overworld with the finite and ever-changing underworld." P. 1297.

317. GOD'S OMNIPOTENCE AND OMNIFICENCE

"The omnipotence of Deity does not imply the power to do the nondoable. Within the time-space frame and from the intellectual reference point of mortal comprehension, even the infinite God cannot create square circles or produce evil that is inherently good. God cannot do the ungodlike thing. Such a contradiction of philosophic terms is the equivalent of nonentity and implies that nothing is thus created. A personality trait cannot at the same time be Godlike and ungodlike. Compossibility is innate in divine power. And all of this is derived from the fact that omnipotence not only creates things with a nature but also gives origin to the nature of all things and beings." *P. 1299*.

"God is truly omnipotent, but he is not omnificent—he does not personally do all that is done. Omnipotence embraces the power-potential of the Almighty Supreme and the Supreme Being, but the volitional acts of God the Supreme are not the personal doings of God the Infinite.

"To advocate the omnificence of primal Deity would be equal to disenfranchising well-nigh a million Creator Sons of Paradise, not to mention the innumerable hosts of various other orders of concurring creative assistants. There is but one uncaused Cause in the whole universe. All other causes are derivatives of this one First Great Source and Center. And none of this philosophy does any violence to the freewillness of the myriads of the children of Deity scattered through a vast universe." *P. 1299*.

318. GOD THE SUPREME AND PROVIDENCE

"God the Supreme is the personalization of all universe experience, the focalization of all finite evolution, the maximation of all creature reality, the consummation of cosmic wisdom, the embodiment of the harmonious beauties of the galaxies of time, the truth of cosmic mind meanings, and the goodness of supreme spirit values. And God the Supreme will, in the eternal future, synthesize these manifold finite diversities into one experientially meaningful whole, even as they are now existentially united on absolute levels in the Paradise Trinity.

"Providence does not mean that God has decided all things for us and in advance. God loves us too much to do that, for that would be nothing short of cosmic tyranny. Man does have relative powers of choice. Neither is the divine love that shortsighted affection which would pamper and spoil the children of men." *P. 1304*.

"The Gods have attributes but the Trinity has functions, and like the Trinity, providence is a function, the composite of the other-than-personal overcontrol of the universe of universes, extending from the evolutionary levels of the Sevenfold synthesizing in the power of the Almighty on up through the transcendental realms of the Ultimacy of Deity." *P. 1304*.

319. MISCONCEPTIONS OF PROVIDENCE

"Nevertheless, the Father as a person may at any time interpose a fatherly hand in the stream of cosmic events all in accordance with the will of God and in consonance with the wisdom of God and as motivated by the love of God.

"But what man calls providence is all too often the product of his own imagination, the fortuitous juxtaposition of the circumstances of chance. There is, however, a real and emerging providence in the finite realm of universe existence, a true and actualizing correlation of the energies of space, the motions of time, the thoughts of intellect, the ideals of character, the desires of spiritual natures, and the purposive volitional acts of evolving personalities. The circumstances of the material realms find final finite integration in the interlocking presences of the Supreme and the Ultimate." P. 1305.

"Some of the amazingly fortuitous conditions occasionally prevailing on the evolutionary worlds may be due to the gradually emerging presence of the Supreme, the foretasting of his future universe activities. Most of what a mortal would call providential is not; his judgment of such matters is very handicapped by lack of farsighted vision into the true meanings of the circumstances of life. Much of what a mortal would call good luck might really be bad luck; the smile of fortune that bestows unearned leisure and undeserved wealth may be the greatest of human afflictions; the apparent cruelty of a perverse fate that heaps tribulation upon some suffering mortal may in reality be the tempering fire that is transmuting the soft iron of immature personality into the tempered steel of real character." P. 1305.

"When men pray for providential intervention in the circumstances of life, many times the answer to their prayer is their own changed attitudes toward life. But providence is not whimsical, neither is it fantastic nor magical. It is the slow and sure emergence of the mighty sovereign of the finite universes, whose majestic presence the evolving creatures occasionally detect in their universe progressions. Providence is the sure and certain march of the galaxies of space and the personalities of time toward the goals of eternity, first in the Supreme, then in the Ultimate, and perhaps in the Absolute. And in infinity we belive there is the same providence, and this is the will, the actions, the purpose of the Paradise Trinity thus motivating the cosmic panorama of universes upon universes." P. 1307.

320. THE BESTOWALS OF MICHAEL

"It required almost one billion years of Urantia time to complete the bestowal career of Michael and to effect the final establishment of his supreme authority in the universe of his own creation. Michael was born a creator, educated an administrator, trained an executive, but he was required to earn his sovereignty by experience. And thus has your little world become known throughout all Nebadon as the arena wherein Michael completed the experience which is required of every Paradise Creator Son before he is given unlimited control and direction of the universe of his own making. As you ascend the local universe, you will learn more about the ideals of the personalities concerned in Michael's previous bestowals.

"In completing his creature bestowals, Michael was not only establishing his own sovereignty but also was augmenting the evolving sovereignty of God the Supreme. In the course of these bestowals the Creator Son not only engaged in a descending exploration of the various natures of creature personality, but he also achieved the revelation of the variously diversified wills of the Paradise Deities, whose synthetic unity, as revealed by the Supreme Creators, is revelatory of the will of the Supreme Being." *P. 1318.*

"The completion of these seven bestowals resulted in the liberation of Michael's supreme sovereignty and also in the creation of the possibility for the sovereignty of the Supreme in Nebadon. On none of Michael's bestowals did he reveal God the Supreme, but the sum total of all seven bestowals is a new Nebadon revelation of the Supreme Being." *P. 1318.*

321. URANTIA A SENTIMENTAL SHRINE

"Urantia is the sentimental shrine of all Nebadon, the chief of ten million inhabited worlds, the mortal home of Christ Michael, sovereign of all Nebadon, a Melchizedek minister to the realms, a system savior, an Adamic redeemer, a seraphic fellow, an associate of ascending spirits, a morontia progressor, a Son of Man in the likeness of mortal flesh, and the Planetary Prince of Urantia. And your record tells the truth when it says that this same Jesus has promised some time to return to the world of his terminal bestowal, the World of the Cross." *P. 1319.*

Part IV

THE LIFE AND TEACHINGS OF JESUS

322. MYSTERY OF THE INCARNATION

"And so certain unworthy children of Michael, who had accused their Creator-father of selfishly seeking rulership and indulged the insinuation that the Creator Son was arbitrarily and autocratically upheld in power by virtue of the unreasoning loyalty of a deluded universe of subservient creatures, were to be silenced forever and left confounded and disillusioned by the life of self-forgetful service which the Son of God now entered upon as the Son of Man—all the while subject to 'the will of the Paradise Father.'

"But make no mistake; Christ Michael, while truly a dual-origin being, was not a double personality. He was not God in association *with* man but, rather, God *incarnate* in man. And he was always just that combined being. The only progressive factor in such a nonunderstandable relationship was the progressive self-conscious realization and recognition (by the human mind) of this fact of being God and man.

"Christ Michael did not progressively become God. God did not, at some vital moment in the earth life of Jesus, become man. Jesus was God *and* man—always and even forevermore. And this God and this man were, and now are, *one*, even as the Paradise Trinity of three beings is in reality *one* Deity.

"Never lose sight of the fact that the supreme spiritual purpose of the Michael bestowal was to enhance the *revelation of God*." P. 1331.

323. JESUS' HEREDITY

"Jesus derived much of his unusual gentleness and marvelous sympathetic understanding of human nature from his father; he inherited his gift as a great teacher and his tremendous capacity for righteous indignation from his mother. In emotional reactions to his adult-life environment, Jesus was at one time like his father, meditative and worshipful, sometimes characterized by apparent sadness; but more often he drove forward in the manner of his mother's optimistic and determined disposition. All in all, Mary's temperament tended to dominate the career of the divine Son as he grew up and swung into the momentous strides of his adult life. In some particulars Jesus was a blending of his parents' traits; in other respects he exhibited the traits of one in contrast with those of the other." P. 1348.

324. BIRTH OF JESUS

"All that night Mary was restless so that neither of them slept much. By the break of day the pangs of childbirth were well in evidence, and at noon, August 21, 7 B.C., with the help and kind ministrations of women fellow travelers, Mary was delivered of a male child. Jesus of Nazareth was born into the world, was wrapped in the clothes which Mary had brought along for such a possible contingency, and laid in a near-by manger." *P. 1351*. **Luke 2:6,7.**

325. JESUS GETS HIS ADJUSTER

"In something more than a year after the return to Nazareth the boy Jesus arrived at the age of his first personal and wholehearted moral decision; and there came to abide with him a Thought Adjuster, a divine gift of the Paradise Father, which had aforetime served with Machiventa Melchizedek, thus gaining the experience of functioning in connection with the incarnation of a supermortal being living in the likeness of mortal flesh. This event occurred on February 11, 2 B.C. Jesus was no more aware of the coming of the divine Monitor than are the millions upon millions of other children who, before and since that day, have likewise received these Thought Adjusters to indwell their minds and work for the ultimate spiritualization of these minds and the eternal survival of their evolving immortal souls." *P. 1357*.

326. TROUBLE ABOUT JESUS' PRAYERS

"During this year Joseph and Mary had trouble with Jesus about his prayers. He insisted on talking to his heavenly Father much as he would talk to Joseph, his earthly father. This departure from the more solemn and reverent modes of communication with Deity was a bit disconcerting to his parents, especially to his mother, but there was no persuading him to change; he would say his prayers just as he had been taught, after which he insisted on having 'just a little talk with my Father in heaven.'" *P. 1360*.

327. TROUBLE OVER JESUS' ARTISTIC EFFORTS

"But trouble was again stirred up at school when one of the more backward pupils discovered Jesus drawing a charcoal picture of the teacher on the floor of the schoolroom. There it was, plain as day, and many of the elders had viewed it before the committee went to call on Joseph to demand that something be done to suppress the lawlessness of his eldest son. And though this was not the first time complaints had come to Joseph and Mary about the doings of their versatile and aggressive child, this was the most serious of all the accusations which had thus far been lodged against him. Jesus listened to the indictment of his artistic efforts for some time, being seated on a large stone just outside the back door. He resented their blaming his father for his alleged misdeeds; so in he marched, fearlessly confronting his accusers. The elders were thrown into confusion. Some were inclined to view the episode humorously, while one or two seemed to think the boy was sacrilegious if not blasphemous. Joseph was nonplused, Mary indignant, but Jesus insisted on being heard. He had his say, courageously defended his viewpoint, and with consummate self-control announced that he would abide by the decision of his father in this as in all other matters controversial. And the committee of elders departed in silence.

"Mary endeavored to influence Joseph to permit Jesus to model in clay at home, provided he promised not to carry on any of these questionable activities at school, but Joseph felt impelled to rule that the rabbinical interpretation of the second commandment should prevail. And so Jesus no more drew or modeled the likeness of anything from that day as long as he lived in his father's house. But he was unconvinced of the wrong of what he had done, and to give up such a favorite pastime constituted one of the great trials of his young life." *Pp. 1366-7.*

328. JESUS' UNWILLINGNESS TO FIGHT

"Perhaps his most unusual and outstanding trait was his unwillingness to fight for his rights. Since he was such a well-developed lad for his age, it seemed strange to his playfellows that he was disinclined to defend himself even from injustice or when subjected to personal abuse. As it happened, he did not suffer much on account of this trait because of the friendship of Jacob, a neighbor boy, who was one year older. He was the son of the stone mason, a business associate of Joseph. Jacob was a great admirer of Jesus and made it his business to see that no one was permitted to impose upon Jesus because of his aversion to physical combat. Several times older and uncouth youths attacked Jesus, relying upon his reputed docility, but they always suffered swift and certain retribution at the hands of his self-appointed champion and ever-ready defender, Jacob the stone mason's son." *P. 1368-9.*

329. JESUS A DIFFICULT CHILD TO REAR

"It was a trying experience for Joseph and Mary to undertake the rearing of this unprecedented combination of divinity and humanity, and they deserve great credit for so faithfully and successfully discharging their parental responsibilities. Increasingly Jesus' parents realized that there was something superhuman resident within this eldest son, but they never even faintly dreamed that this son of promise was indeed and in truth the actual creator of this local universe of things and beings. Joseph and Mary lived and died without ever learning that their son Jesus really was the Universe Creator incarnate in mortal flesh." *P. 1372*.

330. JESUS' FIRST VIEW OF THE TEMPLE

"On the eastern slopes of Olivet they paused for rest in the borders of a little village called Bethany. The hospitable villagers poured forth to minister to the pilgrims, and it happened that Joseph and his family had stopped near the house of one Simon, who had three children about the same age as Jesus—Mary, Martha, and Lazarus. They invited the Nazareth family in for refreshment, and a lifelong friendship sprang up between the two families. Many times afterward, in his eventful life, Jesus stopped in this home.

"They pressed on, soon standing on the brink of Olivet, and Jesus saw for the first time (in his memory) the Holy City, the pretentious palaces, and the inspiring temple of his Father. At no time in his life did Jesus ever experience such a purely human thrill as that which at this time so completely enthralled him as he stood there on this April afternoon on the Mount of Olives, drinking in his first view of Jerusalem. And in after years, on this same spot he stood and wept over the city which was about to reject another prophet, the last and the greatest of her heavenly teachers." *P. 1375*.

331. JESUS' REACTIONS TO THE TEMPLE SERVICES

"Jesus was profoundly impressed by the temple and all the associated services and other activities. For the first time since he was four years old, he was too much preoccupied with his own meditations to ask many questions. He did, however, ask his father several embarrassing questions (as he had on previous occasions) as to why the heavenly Father required the slaughter of so many innocent and helpless animals. And his father well knew from the expression on the lad's face that his answers and attempts at explanation were unsatisfactory to his deep-thinking and keen-reasoning son.

"On the day before the Passover Sabbath, flood tides of spiritual illumination swept through the mortal mind of Jesus and filled his human heart to overflowing with affectionate pity for the spiritually blind and morally ignorant multitudes assembled for the celebration of the ancient Passover commemoration. This was one of the most extraordinary days that the Son of God spent in the flesh; and during the night, for the first time in his earth career, there appeared to him an assigned messenger from Salvington, commissioned by Immanuel, who said: 'The hour has come. It is time that you began to be about your Father's business.'" *Pp. 1375-6*.

"In company with his parents Jesus passed through the temple precincts on his way to join that group of new sons of the law who were about to be consecrated as citizens of Israel. He was a little disappointed by the general demeanor of the temple throngs, but the first great shock of the day came when his mother took leave of them on her way to the women's gallery. It had never occurred to Jesus that his mother was not to accompany him to the consecration ceremonies, and he was thoroughly indignant that she was made to suffer from such unjust discrimination. While he strongly resented this, aside from a few remarks of protest to his father, he said nothing. But he thought, and thought deeply, as his questions to the scribes and teachers a week later disclosed." *P. 1377*.

332. JESUS AND HIS FATHER DISCUSS SACRIFICES

"Though many of the temple rituals very touchingly impressed his sense of the beautiful and the symbolic, he was always disappointed by the explanation of the real meanings of these ceremonies which his parents would offer in answer to his many searching inquiries. Jesus simply would not accept explanations of worship and religious devotion which involved belief in the wrath of God or the anger of the Almighty. In further discussion of these questions, after the conclusion of the temple visit, when his father became mildly insistent that he acknowledge acceptance of the orthodox Jewish beliefs, Jesus turned suddenly upon his parents and, looking appealingly into the eyes of his father, said: 'My father, it cannot be true—the Father in heaven cannot so regard his erring children on earth. The heavenly Father cannot love his children less than you love me. And I well know, no matter what unwise thing I might do, you would never pour out wrath upon me nor vent anger against me. If you, my earthly father, possess such human reflections of the Divine, how much more must the heavenly Father be filled with goodness and overflowing with mercy. I refuse to believe that my Father in heaven loves me less than my father on earth.'

"When Joseph and Mary heard these words of their first-born son, they held their peace. And never again did they seek to change his mind about the love of God and the mercifulness of the Father in heaven." *P. 1378*.

333. JESUS' MEDITATIONS ARE TROUBLED

"Again and again, during the Passover week, his parents would find Jesus sitting off by himself with his youthful head in his hands, profoundly thinking. They had never seen him behave like this, and not knowing how much he was confused in mind and troubled in spirit by the experience through which he was passing, they were sorely perplexed; they did not know what to do.

They welcomed the passing of the days of the Passover week and longed to have their strangely acting son safely back in Nazareth." *P. 1380*.

"After the evening meal at Bethany he again declined to join the merry circle but instead went to the garden, where he lingered long into the night, vainly endeavoring to think out some definite plan of approach to the problem of his lifework and to decide how best he might labor to reveal to his spiritually blinded countrymen a more beautiful concept of the heavenly Father and so set them free from their terrible bondage to law, ritual, ceremonial, and musty tradition. But the clear light did not come to the truth-seeking lad." *P. 1383*.

334. NOTHING EXTRAORDINARY HAPPENED

"By the beginning of this year both Joseph and Mary entertained frequent doubts about the destiny of their first-born son. He was indeed a brilliant and lovable child, but he was so difficult to understand, so hard to fathom, and again, nothing extraordinary or miraculous ever happened. Scores of times had his proud mother stood in breathless anticipation, expecting to see her son engage in some superhuman or miraculous performance, but always were her hopes dashed down in cruel disappointment. And all this was discouraging, even disheartening. The devout people of those days truly believed that prophets and men of promise always demonstrated their calling and established their divine authority by performing miracles and working wonders. But Jesus did none of these things; wherefore was the confusion of his parents steadily increased as they contemplated his future." *P. 1387*.

335. ORIGIN OF "THE LORD'S PRAYER"

"During this year Jesus first formulated the prayer which he subsequently taught to his apostles, and which to many has become known as 'The Lord's Prayer.' In a way it was an evolution of the family altar; they had many forms of praise and several formal prayers. After his father's death Jesus tried to teach the older children to express themselves individually in prayer-much as he so enjoyed doing—but they could not grasp his thought and would invariably fall back upon their memorized prayer forms. It was in this effort to stimulate his older brothers and sisters to say individual prayers that Jesus would endeavor to lead them along by suggestive phrases, and presently, without intention on his part, it developed that they were all using a form of prayer which was largely built up from these suggestive lines which Jesus had taught them.

"At last Jesus gave up the idea of having each member of the family formulate spontaneous prayers, and one evening in October he sat down by the little squat lamp on the low stone table, and, on a piece of smooth cedar board about eighteen inches square, with a piece of charcoal he wrote out the prayer which became from that time on the standard family petition." *P. 1389*.

336. SHOCKS, CONFLICTS, AND DISAPPOINTMENTS

"Apparently all Jesus' plans for a career were thwarted. The future did not look bright as matters now developed. But he did not falter; he was not discouraged. He lived on, day by day, doing well the present duty and faithfully discharging the *immediate* responsibilities of his station in life. Jesus' life is the everlasting comfort of all disappointed idealists." *P. 1393.*

"The great shock of his fifteenth year came when Jesus went over to Sepphoris to receive the decision of Herod regarding the appeal taken to him in the dispute about the amount of money due Joseph at the time of his accidental death. Jesus and Mary had hoped for the receipt of a considerable sum of money when the treasurer at Sepphoris had offered them a paltry amount. Joseph's brothers had taken an appeal to Herod himself, and now Jesus stood in the palace and heard Herod decree that his father had nothing due him at the time of his death. And for such an unjust decision Jesus never again trusted Herod Antipas. It is not surprising that he once alluded to Herod as 'that fox.'" *P. 1393.*

"As he grew up to manhood, he passed through all those conflicts and confusions which the average young persons of previous and subsequent ages have undergone. And the rigorous experience of supporting his family was a sure safeguard against his having overmuch time for idle meditation or the indulgence of mystic tendencies." *P. 1393.*

337. JESUS' ADOLESCENT RESPONSIBILITIES

"As Jesus entered upon his adolescent years, he found himself the head and sole support of a large family. Within a few years after his father's death all their property was gone. As time passed, he became increasingly conscious of his pre-existence; at the same time he began more fully to realize that he was present on earth and in the flesh for the express purpose of revealing his Paradise Father to the children of men.

"No adolescent youth who has lived or ever will live on this world or any other world has had or ever will have more weighty problems to resolve or more intricate difficulties to untangle. No youth of Urantia will ever be called upon to pass through more testing conflicts or more trying situations than Jesus himself endured during those strenuous years from fifteen to twenty.

"Having thus tasted the actual experience of living these adolescent years on a world beset by evil and distraught by sin, the Son of Man became possessed of full knowledge about the life experience of the youth of all the realms of Nebadon, and thus forever he became the understanding refuge for the distressed and perplexed adolescents of all ages and on all worlds throughout the local universe.

"Slowly, but certainly and by actual experience, this divine Son is *earning* the right to become sovereign of his universe, the unquestioned and supreme ruler of all created intelligences on all local universe worlds, the understanding refuge of the beings of all ages and of all degrees of personal endowment and experience." P. 1395.

338. ABOUT JOINING THE ZEALOTS

"But trouble began to brew in Nazareth. Jesus' attitude in these matters had resulted in creating a division among the Jewish youths of the city. About half had joined the nationalist organization, and the other half began the formation of an opposing group of more moderate patriots, expecting Jesus to assume the leadership. They were amazed when he refused the honor offered him, pleading as an excuse his heavy family responsibilities, which they all allowed. But the situation was still further complicated when, presently, a wealthy Jew, Isaac, a money-lender to the gentiles, came forward agreeing to support Jesus' family if he would lay down his tools and assume leadership of these Nazareth patriots.

"Jesus, then scarcely seventeen years of age, was confronted with one of the most delicate and difficult situations of his early life. Patriotic issues, especially when complicated by tax-gathering foreign oppressors, are always difficult for spiritual leaders to relate themselves to, and it was doubly so in this case since the Jewish religion was involved in all this agitation against Rome." P. 1397.

"Something had to be done. He must state his position, and this he did bravely and diplomatically to the satisfaction of many, but not all. He adhered to the terms of his original plea, maintaining that his first duty was to his family, that a widowed mother and eight brothers and sisters needed something more than mere money could buy—the physical necessities of life that they were entitled to a father's watchcare and guidance, and that he could not in clear conscience release himself from the obligation which a cruel accident had thrust upon him. He paid compliment to his mother and eldest brother for being willing to release him but reiterated that loyalty to a dead father forbade his leaving the family no matter how much money was forthcoming for their material support, making his never-to-be-forgotten statement that 'money cannot love.' In the course of this address Jesus made several veiled references to his 'life mission' but explained that, regardless of whether or not it might be inconsistent with the military idea, it, along with everything else in his life, had been given up in order that he might be able to discharge faithfully his obligation to his family. Everyone in Nazareth well knew he was a good father to his family, and this was a matter so near the heart of every noble Jew that Jesus' plea found an appreciative response in the hearts of many of his hearers; and some of those who were not thus minded were disarmed by a speech made by James, which, while not on the program, was delivered at this time." Pp. 1397-8.

339. THE DEATH OF LITTLE AMOS

"On Saturday afternoon, December 3, of this year, death for the second time struck at this Nazareth family. Little Amos, their baby brother, died after a week's illness with a high fever. After passing through this time of sorrow with her first-born son as her only support, Mary at last and in the fullest sense recognized Jesus as the real head of the family; and he was truly a worthy head.

"For four years their standard of living had steadily declined; year by year they felt the pinch of increasing poverty. By the close of this year they faced one of the most difficult experiences of all their uphill struggles. James had not yet begun to earn much, and the expenses of a funeral on top of everything else staggered them. But Jesus would only say to his anxious and grieving mother: 'Mother-Mary, sorrow will not help us; we are all doing our best, and mother's smile, perchance, might even inspire us to do better. Day by day we are strengthened for these tasks by our hope of better days ahead.' His sturdy and practical optimism was truly contagious; all the children lived in an atmosphere of anticipation of better times and better things. And this hopeful courage contributed mightily to the development of strong and noble characters, in spite of the depressiveness of their poverty." P. 1400.

340. THE FIRST BLOODLESS PASSOVER

"On this visit occurred one of those periodic outbreaks of rebellion against tradition—the expression of resentment for those ceremonial practices which Jesus deemed misrepresentative of his Father in heaven. Not knowing Jesus was coming, Lazarus had arranged to celebrate the Passover with friends in an adjoining village down the Jericho road. Jesus now proposed that they celebrate the feast where they were, at Lazarus's house. 'But,' said Lazarus, 'we have no paschal lamb.' And then Jesus entered upon a prolonged and convincing dissertation to the effect that the Father in heaven was not truly concerned with such childlike and meaningless rituals. After solemn and fervent prayer they rose, and Jesus said: 'Let the childlike and darkened minds of my people serve their God as Moses directed; it is better that they do, but let us who have seen the light of life no longer approach our Father by the darkness of death. Let us be free in the knowledge of the truth of our Father's eternal love.'

"That evening about twilight these four sat down and partook of the first Passover feast ever to be celebrated by devout Jews without the paschal lamb. The unleavened bread and the wine had been made ready for this Passover, and these emblems, which Jesus termed 'the bread of life' and 'the water of life,' he served to his companions, and they ate in solemn conformity with the teachings just imparted. It was his custom to engage in this sacramental ritual whenever he paid subsequent visits to Bethany. When he returned home, he told all this to his mother. She was shocked at first but came gradually to see his viewpoint; nevertheless, she was greatly relieved when Jesus assured her that he did not intend to introduce this new idea of the Passover in their family. At home with the children he continued, year by year, to eat the Passover 'according to the law of Moses.'" P. 1404.

341. JESUS MASTERING THE ART OF LIVING

"Jesus is rapidly becoming a man, not just a young man but an adult. He has learned well to bear responsibility. He knows how to carry on in the face of disappointment. He bears up bravely when his plans are thwarted and his purposes temporarily defeated. He has learned how to be fair and just even in the face of injustice. He is learning how to adjust his ideals of spiritual living to the practical demands of earthly existence. He is learning how to plan for the achievement of a higher and distant goal of idealism while he toils earnestly for the attainment of a nearer and immediate goal of necessity. He is steadily acquiring the art of adjusting his aspirations to the commonplace demands of the human occasion. *He has very nearly mastered the technique of utilizing the energy of the spiritual drive* to turn the mechanism of material achievement. He is slowly learning how to live the heavenly life while he continues on with the earthly existence. More and more he depends upon the ultimate guidance of his heavenly Father while he assumes the fatherly role of guiding and directing the children of his earth family. He is becoming experienced in the skillful wresting of victory from the very jaws of defeat; he is learning how to transform the difficulties of time into the triumphs of eternity." P. 1405.

"Born into the world a babe of the realm, he has lived his childhood life and passed through the successive stages of youth and young manhood; he now stands on the threshold of full manhood, rich in the experience of human living, replete in the understanding of human nature, and full of sympathy for the frailties of human nature. He is becoming expert in the divine art of revealing his Paradise Father to all ages and stages of mortal creatures.

"And now as a full-grown man—an adult of the realm—he prepares to continue his supreme mission of revealing God to men and leading men to God." Pp. 1405-6.

342. THE HUMANITY OF JESUS

"It is forever and gloriously true: 'We have a high ruler who can be touched with the feeling of our infirmities. We have a Sovereign who was in all points tested and tempted like as we are, yet without sin.' And since he himself has suffered, being tested and tried, he is abundantly able to understand and minister to those who are confused and distressed." *P. 1408*.

"He lived his mortal life just as all others of the human family may live theirs, 'who in the days of the flesh so frequently offered up prayers and supplications, even with strong feelings and tears, to Him who is able to save from all evil, and his prayers were effective because he believed.' Wherefore it behooved him *in every respect* to be made like his brethren that he might become a merciful and understanding sovereign ruler over them." *P. 1408*.

"Between these two celestial visitations, one in his thirteenth year and the other at his baptism, there occurred nothing supernatural or superhuman in the life of this incarnated Creator Son. Notwithstanding this, the babe of Bethlehem, the lad, youth, and man of Nazareth, was in reality the incarnated Creator of a universe; but he never once used aught of this power, nor did he utilize the guidance of celestial personalities, aside from that of his guardian seraphim, in the living of his human life up to the day of his baptism by John. And we who thus testify know whereof we speak." *P. 1408*.

343. THE DIVINITY OF JESUS

"After his baptism he thought nothing of permitting his sincere believers and grateful followers to worship him. Even while he wrestled with poverty and toiled with his hands to provide the necessities of life for his family, his awareness that he was a Son of God was growing; he knew that he was the maker of the heavens and this very earth whereon he was now living out his human existence. And the hosts of celestial beings throughout the great and onlooking universe likewise knew that this man of Nazareth was their beloved Sovereign and Creator-father. A profound suspense pervaded the universe of Nebadon throughout these years; all celestial eyes were continuously focused on Urantia—on Palestine." *P. 1409*.

344. JESUS' LOVE FOR CHILDREN

"This year his seasons of deep meditation were often broken into by Ruth and her playmates. And always was Jesus ready to postpone the contemplation of his future work for the world and the universe that he might share in the childish joy and youthful gladness of these youngsters, who never tired of listening to Jesus relate the experiences of his various trips to Jerusalem. They also greatly enjoyed his stories about animals and nature.

"The children were always welcome at the repair shop. Jesus provided sand, blocks, and stones by the side of the shop, and bevies of youngsters flocked there to amuse themselves. When they tired of their play, the more intrepid ones would peek into the shop, and if its keeper were not busy, they would make bold to go in and say, 'Uncle Joshua, come out and tell us a big story.' Then they would lead him out by tugging at his hands until he was seated on the favorite rock by the corner of the shop, with the children on the ground in a semicircle before him. And how the little folks did enjoy their Uncle Joshua. They were learning to laugh, and to laugh heartily. It was customary for one or two of the smallest of the children to climb upon his knees and sit there, looking up in wonderment at his expressive features as he told his stories. The children loved Jesus, and Jesus loved the children.

"It was difficult for his friends to comprehend the range of his intellectual activities, how he could so suddenly and so completely swing from the profound discussion of politics, philosophy, or religion to the lighthearted and joyous playfulness of these tots of from five to ten years of age. As his own brothers and sisters grew up, as he gained more leisure, and before the grandchildren arrived, he paid a great deal of attention to these little ones. But he did not live on earth long enough to enjoy the grandchildren very much." *P. 1416.*

345. JESUS MEETS GONAD AND GANID

"Before the end of this Passover week, by apparent chance, Jesus met a wealthy traveler and his son, a young man about seventeen years of age. These travelers hailed from India, and being on their way to visit Rome and various other points on the Mediterranean, they had arranged to arrive in Jerusalem during the Passover, hoping to find someone whom they could engage as interpreter for both and tutor for the son. The father was insistent that Jesus consent to travel with them. Jesus told him about his family and that it was hardly fair to go away for almost two years, during which time they might find themselves in need. Whereupon, this traveler from the Orient proposed to advance to Jesus the wages of one year so that he could intrust such funds to his friends for the safeguarding of his family against want. And Jesus agreed to make the trip." *Pp. 1422-3.*

346. PURPOSE OF THE TRIP TO ROME

"The real purpose of his trip around the Mediterranean basin was to *know men*. He came very close to hundreds of humankind on this journey. He met and loved all manner of men, rich and poor, high and low, black and white, educated and uneducated, cultured and uncultured, animalistic and spiritual, religious and irreligious, moral and immoral.

"On this Mediterranean journey Jesus made great advances in his human task of mastering the material and mortal mind, and his indwelling Adjuster made great progress in the ascension and spiritual conquest of this same human intellect. By the end of this tour Jesus virtually knew—with all human certainty—that he was a Son of God, a Creator Son of the Universal Father. The Adjuster more and more was able to bring up in the mind of the Son of Man shadowy memories of his Paradise experience in association with his divine Father ere he ever came to organize and administer this local universe of Nebadon. Thus did the Adjuster, little by little, bring to Jesus' human consciousness those necessary memories of his former and divine existence in the various epochs of the well-nigh eternal past. The last episode of his prehuman experience to be brought forth by the Adjuster was his farewell conference with Immanuel of Salvington just before his surrender of conscious personality to embark upon the Urantia incarnation. And this final memory picture of prehuman existence was made clear in Jesus' consciousness on the very day of his baptism by John in the Jordan." P. 1424.

347. JESUS KNOWS ALL ABOUT US

"The Son of Man experienced those wide ranges of human emotion which reach from superb joy to profound sorrow. He was a child of joy and a being of rare good humor; likewise was he a 'man of sorrows and acquainted with grief.' In a spiritual sense, he did live through the mortal life from the bottom to the top, from the beginning to the end. From a material point of view, he might appear to have escaped living through both social extremes of human existence, but intellectually he became wholly familiar with the entire and complete experience of humankind.

"Jesus knows about the thoughts and feelings, the urges and impulses, of the evolutionary and ascendant mortals of the realms, from birth to death. He has lived the human life from the beginnings of physical, intellectual, and spiritual selfhood up through infancy, childhood, youth, and adulthood—even to the human experience of death. He not only passed through these usual and familiar human periods of intellectual and spiritual advancement, but he *also* fully experienced those higher and more advanced phases of human and Adjuster reconciliation which so few Urantia mortals ever attain. And thus he experienced the full life of mortal man, not only as it is lived on your world, but also as it is lived on all other evolutionary worlds of time and space, even on the highest and most advanced of all the worlds settled in light and life." P. 1425.

348. "OUR RELIGION"

"After the arduous labor of effecting this compilation of the teachings of the world religions concerning the Paradise Father, Ganid set himself to the task of formulating what he deemed to be a summary of the belief he had arrived at regarding God as a result of Jesus' teaching. This young man was in the habit of referring to such beliefs as 'our religion.' This was his record:

"'The Lord our God is one Lord, and you should love him with all your mind and heart while you do your very best to love all his children as you love yourself. This one God is our heavenly Father, in whom all things consist, and who dwells, by his spirit, in every sincere human soul. And we who are the children of God should learn how to commit the keeping of our souls to him as to a faithful Creator. With our heavenly Father all things are possible. Since he is the Creator, having made all things and all beings, it could not be otherwise. Though we cannot see God, we can know him. And by daily living the will of the Father in heaven, we can reveal him to our fellow men.

"'The divine riches of God's character must be infinitely deep and eternally wise. We cannot search out God by knowledge, but we can know him in our hearts by personal experience. While his justice may be past finding out, his mercy may be received by the humblest being on earth. While the Father fills the universe, he also lives in our hearts. The mind of man is human, mortal, but the spirit of man is divine, immortal. God is not only all-powerful but also all-wise. If our earth parents, being of evil tendency, know how to love their children and bestow good gifts on them, how much more must the good Father in heaven know how wisely to love his children on earth and to bestow suitable blessings upon them.

"'The Father in heaven will not suffer a single child on earth to perish if that child has a desire to find the Father and truly longs to be like him. Our Father even loves the wicked and is always kind to the ungrateful. If more human beings could only know about the goodness of God, they would certainly be led to repent of their evil ways and forsake all known sin. All good things come down from the Father of light, in whom there is no variableness neither shadow of changing. The spirit of the true God is in man's heart. He intends that all men should be brothers. When men begin to feel after God, that is evidence that God has found them, and that they are in quest of knowledge about him. We live in God and God dwells in us.

"'I will no longer be satisfied to believe that God is the Father of all my people; I will henceforth believe that he is also *my* Father. Always will I try to worship God with the help of the Spirit of Truth, which is my helper when I have become really God-knowing. But first of all I am going to practice worshiping God by learning how to do the will of God on earth; that is, I am going to do my best to treat each of my fellow mortals just as I think God would like to have him treated. And when we live this sort of a life in the flesh, we may ask many things of God, and he will give us the desire of our hearts that we may be the better prepared to serve our fellows. And all of this loving service of the children of God enlarges our capacity to receive and experience the joys of heaven, the high pleasures of the ministry of the spirit of heaven.'" *Pp. 1453-4.*

349. THE STORY ABOUT WEALTH

"A certain rich man, a Roman citizen and a Stoic, became greatly interested in Jesus' teaching, having been introduced by Angamon. After many intimate conferences this wealthy citizen asked Jesus what he would do with wealth if he had it, and Jesus answered him: 'I would bestow material wealth for the enhancement of material life, even as I would minister knowledge, wisdom, and spiritual service for the enrichment of the intellectual life, the ennoblement of the social life, and the advancement of the spiritual life. I would administer material wealth as a wise and effective trustee of the resources of one generation for the benefit and ennoblement of the next and succeeding generations.'

"But the rich man was not fully satisfied with Jesus' answer. He made bold to ask again: 'But what do you think a man in my position should do with his wealth? Should I keep it, or should I give it away?' And when Jesus perceived that he really desired to know more of the truth about his loyalty to God and his duty to men, he further answered: 'My good friend, I discern that you are a sincere seeker after wisdom and an honest lover of truth; therefore am I minded to lay before you my view of the solution of your problems having to do with the responsibilities of wealth. I do this because you have *asked* for my counsel, and in giving you this advice, I am not concerned with the wealth of any other rich man; I am offering advice only to you and for your personal guidance. If you honestly desire to regard your wealth as a trust, if you really wish to become a wise and efficient steward of your accumulated wealth, then would I counsel you to make the following analysis of the sources of your riches: Ask yourself, and do your best to find the honest answer, whence came this wealth? And as a help in the study of the sources of your great fortune, I would suggest that you bear in mind the following ten different methods of amassing material wealth:

"'1. Inherited wealth—riches derived from parents and other ancestors.

"'2. Discovered wealth—riches derived from the uncultivated resources of mother earth.

"'3. Trade wealth—riches obtained as a fair profit in the exchange and barter of material goods.

"'4. Unfair wealth—riches derived from the unfair exploitation or the enslavement of one's fellows.

"'5. Interest wealth—income derived from the fair and just earning possibilities of invested capital.

"'6. Genius wealth—riches accruing from the rewards of the creative and inventive endowments of the human mind.

"'7. Accidental wealth—riches derived from the generosity of one's fellows or taking origin in the circumstances of life.

"'8. Stolen wealth—riches secured by unfairness, dishonesty, theft, or fraud.

"'9. Trust funds—wealth lodged in your hands by your fellows for some specific use, now or in the future.

"'10. Earned wealth—riches derived directly from your own personal labor, the fair and just reward of your own daily efforts of mind and body.'" *Pp. 1462-3.*

350. GANID WANTS TO MAKE A NEW RELIGION

"Then exclaimed Ganid: 'Teacher, let's you and I make a new religion, one good enough for India and big enough for Rome, and maybe we can trade it to the Jews for Yahweh.' And Jesus replied: 'Ganid, religions are not made. The religions of men grow up over long periods of time, while the revelations of God flash upon earth in the lives of the men who reveal God to their fellows.' But they did not comprehend the meaning of these prophetic words.

"That night after they had retired, Ganid could not sleep. He talked a long time with his father and finally said, 'You know, father, I sometimes think Joshua is a prophet.' And his father only sleepily replied, 'My son, there are others—'" *P. 1467.*

351. SAYING GOODBYE TO THE INDIANS

"At last the day came for the separation. They were all brave, especially the lad, but it was a trying ordeal. They were tearful of eye but courageous of heart. In bidding his teacher farewell, Ganid said: 'Farewell, Teacher, but not forever. When I come again to Damascus, I will look for you. I love you, for I think the Father in heaven must be something like you; at least I know you are much like what you have told me about him. I will remember your teaching, but most of all, I will never forget you.' Said the father, 'Farewell to a great teacher, one who has made us better and helped us to know God.' And

Jesus replied, 'Peace be upon you, and may the blessing of the Father in heaven ever abide with you.' And Jesus stood on the shore and watched as the small boat carried them out to their anchored ship. Thus the Master left his friends from India at Charax, never to see them again in this world; nor were they, in Nazareth was this same friend they had just taken leave of—Joshua their teacher." *P. 1481.*

352. JESUS' TALKS AT URMIA

"Peace will not come to Urantia until every so-called sovereign nation surrenders its power to make war into the hands of a representative government of all mankind. Political sovereignty is innate with the peoples of the world. When all the peoples of Urantia create a world government, they have the right and the power to make such a government SOVEREIGN; and when such a representative or democratic world power controls the world's land, air, and naval forces, peace on earth and good will among men can prevail—but not until then." *P. 1489.*

"There shall be wars and rumors of wars—nation will rise against nation just as long as the world's political sovereignty is divided up and unjustly held by a group of nation-states. England, Scotland, and Wales were always fighting each other until they gave up their respective sovereignties, reposing them in the United Kingdom." *P. 1490.*

"Urantia will not enjoy lasting peace until the so-called sovereign nations intelligently and fully surrender their sovereign powers into the hands of the brotherhood of men—mankind government. Internationalism—Leagues of Nations—can never bring permanent peace to mankind. World-wide confederations of nations will effectively prevent minor wars and acceptably control the smaller nations, but they will not prevent world wars nor control the three, four, or five most powerful governments. In the face of real conflicts, one of these world powers will withdraw from the League and declare war. You cannot prevent nations going to war as long as they remain infected with the delusional virus of national sovereignty. Internationalism is a step in the right direction. An international police force will prevent many minor wars, but it will not be effective in preventing major wars, conflicts between the great military governments of earth." *P. 1489.*

"World peace cannot be maintained by treaties, diplomacy, foreign policies, alliances, balances of power, or any other type of makeshift juggling with the sovereignties of nationalism. World law must come into being and must be enforced by world government—the sovereignty of all mankind.

"The individual will enjoy far more liberty under world government. Today, the citizens of the great powers are taxed, regulated, and controlled almost oppressively, and much of this present interference with this world, ever to know that the man who later appeared as Jesus of individual liberties will vanish when the national governments are willing to trustee their sovereignty as regards international affairs into the hands of global government." *P. 1491*.

353. WINNING THE SOVEREIGNTY OF A UNIVERSE

"On an afternoon in late summer, amid the trees and in the silence of nature, Michael of Nebadon won the unquestioned sovereignty of his universe. On that day he completed the task set for Creator Sons to live to the full the incarnated life in the likeness of mortal flesh on the evolutionary worlds of time and space. The universe announcement of this momentous achievement was not made until the day of his baptism, months afterward, but it all really took place that day on the mountain. And when Jesus came down from his sojourn on Mount Hermon, the Lucifer rebellion in Satania and the Caligastia secession on Urantia were virtually settled. Jesus had paid the last price required of him to attain the sovereignty of his universe, which in itself regulates the status of all rebels and determines that all such future upheavals (if they ever occur) may be dealt with summarily and effectively. Accordingly, it may be seen that the so-called 'great temptation' of Jesus took place some time before his baptism and not just after that event." *P. 1494*.

354. JESUS LAYS DOWN HIS TOOLS

"Just before the noon rest, Jesus laid down his tools, removed his work apron, and merely announced to the three workmen in the room with him, 'My hour has come.' He went out to his brothers James and Jude, repeating, 'My hour has come—let us go to John.' And they started immediately for Pella, eating their lunch as they journeyed. This was on Sunday, January 13. They tarried for the night in the Jordan valley and arrived on the scene of John's baptizing about noon of the next day." *P. 1504*.

355. BAPTISM OF JESUS

"Being engrossed with the details of rapidly baptizing such a large number of converts, John did not look up to see Jesus until the Son of Man stood in his immediate presence. When John recognized Jesus, the ceremonies were halted for a moment while he greeted his cousin in the flesh and asked, 'But why do you come down into the water to greet me?' And Jesus answered, 'To be subject to your baptism.' John replied: 'But I have need to be baptized by you. Why do you come to me?' And Jesus whispered to John: 'Bear with me now, for it becomes us to set this example for my brothers standing here with me,

"There was a tone of finality and authority in Jesus' voice. John was atremble with emotion as he made ready to baptize Jesus of Nazareth in the Jordan at noon on Monday, January 14, A.D. 26. Thus did John baptize Jesus and his two brothers James and Jude. And when John had baptized these three, he dismissed the others for the day, announcing that he would resume baptisms at noon the next day. As the people were departing, the four men still standing in the water heard a strange sound, and presently there appeared for a moment an apparition immediately over the head of Jesus, and they heard a voice saying, 'This is my beloved Son in whom I am well pleased.' A great change came over the countenance of Jesus, and coming up out of the water in silence he took leave of them, going toward the hills to the east. And no man saw Jesus again for forty days." P. 1504.

356. JESUS AND HIS ADJUSTER

"When Jesus of Nazareth went down into the Jordan to be baptized, he was a mortal of the realm who had attained the pinnacle of human evolutionary ascension in all matters related to the conquest of mind and to self-identification with the spirit. He stood in the Jordan that day a perfected mortal of the evolutionary worlds of time and space. Perfect synchrony and full communication had become established between the mortal mind of Jesus and the indwelling spirit Adjuster, the divine gift of his Father in Paradise. And just such an Adjuster indwells all normal beings living on Urantia since the ascension of Michael to the headship of his universe, except that Jesus' Adjuster had been previously prepared for this special mission by similarly indwelling another superhuman incarnated in the likeness of mortal flesh, Machiventa Melchizedek.

"Ordinarily, when a mortal of the realm attains such high levels of personality perfection, there occur those preliminary phenomena of spiritual elevation which terminate in eventual fusion of the matured soul of the mortal with its associated divine Adjuster. And such a change was apparently due to take place in the personality experience of Jesus of Nazareth on that very day when he went down into the Jordan with his two brothers to be baptized by John. This ceremony was the final act of his purely human life on Urantia, and many superhuman observers expected to witness the fusion of the Adjuster with its indwelt mind, but they were all destined to suffer disappointment. Something new and even greater occurred. As John laid his hands upon Jesus to baptize him, the indwelling Adjuster took final leave of the perfected human soul of Joshua ben Joseph. And in a few moments this divine entity returned from Divinington as a Personalized Adjuster and chief of his kind throughout the entire local universe of Nebadon. Thus did Jesus observe his own former divine spirit descending on its return to him in personalized form. And he heard this same spirit of Paradise origin now speak, saying, 'This is my beloved Son in whom I am well pleased.' And John, with Jesus' two brothers, also heard these words. John's disciples, standing by the water's edge, did not hear these words, neither did they see the apparition of the Personalized Adjuster. Only the eyes of Jesus beheld the Personalized Adjuster." P. 1511.

357. JUST AFTER THE BAPTISM

"While wandering about in the hills, seeking a suitable shelter, Jesus encountered his universe chief executive, Gabriel, the Bright and Morning Star of Nebadon. Gabriel now re-established personal communication with the Creator Son of the universe; they met directly for the first time since Michael took leave of his associates on Salvington when he went to Edentia preparatory to entering upon the Urantia bestowal. Gabriel, by direction of Immanuel and on authority of the Uversa Ancients of Days, now laid before Jesus information indicating that his bestowal experience on Urantia was practically finished so far as concerned the earning of the perfected sovereignty of his universe and the termination of the Lucifer rebellion. The former was achieved on the day of his baptism when the personalization of his Adjuster demonstrated the perfection and completion of his bestowal in the likeness of mortal flesh, and the latter was a fact of history on that day when he came down from Mount Hermon to join the waiting lad, Tiglath. Jesus was now informed, upon the highest authority of the local universe and the superuniverse, that his bestowal work was finished in so far as it affected his personal status in relation to sovereignty and rebellion. He had already had this assurance direct from Paradise in the baptismal vision and in the phenomenon of the personalization of his indwelling Thought Adjuster." P. 1513.

358. JESUS REFUSES TO BE A WONDER-WORKER

"Jesus portrayed to all the worlds of his vast universe the folly of creating artificial situations for the purpose of exhibiting arbitrary authority or of indulging exceptional power for the purpose of enhancing moral values or accelerating spiritual progress. Jesus decided that he would not lend his mission on earth to a repetition of the disappointment of the reign of the Maccabees. He refused to prostitute his divine attributes for the purpose of acquiring unearned popularity or for gaining political prestige. He would not countenance the transmutation of divine and creative energy into national power or international prestige. Jesus of Nazareth refused to compromise with *evil*, much less to consort with sin. The Master triumphantly put loyalty to his Father's will above every other earthly and temporal consideration." P. 1521.

"You can hardly imagine what would have happened on Urantia had this God-man, now in potential possession of all power in heaven and on earth, once decided to unfurl the banner of sovereignty, to marshal his wonder-working battalions in militant array! But he would not compromise. He would not serve evil that the worship of God might presumably be derived therefrom. He would abide by the Father's will. He would proclaim to an onlooking universe, 'You shall worship the Lord your God and him only shall you serve.'" *P. 1522.*

"By these decisions Jesus set a worthy example for every person on every world throughout a vast universe when he refused to apply material tests to prove spiritual problems, when he refused presumptuously to defy natural laws. And he set an inspiring example of universe loyalty and moral nobility when he refused to grasp temporal power as the prelude to spiritual glory." *P. 1523.*

359. PHILIP LEADS NATHANIEL TO JESUS

"Philip now motioned to the group to remain where they were while he hurried back to break the news of his decision to his friend Nathaniel, who still tarried behind under the mulberry tree, turning over in his mind the many things which he had heard concerning John the Baptist, the coming kingdom, and the expected Messiah. Philip broke in upon these meditations, exclaiming, 'I have found the Deliverer, him of whom Moses and the prophets wrote and whom John has proclaimed.' Nathaniel, looking up, inquired, 'Whence comes this teacher?' And Philip replied, 'He is Jesus of Nazareth, the son of Joseph, the carpenter, more recently residing at Capernaum.' And then, somewhat shocked, Nathaniel asked, 'Can any such good thing come out of Nazareth?' But Philip, taking him by the arm, said, 'Come and see.'

"Philip led Nathaniel to Jesus, who, looking benignly into the face of the sincere doubter, said: 'Behold a genuine Israelite, in whom there is no deceit. Follow me.' And Nathaniel, turning to Philip, said: 'You are right. He is indeed a master of men. I will also follow, if I am worthy.' And Jesus nodded to Nathaniel, again saying, 'Follow me.'" *Pp. 1526-7.* **John 1:45-49.**

360. MARY ON THE WAY TO CANA

"Mary had not been so joyous in years. She journeyed to Cana in the spirit of the queen mother on the way to witness the coronation of her son. Not since he was thirteen years old had Jesus' family and friends seen him so carefree and happy, so thoughtful and understanding of the wishes and desires of his associates, so touchingly sympathetic. And so they all whispered among themselves, in small groups, wondering what was going to happen. What would this strange person do next? How would he usher in the glory of the coming kingdom? And they were all thrilled with the thought that they were to be present to see the revelation of the might and power of Israel's God." *P. 1528*.

361. THE WATER AND THE WINE

"Throughout a period of many years, Mary had always turned to Jesus for help in every crisis of their home life at Nazareth so that it was only natural for her to think of him at this time. But this ambitious mother had still other motives for appealing to her eldest son on this occasion. As Jesus was standing alone in a corner of the garden, his mother approached him, saying, 'My son, they have no wine.' And Jesus answered, 'My good woman, what have I to do with that?' Said Mary, 'But I believe your hour has come; cannot you help us?' Jesus replied: 'Again I declare that I have not come to do things, in this wise. Why do you trouble me again with these matters?' And then, breaking down in tears, Mary entreated him, 'But, my son, I promised them that you would help us; won't you please do something for me?' And then spoke Jesus: 'Woman, what have you to do with making such promises? See that you do it not again. We must in all things wait upon the will of the Father in heaven.'

"Mary the mother of Jesus was crushed; she was stunned! As she stood there before him motionless, with the tears streaming down her face, the human heart of Jesus was overcome with compassion for the woman who had borne him in the flesh; and bending forward, he laid his hand tenderly upon her head, saying: 'Now, now, Mother Mary, grieve not over my apparently hard sayings, for have I not many times told you that I have come only to do the will of my heavenly Father? Most gladly would I do what you ask of me if it were a part of the Father's will—' and Jesus stopped short, he hesitated. Mary seemed to sense that something was happening. Leaping up, she threw her arms around Jesus' neck, kissed him, and rushed off to the servants' quarters, saying, 'Whatever my son says, that do.' But Jesus said nothing. He now realized that he had already said—or rather desirefully thought—too much.

"Mary was dancing with glee. She did not know how the wine would be produced, but she confidently believed that she had finally persuaded her first-born son to assert his authority, to dare to step forth and claim his position and exhibit his Messianic power. And, because of the presence and association of certain universe powers and personalities, of which all those present were wholly ignorant, she was not to be disappointed. The wine Mary desired and which Jesus, the God-man, humanly and sympathetically wished for, was forth-coming.

"Near at hand stood six waterpots of stone, filled with water, holding about twenty gallons apiece. This water was intended for subsequent use in the final purification ceremonies of the wedding celebration. The commotion of the servants about these huge stone vessels, under the busy direction of his mother, attracted Jesus' attention, and going over, he observed that they were drawing wine out of them by the pitcherful.

"It was gradually dawning upon Jesus what had happened. Of all persons present at the marriage feast of Cana, Jesus was the most surprised. Others had expected him to work a wonder, but that was just what he had purposed not to do. And then the Son of Man recalled the admonition of his Personalized Thought Adjuster in the hills. He recounted how the Adjuster had warned him about the inability of any power or any personality to deprive him of the creator prerogative of independence of time. On this occasion power transformers, midwayers, and all other required personalities were assembled near the water and other necessary elements, and in the face of the expressed wish of the Universe Creator Sovereign, there was no escaping the instantaneous appearance of *wine*. And this occurrence was made doubly certain since the Personalized Adjuster had signified that the execution of the Son's desire was in no way a contravention of the Father's will." *Pp. 1529-30.* **John 2:3-10.**

362. JESUS REALIZES THAT HE MUST BE ON GUARD

"Jesus now fully comprehended that he must constantly be on guard lest his indulgence of sympathy and pity become responsible for repeated episodes of this sort. Nevertheless, many similar events occurred before the Son of Man took final leave of his mortal life in the flesh." *P. 1531.*

"That night Jesus did not sleep. Donning his evening wraps, he sat out on the lake shore thinking, thinking until the dawn of the next day. In the long hours of that night of meditation Jesus came clearly to comprehend that he never would be able to make his followers see him in any other light than as the long-expected Messiah. At last he recognized that there was no way to launch his message of the kingdom except as the fulfillment of John's prediction and as the one for whom the Jews were looking. After all, though he was not the Davidic type of Messiah, he was truly the fulfillment of the prophetic utterances of the more spiritually minded of the olden seers. Never again did he wholly deny that he was the Messiah. He decided to leave the final untangling of this complicated situation to the outworking of the Father's will." *P. 1532.*

363. BANQUET AT MATTHEW'S HOUSE

"As the dinner progressed, the joy of the diners mounted to heights of good cheer, and everybody was having such a splendid time that the onlooking Pharisees began, in their hearts, to criticize Jesus for his participation in such a lighthearted and carefree affair. Later in the evening, when they were making speeches, one of the more malignant of the Pharisees went so far as to criticize Jesus' conduct to Peter, saying: 'How dare you to teach that this man is righteous when he eats with publicans and sinners and thus lends his presence to such scenes of careless pleasure making.' Peter whispered this criticism to Jesus before he spoke the parting blessing upon those assembled. When Jesus began to speak, he said: 'In coming here tonight to welcome Matthew and Simon to our fellowship, I am glad to witness your lightheartedness and social good cheer, but you should rejoice still more because many of you will find entrance into the coming kingdom of the spirit, wherein you shall more abundantly enjoy the good things of the kingdom of heaven. And to you who stand about criticizing me in your hearts because I have come here to make merry with these friends, let me say that I have come to proclaim joy to the socially downtrodden and spiritual liberty to the moral captives. Need I remind you that they who are whole need not a physician, but rather those who are sick? I have come, not to call the righteous, but sinners.'

"And truly this was a strange sight in all Jewry: to see a man of righteous character and noble sentiments mingling freely and joyously with the common people, even with an irreligious and pleasure-seeking throng of publicans and reputed sinners. Simon Zelotes desired to make a speech at this gathering in Matthew's house, but Andrew, knowing that Jesus did not want the coming kingdom to become confused with the Zealots' movement, prevailed upon him to refrain from making any public remarks." *Pp. 1540-1*. **Matt. 9:10-13**.

364. THE WEDNESDAY PLAY DAY

"It was at this time that Jesus established the mid-week holiday for rest and recreation. And they pursued this plan of relaxation for one day each week throughout the remainder of his material life. As a general rule, they never prosecuted their regular activities on Wednesday. On this weekly holiday Jesus would usually take himself away from them, saying: 'My children, go for a day of play. Rest yourselves from the arduous labors of the kingdom and enjoy the refreshment that comes from reverting to your former vocations or from discovering new sorts of recreational activity.' While Jesus, at this period of his earth life, did not actually require this day of rest, he conformed to this plan because he knew it was best for his human associates. Jesus was the teacher— the Master; his associates were his pupils—disciples." *Pp. 1542-3.*

365. WARNING AGAINST RELIGION ABOUT JESUS

"Jesus endeavored to make clear to his apostles the difference between his teachings and his *life among them* and the teachings which might subsequently spring up *about* him. Said Jesus: 'My kingdom and the gospel related thereto shall be the burden of your message. Be not sidetracked into preaching *about* me and *about* my teachings. Proclaim the gospel of the kingdom and portray my revelation of the Father in heaven but do not be misled into the bypaths of creating legends and building up a cult having to do with beliefs and teachings *about* my beliefs and teachings.' But again they did not understand why he thus spoke, and no man dared to ask why he so taught them." P. 1543.

366. THE APOSTLES BELIEVED IN JESUS

"Jesus now recounted for them the coming of John, the baptism in the Jordan, the marriage feast at Cana, the recent choosing of the six, and the withdrawal from them of his own brothers in the flesh, and warned them that the enemy of the kingdom would seek also to draw them away. After this short but earnest talk the apostles all arose, under Peter's leadership, to declare their undying devotion to their Master and to pledge their unswerving loyalty to the kingdom, as Thomas expressed it, 'To this coming kingdom, no matter what it is and even if I do not fully understand it.' They all truly *believed in Jesus*, even though they did not fully comprehend his teaching." P. 1544.

367. FAITH VS. WORKS

"Jesus made plain to his apostles the difference between the repentance of so-called good works as taught by the Jews and the change of mind by faith—the new birth—which he required as the price of admission to the kingdom. He taught his apostles that *faith* was the only requisite to entering the Father's kingdom. John had taught them 'repentance—to flee from the wrath to come.' Jesus taught, 'Faith is the open door for entering into the present, perfect, and eternal love of God.' Jesus did not speak like a prophet, one who comes to declare the word of God. He seemed to speak of himself as one having authority. Jesus sought to divert their minds from miracle seeking to the finding of a real and personal experience in the satisfaction and assurance of the indwelling of God's spirit of love and saving grace." P. 1545. **Matt. 3:7; Luke 3:7.**

368. JESUS' RESPECT FOR THE INDIVIDUAL

"The disciples early learned that the Master had a profound respect and sympathetic regard for *every* human being he met, and they were tremendously impressed by this uniform and unvarying consideration which he so consistently gave to all sorts of men, women, and children. He would pause in the midst of a profound discourse that he might go out in the road to speak good cheer to a passing woman laden with her burden of body and soul. He would interrupt a serious conference with his apostles to fraternize with an intruding child. Nothing ever seemed so important to Jesus as the *individual human* who chanced to be in his immediate presence. He was master and teacher, but he was more—he was also a friend and neighbor, an understanding comrade." *Pp. 1545-6.*

369. CHARACTERISTICS OF THE APOSTLES

"It is an eloquent testimony to the charm and righteousness of Jesus' earth life that, although he repeatedly dashed to pieces the hopes of his apostles and tore to shreds their every ambition for personal exaltation, only one deserted him.

"The apostles learned from Jesus about the kingdom of heaven, and Jesus learned much from them about the kingdom of men, human nature as it lives on Urantia and on the other evolutionary worlds of time and space. There twelve men represented many different types of human temperament, and they had not been made *alike* by schooling. Many of these Galilean fishermen carried heavy strains of gentile blood as a result of the forcible conversion of the gentile population of Galilee one hundred years previously." *P. 1548.*

370. FROM THE ORDINATION SERMON

"'I send you forth to proclaim liberty to the spiritual captives, joy to those in the bondage of fear, and to heal the sick in accordance with the will of my Father in heaven. When you find my children in distress, speak encouragingly to them, saying:

"'Happy are the poor in spirit, the humble, for theirs are the treasures of the kingdom of heaven.

"'Happy are they who hunger and thirst for righteousness, for they shall be filled.

"'Happy are the meek, for they shall inherit the earth.

"'Happy are the pure in heart, for they shall see God.

"'And even so speak to my children these further words of spiritual comfort and promise:

"'Happy are they who mourn, for they shall be comforted. Happy are they who weep, for they shall receive the spirit of rejoicing.

"'Happy are the merciful, for they shall obtain mercy.

"'Happy are the peacemakers, for they shall be called the sons of God.

"'Happy are they who are persecuted for righteousness' sake, for theirs is the kingdom of heaven. Happy are you when men shall revile you and persecute you and shall say all manner of evil against you falsely. Rejoice and be exceedingly glad, for great is your reward in heaven.

"'My brethren, as I send you forth, you are the salt of the earth, salt with a saving savor. But if this salt has lost its savor, wherewith shall it be salted? It is henceforth good for nothing but to be cast out and trodden under foot of men.

"'You are the light of the world. A city set upon a hill cannot be hid. Neither do men light a candle and put it under a bushel, but on a candlestick; and it gives light to all who are in the house. Let your light so shine before men that they may see your good works and be led to glorify your Father who is in heaven.

"'I am sending you out into the world to represent me and to act as ambassadors of my Father's kingdom, and as you go forth to proclaim the glad tidings, put your trust in the Father whose messengers you are. Do not forcibly resist injustice; put not your trust in the arm of the flesh. If your neighbor smites you on the right cheek, turn to him the other also. Be willing to suffer injustice rather than to go to law among yourselves. In kindness and with mercy minister to all who are in distress and in need.

"'I say to you: Love your enemies, do good to those who hate you, bless those who curse you, and pray for those who despitefully use you. And whatsoever you believe that I would do to men, do you also to them.

"'Your Father in heaven makes the sun to shine on the evil as well as upon the good; likewise he sends rain on the just and the unjust. You are the sons of God; even more, you are now the ambassadors of my Father's kingdom. Be merciful, even as God is merciful, and in the eternal future of the kingdom you shall be perfect, even as your heavenly Father is perfect.'" *Pp. 1570-1*.

"Strong characters are not derived from *not* doing wrong but rather from actually doing right. Unselfishness is the badge of human greatness. The highest levels of self-realization are attained by worship and service. The happy and effective person is motivated, not by fear of wrongdoing, but by love of right doing." *P. 1572*.

"An effective philosophy of living is formed by a combination of cosmic insight and the total of one's emotional reactions to the social and economic environment. Remember; While inherited urges cannot be fundamentally modified, emotional responses to such urges can be changed; therefore the moral nature can be modified, character can be improved. In the strong character emotional responses are integrated and co-ordinated, and thus is produced a unified personality. Deficient unification weakens the moral nature and engenders unhappiness." *P. 1572*. **Matt. 5:1-16; Luke 6:20-37.**

371. FATHERLY VS. BROTHERLY LOVE

"From the Sermon on the Mount to the discourse of the Last Supper, Jesus taught his followers to manifest *fatherly* love rather than *brotherly* love. Brotherly love would love your neighbor as you love yourself, and that would be adequate fulfillment of the 'golden rule.' But fatherly affection would require that you should love your fellow mortals as Jesus loves you.

"Jesus loves mankind with a dual affection. He lived on earth as a twofold personality—human and divine. As the Son of God he loves man with a fatherly love—he is man's Creator, his universe Father. As the Son of Man, Jesus loves mortals as a brother—he was truly a man among men." *P. 1573.*

372. THE FUTILITY OF HATE AND VENGEANCE

"He never ceased to warn his disciples against the evil practice of *retaliation*; he made no allowance for revenge, the idea of getting even. He deplored the holding of grudges. He disallowed the idea of an eye for an eye and a tooth for a tooth. He discountenanced the whole concept of private and personal revenge, assigning these matters to civil government, on the one hand, and to the judgment of God, on the other. He made it clear to the three that his teachings applied to the *individual*, not the state. He summarized his instructions up to that time regarding these matters, as:

"Love your enemies—remember the moral claims of human brotherhood.

"The futility of evil: A wrong is not righted by vengeance. Do not make the mistake of fighting evil with its own weapons.

"Have faith—confidence in the eventual triumph of divine justice and eternal goodness." *Pp. 1579-80.*

373. JESUS' ATTITUDE TOWARD SOCIETY

"Jesus frequently warned his listeners against covetousness, declaring that 'a man's happiness consists not in the abundance of his material possessions.' He constantly reiterated, 'What shall it profit a man if he gain the whole world and lose his own soul?' He made no direct attack on the possession of property, but he did insist that it is eternally essential that spiritual values come first. In his later teachings he sought to correct many erroneous Urantia views of life by narrating numerous parables which he presented in the course of his public ministry. Jesus never intended to formulate economic theories; he well knew that each age must evolve its own remedies for existing troubles. And if Jesus were on earth today, living his life in the flesh, he would be a great disappointment to the majority of good men and women for the simple reason that he would not take sides in present-day political, social, or economic disputes. He would remain grandly aloof while teaching you how to perfect your inner spiritual life so as to render you manyfold more competent to attack the solution of your purely human problems." P. 1581.

374. WRONG IDEAS OF JESUS AND HIS RELIGION

"Jesus did not attack the teachings of the Hebrew prophets or the Greek moralists. The Master recognized the many good things which these great teachers stood for, but he had come down to earth to teach something *additional*' 'the voluntary conformity of man's will to God's will.' Jesus did not want simply to produce a *religious man*, a mortal wholly occupied with religious feelings and actuated only by spiritual impulses. Could you have had but one look at him, you would have known that Jesus was a real man of great experience in the things of this world. The teachings of Jesus in this respect have been grossly perverted and much misrepresented all down through the centuries of the Christian era; you have also held perverted ideas about the Master's meekness and humility. What he aimed at in his life appears to have been a *superb self-respect*. He only advised man to humble himself that he might become truly exalted; what he really aimed at was true humility toward God. He placed great value upon sincerity—a pure heart. Fidelity was a cardinal virtue in his estimate of character, while *courage* was the very heart of his teachings. 'Fear not' was his watchword, and patient endurance his ideal of strength of character. The teachings of Jesus constitute a religion of valor, courage, and heroism. And this is just why he chose as his personal representatives twelve commonplace men, the majority of whom were rugged, virile, and manly fishermen." P. 1582.

375. GROWTH VS. SELF-EXAMINATION

"The three apostles were shocked this afternoon when they realized that their Master's religion made no provision for spiritual self-examination. All religions before and after the times of Jesus, even Christianity, carefully provide for conscientious self-examination. But not so with the religion of Jesus of Nazareth. Jesus' philosophy of life is without religious introspection. The carpenter's son never taught character *building*; he taught character *growth*, declaring that the kingdom of heaven is like a mustard seed. But Jesus said nothing which would proscribe self-analysis as a prevention of conceited egotism." P. 1583.

376. JESUS NOT A SOCIAL REFORMER

"The Master offered no solutions for the nonreligious problems of his own age nor for any subsequent age. Jesus wished to develop spiritual insight into eternal realties and to stimulate initiative in the originality of living; he concerned himself exclusively with the underlying and permanent spiritual needs of the human race. He revealed a goodness equal to God. He exalted love—truth, beauty, and goodness—as the divine ideal and the eternal reality.

"The Master came to create in man a new spirit, a new will—to impart a new capacity for knowing the truth, experiencing compassion, and choosing goodness—the will to be in harmony with God's will, coupled with the eternal urge to become perfect, even as the Father in heaven is perfect." *P. 1583*.

377. JESUS' LIFE AN INSPIRATIONAL IDEAL

"It was not apparent to the apostles that their Master was engaged in living a life of spiritual inspiration for every person of every age on every world of a far-flung universe. Notwithstanding what Jesus told them from time to time, the apostles did not grasp the idea that he was doing a work *on* this world but *for* all other worlds in his vast creation. Jesus lived his earth life on Urantia, not to set a personal example of mortal living for the men and women of this world, but rather to create *a high spiritual and inspirational ideal* for all mortal beings on all worlds." *P. 1585*.

378. ALL MEN ARE SONS OF GOD

"After Jesus and Matthew had finished talking, Simon Zelotes asked, 'But, Master, are *all* men the sons of God?' And Jesus answered: 'Yes, Simon, all men are the sons of God, and that is the good news you are going to proclaim.' But the apostles could not grasp such a doctrine; it was a new, strange, and startling announcement. And it was because of his desire to impress this truth upon them that Jesus taught his followers to treat all men as their brothers.

"In response to a question asked by Andrew, the Master made it clear that the morality of his teaching was inseparable from the religion of his living. He taught morality, not from the *nature* of man, but from the *relation* of man to God." *P. 1585*.

379. JESUS CRAVED FAMILY AFFECTION

"Just before leaving, the apostles missed the Master, and Andrew went out to find him. After a brief search he found Jesus sitting in a boat down the beach, and he was weeping. The twelve had often seen their Master when he seemed to grieve, and they had beheld his brief seasons of serious preoccupation of mind, but none of them had ever seen him weep. Andrew was somewhat startled to see the Master thus affected on the eve of their departure for Jerusalem, and he ventured to approach Jesus and ask: 'On this great day,

Master, when we are to depart for Jerusalem to proclaim the Father's kingdom, why is it that you weep? Which of us has offended you?' And Jesus, going back with Andrew to join the twelve, answered him: 'No one of you has grieved me. I am saddened only because none of my father Joseph's family have remembered to come over to bid us Godspeed.' At this time Ruth was on a visit to her brother Joseph at Nazareth. Other members of his family were kept away by pride, disappointment, misunderstanding, and petty resentment indulged as a result of hurt feelings." *P. 1587.*

380. JESUS WAS A COMMANDING PERSONALITY

"The Master displayed great wisdom and manifested perfect fairness in all of his dealings with his apostles and with all of his disciples. Jesus was truly a master of men; he exercised great influence over his fellow men because of the combined charm and force of his personality. There was a subtle commanding influence in his rugged, nomadic, and homeless life. There was intellectual attractiveness and spiritual drawing power in his authoritative manner of teaching, in his lucid logic, his strength of reasoning, his sagacious insight, his alertness of mind, his matchless poise, and his sublime tolerance. He was simple, manly, honest, and fearless. With all of this physical and intellectual influence manifest in the Master's presence, there were also all those spiritual charms of being which have become associated with his personality—patience, tenderness, meekness, gentleness, and humility.

"Jesus of Nazareth was indeed a strong and forceful personality; he was an intellectual power and a spiritual stronghold. His personality not only appealed to the spiritually minded women among his followers, but also to the educated and intellectual Nicodemus and to the hardy Roman soldier, the captain stationed on guard at the cross, who, when he had finished watching the Master die, said, 'Truly, this was a Son of God.' And red-blooded, rugged Galilean fishermen called him Master.

"The pictures of Jesus have been most unfortunate. These paintings of the Christ have exerted a deleterious influence on youth; the temple merchants would hardly have fled before Jesus if he had been such a man as your artists usually have depicted. His was a dignified manhood; he was good, but natural. Jesus did not pose as a mild, sweet, gentle, and kindly mystic. His teaching was thrillingly dynamic. He not only *meant well*, but he went about actually *doing good*." *Pp. 1589-90.*

381. WARNINGS AGAINST CREEDS

"Many times during the training of the twelve Jesus reverted to this theme. Repeatedly he told them it was not his desire that those who believed in him should become dogmatized and standardized in accordance with the religious interpretations of even good men. Again and again he warned his apostles against the formulation of creeds and the establishment of traditions as a means of guiding and controlling believers in the gospel of the kingdom." *P. 1592.*

382. THE STORY OF TEHERMA

"Near the end of the last week at Amathus, Simon Zelotes brought to Jesus one Teherma, a Persian doing business at Damascus. Teherma had heard of Jesus and had come to Capernaum to see him, and there learning that Jesus had gone with his apostles down the Jordan on the way to Jerusalem, he set out to find him. Andrew had presented Teherma to Simon for instruction. Simon looked upon the Persian as a 'fire worshiper,' although Teherma took great pains to explain that fire was only the visible symbol of the Pure and Holy one. After talking with Jesus, the Persian signified his intention of remaining for several days to hear the teaching and listen to the preaching.

"When Simon Zelotes and Jesus were alone, Simon asked the Master: 'Why is it that I could not persuade him? Why did he so resist me and so readily lend an ear to you?' Jesus answered: 'Simon, Simon, how many times have I instructed you to refrain from all efforts to take something *out* of the hearts of those who seek salvation? How often have I told you to labor only to put something *into* these hungry souls? Lead men into the kingdom, and the great and living truths of the kingdom will presently drive out all serious error. When you have presented to mortal man the good news that God is his Father, you can the easier persuade him that he is in reality a son of God. And having done that, you have brought the light of salvation to the one who sits in darkness. Simon, when the Son of Man came first to you, did he come denouncing Moses and the prophets and proclaiming a new and better way of life? No. I came not to take away that which you had from your forefathers but to show you the perfected vision of that which your fathers saw only in part. Go then, Simon, teaching and preaching the kingdom, and when you have a man safely and securely within the kingdom, then is the time, when such a one shall come to you with inquiries, to impart instruction having to do with the progressive advancement of the soul within the divine kingdom.'

"Simon was astonished at these words, but he did as Jesus had instructed him, and Teherma, the Persian, was numbered among those who entered the kingdom." *P. 1592.*

383. JESUS' UNPERTURBED CHARACTER

"The apostles were beginning to recognize the unaffected friendliness of Jesus. Though the Master was easy of approach, he always lived independent of, and above, all human beings. Not for one moment was he ever dominated by any purely mortal influence or subject to frail human judgment. He paid no attention to public opinion, and he was uninfluenced by praise. He seldom paused to correct misunderstandings or to resent misrepresentation. He never asked any man for advice; he never made requests for prayers.

"James was astonished at how Jesus seemed to see the end from the beginning. The Master rarely appeared to be surprised. He was never excited, vexed, or disconcerted. He never apologized to any man. He was at times saddened, but never discouraged." *P. 1594.*

384. THE HEROIC AND MILITANT GOSPEL

"'I have come into this world to do the will of my Father and to reveal his loving character to all mankind. That, my brethren, is my mission. And this one thing I will do, regardless of the misunderstanding of my teachings by Jews or gentiles of this day or of another generation. But you should not overlook the fact that even divine love has its severe disciplines. A father's love for his son oftentimes impels the father to restrain the unwise acts of his thoughtless offspring. The child does not always comprehend the wise and loving motives of the father's restraining discipline. But I declare to you that my Father in Paradise does rule a universe of universes by the compelling power of his love. Love is the greatest of all spirit realities. Truth is a liberating revelation, but love is the supreme relationship. And no matter what blunders your fellow men make in their world management of today, in an age to come the gospel which I declare to you will rule this very world. The ultimate goal of human progress is the reverent recognition of the fatherhood of God and the loving materialization of the brotherhood of man.

"'But who told you that my gospel was intended only for slaves and weaklings? Do you, my chosen apostles, resemble weaklings? Did John look like a weakling? Do you observe that I am enslaved by fear? True, the poor and oppressed of this generation have the gospel preached to them. The religions of this world have neglected the poor, but my Father is no respecter of persons. Besides, the poor of this day are the first to heed the call to repentance and acceptance of sonship. The gospel of the kingdom is to be preached to all men—Jew and gentile, Greek and Roman, rich and poor, free and bond—and equally to young and old, male and female.

"'Because my Father is a God of love and delights in the practice of mercy, do not imbibe the idea that the service of the kingdom is to be one of monotonous ease. The Paradise ascent is the supreme adventure of all time, the rugged achievement of eternity. The service of the kingdom on earth will call for all the courageous manhood that you and your coworkers can muster. Many of you will be put to death for your loyalty to the gospel of this kingdom. It is easy to die in the line of physical battle when your courage is strengthened by the presence of your fighting comrades, but it requires a higher and more profound form of human courage and devotion calmly and all alone to lay down your life for the love of a truth enshrined in your mortal heart.

"'Today, the unbelievers may taunt you with preaching a gospel of nonresistance and with living lives of nonviolence, but you are the first volunteers of a long line of sincere believers in the gospel of this kingdom who will astonish all mankind by their heroic devotion to these teachings. No armies of the world have ever displayed more courage and bravery than will be portrayed by you and your loyal successors who shall go forth to all the world proclaiming the good news—the fatherhood of God and the brotherhood of men. The courage of the flesh is the lowest form of bravery. Mind bravery is a higher type of human courage, but the highest and supreme is uncompromising loyalty to the enlightened convictions of profound spiritual realities. And such courage constitutes the heroism of the God-knowing man. And you are all God-knowing men; you are in very truth the personal associates of the Son of Man.'" P. 1608.

385. SELF-MASTERY

"'Verily, verily, I say to you, he who rules his own self is greater than he who captures a city. Self-mastery is the measure of man's moral nature and the indicator of his spiritual development. In the old order you fasted and prayed; as the new creature of the rebirth of the spirit, you are taught to believe and rejoice. In the Father's kingdom you are to become new creatures; old things are to pass away; behold I show you how all things are to become new. And by your love for one another you are to convince the world that you have passed from bondage to liberty, from death into life everlasting.

"'By the old way you seek to suppress, obey, and conform to the rules of living; by the new way you are first transformed by the Spirit of Truth and thereby strengthened in your inner soul by the constant spiritual renewing of your mind, and so are you endowed with the power of the certain and joyous performance of the gracious, acceptable, and perfect will of God. Forget not—it is your personal faith in the exceedingly great and precious promises of God that ensures your becoming partakers of the divine nature. Thus by your faith and the spirit's transformation, you become in reality the temples of God, and his spirit actually dwells within you. If, then, the spirit dwells within you, you are no longer bondslaves of the flesh but free and liberated sons of the spirit. The new law of the spirit endows you with the liberty of self-mastery in place of the old law of the fear of selfbondage and the slavery of self-denial.'" P. 1609.

386. FIRST STATEMENT OF HIS DIVINITY

"But Nalda would make one more effort to avoid the discussion of the embarrassing question of her personal life on earth and the status of her soul before God. Once more she resorted to questions of general religion, saying: 'Yes, I know, Sir, that John has preached about the coming of the Converter, he who will be called the Deliverer, and that, when he shall come, he will declare to us all things'—and Jesus, interrupting Nalda, said with startling assurance, 'I who speak to you am he.'

"This was the first direct, positive, and undisguised pronouncement of his divine nature and sonship which Jesus had made on earth; and it was made to a woman, a Samaritan woman, and a woman of questionable character in the eyes of men up to this moment, but a woman whom the divine eye beheld as having been sinned against more than as sinning of her own desire and as *now* being a human soul who desired salvation, desired it sincerely and wholeheartedly, and that was enough." P. 1614.

387. THE LORD'S PRAYER

"But the apostles were not yet satisfied; they desired Jesus to give them a model prayer which they could teach the new disciples. After listening to this discourse on prayer, James Zebedee said: 'Very good, Master, but we do not desire a form of prayer for ourselves so much as for the newer believers who so frequently beseech us, "Teach us how acceptably to pray to the Father in heaven."'

"When James had finished speaking, Jesus said: 'If, then, you still desire such a prayer, I would present the one which I taught my brothers and sisters in Nazareth':

> "Our Father who is in heaven,
>   Hallowed be your name.
> Your kingdom come; your will be done
>   On earth as it is in heaven.
> Give us this day our bread for tomorrow;
>   Refresh our souls with the water of life.
> And forgive us every one our debts
>   As we also have forgiven our debtors.
> Save us in temptation, deliver us from evil,
>   And increasingly make us perfect like yourself."
>   P. 1619-20. **Matt. 6:7-13; Luke 11:1-4.**

388. THE STEADFASTNESS OF RUTH

"Late on Friday evening Jesus' baby sister, Ruth, secretly paid him a visit. They spent almost an hour together in a boat anchored a short distance from the shore. No human being, save John Zebedee, ever knew of this visit, and he was admonished to tell no man. Ruth was the only member of Jesus' family who consistently and unwaveringly believed in the divinity of his earth mission from the times of her earliest spiritual consciousness right on down through his eventful ministry, death, resurrection, and ascension; and she finally passed on to the worlds beyond never having doubted the supernatural character of her father-brother's mission in the flesh. Baby Ruth was the chief comfort of Jesus, as regards his earth family, throughout the trying ordeal of his trial, rejection, and crucifixion." P. 1628.

389. HATE IS THE SHADOW OF FEAR

"That Sabbath was a great day in the earth life of Jesus, yes, in the life of a universe. To all local universe intents and purposes the little Jewish city of Capernaum was the real capital of Nebadon. The handful of Jews in the Capernaum synagogue were not the beings to hear that momentous closing statement of Jesus' sermon: 'Hate is the shadow of fear; revenge the mask of cowardice.' Neither could his hearers forget his blessed words, declaring, 'Man is the son of God, not a child of the devil'" P. 1632.

390. SPONTANEOUS HEALING

"But of all the beings who were astonished at this sudden and unexpected outbreak of supernatural healing, Jesus was the most surprised. In a moment when his human interests and sympathies were focused upon the scene of suffering and affliction there spread out before him, he neglected to bear in his human mind the admonitory warnings of his Personalized Adjuster regarding the impossibility of limiting the time element of the creator prerogatives of a Creator Son under certain conditions and in certain circumstances. Jesus desired to see these suffering mortals made whole if his Father's will would not thereby be violated. The Personalized Adjuster of Jesus instantly ruled that such an act of creative energy at that time would not transgress the will of the Paradise Father, and by such a decision—in view of Jesus' preceding expression of healing desire—the creative act *was*. What a *Creator Son* desires and his Father *wills* IS. Not in all of Jesus' subsequent earth life did another such en masse physical healing of mortals take place." P. 1633.

PART IV: *The Life of Jesus*

391. EVIL IS NOT SIN

"'Men are, indeed, by nature evil, but not necessarily sinful. The new birth—the baptism of the spirit—is essential to deliverance from evil and necessary for entrance into the kingdom of heaven, but none of this detracts from the fact that man is the son of God. Neither does this inherent presence of potential evil mean that man is in some mysterious way estranged from the Father in heaven so that, as an alien, foreigner, or stepchild, he must in some manner seek for legal adoption by the Father. All such notions are born, first, of your misunderstanding of the Father and, second, of your ignorance of the origin, nature, and destiny of man.'" P. 1660.

392. AFFLICTION NOT PUNISHMENT

"'But, my son, you should know that the Father does not purposely afflict his children. Man brings down upon himself unnecessary affliction as a result of his persistent refusal to walk in the better ways of the divine will. Affliction is potential in evil, but much of it has been produced by sin and iniquity. Many unusual events have transpired on this world, and it is not strange that all thinking men should be perplexed by the scenes of suffering and affliction which they witness. But of one thing you may be sure: The Father does not send affliction as an arbitrary punishment for wrongdoing. The imperfections and handicaps of evil are inherent; the penalties of sin are inevitable; the destroying consequences of iniquity are inexorable. Man should not blame God for those afflictions which are the natural result of the life which he chooses to live; neither should man complain of those experiences which are a part of life as it is lived on this world. It is the Father's will that mortal man should work persistently and consistently toward the betterment of his estate on earth. Intelligent application would enable man to overcome much of his earthly misery.'" P. 1661.

"'Nathaniel, it is our mission to help men solve their spiritual problems and in this way to quicken their minds so that they may be the better prepared and inspired to go about solving their manifold material problems. I know of your confusion as you have read the Scriptures. All too often there has prevailed a tendency to ascribe to God the responsibility for everything which ignorant man fails to understand. The Father is not personally responsible for all you may fail to comprehend. Do not doubt the love of the Father just because some just and wise law of his ordaining chances to afflict you because you have innocently or deliberately transgressed such a divine ordinance.'" P. 1662.

"Then Jesus made this final statement: 'The Father in heaven does not willingly afflict the children of men. Man suffers, first, from the accidents of time and the imperfections of the evil of an immature physical existence. Next, he suffers the inexorable consequences of sin—the transgression of the laws of life and light. And finally, man reaps the harvest of his own iniquitous persistence in rebellion against the righteous rule of heaven on earth. But man's miseries are not a *personal* visitation of divine judgment. Man can, and will, do much to lessen his temporal sufferings. But once and for all be delivered from the superstition that God afflicts man at the behest of the evil one. Study the Book of Job just to discover how many wrong ideas of God even good men may honestly entertain; and then note how even the painfully afflicted Job found the God of comfort and salvation in spite of such erroneous teachings. At last his faith pierced the clouds of suffering to discern the light of life pouring forth from the Father as healing mercy and everlasting righteousness.'" P. 1664. **Lam. 3:33**.

393. THE LIBERATION OF WOMEN

"The most astonishing and the most revolutionary feature of Michael's mission on earth was his attitude toward women. In a day and generation when a man was not supposed to salute even his own wife in a public place, Jesus dared to take women along as teachers of the gospel in connection with his third tour of Galilee. And he had the consummate courage to do this in the face of the rabbinic teaching which declared that it was 'better that the words of the law should be burned than delivered to women.'

"In one generation Jesus lifted women out of the disrespectful oblivion and the slavish drudgery of the ages. And it is the one shameful thing about the religion that presumed to take Jesus' name that it lacked the moral courage to follow this noble example in its subsequent attitude toward women." P. 1671.

394. THE SECRET OF HAPPINESS

"'Simon, some persons are naturally more happy than others. Much, very much, depends upon the willingness of man to be led and directed by the Father's spirit which lives within him. Have you not read in the Scriptures the words of the wise man, "The spirit of man is the candle of the Lord, searching all the inward parts"? And also that such spirit-led mortals say: "The lines are fallen to me in pleasant places; yes, I have a goodly heritage." "A little that a righteous man has is better than the riches of many wicked," for "a good man shall be satisfied from within himself." "A merry heart makes a cheerful countenance and is a continual feast. Better is a little with the reverence of the Lord than great treasure and trouble therewith. Better is a dinner of herbs where love is than a fatted ox and hatred therewith. Better is a little with righteousness than great revenues without rectitude." "A merry heart does good like a medicine." "Better is a handful with composure than a superabundance with sorrow and vexation of spirit."

"'Much of man's sorrow is born of the disappointment of his ambitions and the wounding of his pride. Although men owe a duty to themselves to make the best of their lives on earth, having thus sincerely exerted themselves, they should cheerfully accept their lot and exercise ingenuity in making the most of that which has fallen to their hands. All too many of man's troubles take origin in the fear soil of his own natural heart. "The wicked flee when no man pursues.""The wicked are like the troubled sea, for it cannot rest, but its waters cast up mire and dirt; there is no peace, says God, for the wicked."

"'Seek not, then, for false peace and transient joy but rather for the assurance of faith and the sureties of divine sonship which yield composure, contentment, and supreme joy in the spirit.'" *P. 1674*. **Prov. 20:27; Ps. 16:6; Ps. 37:16; Prov. 14:14; Prov. 15:13,16,17; Prov. 16:8; Prov. 17:22; Eccl. 4:6; Prov. 28:1; Isa. 57:20,21.**

395. LOVE IN THE PLACE OF FEAR

"'Your forebears feared God because he was mighty and mysterious. You shall adore him because he is magnificent in love, plenteous in mercy, and glorious in truth. The power of God engenders fear in the heart of man, but the nobility and righteousness of his personality beget, reverence, love, and willing worship. A dutiful and affectionate son does not fear or dread even a mighty and noble father. I have come into the world to put love in the place of fear, joy in the place of sorrow, confidence in the place of dread, loving service and appreciative worship in the place of slavish bondage and meaningless ceremonies. But it is still true of those who sit in darkness that "the fear of the Lord is the beginning of wisdom." But when the light has more fully come, the sons of God are led to praise the Infinite for what he *is* rather than to fear him for what he *does*.'" *P. 1675*. **Ps. 111:10.**

396. WHAT SHALL WE DO TO BE SAVED?

"'When men and women ask what shall we do to be saved, you shall answer, Believe this gospel of the kingdom; accept divine forgiveness. By faith recognize the indwelling spirit of God, whose acceptance makes you a son of God. Have you not read in the Scriptures where it says, "In the Lord have I righteousness and strength." Also where the Father says, "My righteousnes is near; my salvation has gone forth, and my arms shall enfold my people." "My soul shall be joyful in the love of my God, for he has clothed me with the garments of salvation and has covered me with the robe of his righteousness." Have you not also read of the Father that his name "shall be called the Lord our righteousness." "Take away the filthy rags of self-righteousness and clothe my son with the robe of divine righteousness and eternal salvation." It is forever true, "the just shall live by faith." Entrance into the Father's kingdom is wholly free, but progress—growth in grace—is essential to continuance therein.'" P. 1682.

"In summing up his final statement, Jesus said: 'You cannot buy salvation; you cannot earn righteousness. Salvation is the gift of God, and righteousness is the natural fruit of the spirit-born life of sonship in the kingdom. You are not to be saved because you live a righteous life; rather is it that you live a righteous life because you have already been saved, have recognized sonship as the gift of God and service in the kingdom as the supreme delight of life on earth. When men believe this gospel, which is a revelation of the goodness of God, they will be led to voluntary repentance of all known sin. Realization of sonship is incompatible with the desire to sin. Kingdom believers hunger for righteousness and thirst for divine perfection.'" P. 1683.

397. MISSION OF ADVERSITY

"Universe difficulties must be met and planetary obstacles must be encountered as a part of the experience training provided for the growth and development, the progressive perfection, of the evolving souls of mortal creatures. The spiritualization of the human soul requires intimate experience with the educational solving of a wide range of real universe problems. The animal nature and the lower forms of will creatures do not progress favorably in environmental ease. Problematic situations, coupled with exertion stimuli, conspire to produce those activities of mind, soul, and spirit which contribute mightily to the achievement of worthy goals of mortal progression and to the attainment of higher levels of spirit destiny." P. 1719.

398. THE RELIGION OF THE SPIRIT

"The religion of the spirit means effort, struggle, conflict, faith, determination, love, loyalty, and progress. The religion of the mind—the theology of authority—requires little or none of these exertions from its formal believers. Tradition is a safe refuge and an easy path for those fearful and halfhearted souls who instinctively shun the spirit struggles and mental uncertainties associated with those faith voyages of daring adventure out upon the high seas of unexplored truth in search for the farther shores of spiritual realities as they may be discovered by the progressive human mind and experienced by the evolving human soul." P. 1729.

399. DOING THE WILL OF GOD

"Never forget there is only one adventure which is more satisfying and thrilling than the attempt to discover the will of the living God, and that is the supreme experience of honestly trying to do that divine will. And fail not to remember that the will of God can be done in any earthly occupation. Some callings are not holy and others secular. All things are sacred in the lives of those who are spirit led; that is, subordinated to truth, ennobled by love, dominated by mercy, and restrained by fairness—justice. The spirit which my Father and I shall send into the world is not only the Spirit of Truth but also the spirit of idealistic beauty." *P. 1732.*

400. THE FAINTEST FLICKER OF FAITH

"Now, mistake not, my Father will ever respond to the faintest flicker of faith. He takes note of the physical and superstitious emotions of the primitive man. And with those honest but fearful souls whose faith is so weak that it amounts to little more than an intellectual conformity to a passive attitude of assent to religions of authority, the Father is ever alert to honor and foster even all such feeble attempts to reach out for him. But you who have been called out of darkness into the light are expected to believe with a whole heart; your faith shall dominate the combined attitudes of body, mind, and spirit.

"You are my apostles, and to you religion shall not become a theologic shelter to which you may flee in fear of facing the rugged realities of spiritual progress and idealistic adventure; but rather shall your religion become the fact of real experience which testifies that God has found you, idealized, ennobled, and spiritualized you, and that you have enlisted in the eternal adventure of finding the God who has thus found and sonshipped you." *P. 3733.*

401. THIS LIFE IS ONLY A BRIDGE

"In entering Sidon, Jesus and his associates passed over a bridge, the first one many of them had ever seen. As they walked over this bridge, Jesus, among other things, said: 'This world is only a bridge; you may pass over it, but you should not think to build a dwelling place upon it.'" *P. 1735.*

402. HUMOR AND FAITH

"Jesus greatly enjoyed the keen sense of humor which these gentiles exhibited. It was the sense of humor displayed by Norana, the Syrian woman, as well as her great and persistent faith, that so touched the Master's heart and appealed to his mercy. Jesus greatly regretted that his people—the Jews—were so lacking in humor. He once said to Thomas: 'My people take themselves too seriously; they are just about devoid of an appreciation of humor. The burdensome religion of the Pharisees could never have had origin among a people with a sense of humor. They also lack consistency; they strain at gnats and swallow camels.'" *P. 1736.*

403. LEADERSHIP AND HUMAN FRAILTIES

"Forceful ambition, intelligent judgment, and seasoned wisdom are the essentials of material success. Leadership is dependent on natural ability, discretion, will power, and determination. Spiritual destiny is dependent on faith, love, and devotion to truth—hunger and thirst for righteousness—the wholehearted desire to find God and to be like him.

"Do not become discouraged by the discovery that you are human. Human nature may tend toward evil, but it is not inherently sinful. Be not downcast by your failure wholly to forget some of your regrettable experiences. The mistakes which you fail to forget in time will be forgotten in eternity. Lighten your burdens of soul by speedily acquiring a long-distance view of your destiny, a universe expansion of your career." P. 1739.

404. CERTAINTY OF SALVATION

"The God-conscious mortal is certain of salvation; he is unafraid of life; he is honest and consistent. He knows how bravely to endure unavoidable suffering; he is uncomplaining when faced by inescapable hardship.

"The true believer does not grow weary in well-doing just because he is thwarted. Difficulty whets the ardor of the truth lover, while obstacles only challenge the exertions of the undaunted kingdom builder." P. 1740.

405. THE KEYS OF THE KINGDOM

"Jesus, still standing, then said to the twelve: 'You are my chosen ambassadors, but I know that, in the circumstances, you could not entertain this belief as a result of mere human knowledge. This is a revelation of the spirit of my Father to your inmost souls. And when, therefore, you make this confession by the insight of the spirit of my Father which dwells within you, I am led to declare that upon this foundation will I build the brotherhood of the kingdom of heaven. Upon this rock of spiritual reality will I build the living temple of spiritual fellowship in the eternal realities of my Father's kingdom. All the forces of evil and the hosts of sin shall not prevail against this human fraternity of the divine spirit. And while my Father's spirit shall ever be the divine guide and mentor of all who enter the bonds of this spirit fellowship, to you and your successors I now deliver the keys of the outward kingdom—the authority over things temporal—the social and economic features of this association of men and women as fellows of the kingdom.' And again he charged them, for the time being, that they should tell no man that he was the Son of God." P. 1747.

"Jesus had sincerely endeavored to lead his followers into the spiritual kingdom as a teacher, then as a teacher-healer, but they would not have it so. He well knew that his earth mission could not possibly fulfill the Messianic expectations of the Jewish people; the olden prophets had portrayed a Messiah which he could never be. He sought to establish the Father's kingdom as the Son of Man, but his followers would not go forward in the adventure. Jesus, seeing this, then elected to meet his believers part way and in so doing prepared openly to assume the role of the bestowal Son of God." P. 1749. **Matt. 16:15-20.**

406. JUDGEMENT BELONGS TO THE GROUP

"Thus did Jesus teach the dangers and illustrate the unfairness of sitting in personal judgment upon one's fellows. Discipline must be maintained, justice must be administered, but in all these matters the wisdom of the brotherhood should prevail. Jesus invested legislative and judicial authority in the *group*, not in the *individual*. Even this investment of authority in the group must not be exercised as personal authority. There is always danger that the verdict of an individual may be warped by prejudice or distorted by passion. Group judgment is more likely to remove the dangers and eliminate the unfairness of personal bias. Jesus sought always to minimize the elements of unfairness, retaliation, and vengeance." P. 1764.

407. AVOID FRIGHTENING PEOPLE

"Never be guilty of such unworthy tactics as endeavoring to frighten men and women into the kingdom. A loving father does not frighten his children into yielding obedience to his just requirements." P. 1766.

408. JESUS NOT A MAN OF SORROWS

"You shall not portray your teacher as a man of sorrows. Future generations shall know also the radiance of our joy, the buoyancy of our good will, and the inspiration of our good humor. We proclaim a message of good news which is infectious in its transforming power. Our religion is throbbing with new life and new meanings. Those who accept this teaching are filled with joy and in their hearts are constrained to rejoice evermore. Increasing happiness is always the experience of all who are certain about God." P. 1766.

409. DANGERS OF FALSE SYMPATHY

"Teach all believers to avoid leaning upon the insecure props of false sympathy. You cannot develop strong characters out of the indulgence of self-pity; honestly endeavor to avoid the deceptive influence of mere fellowship in misery. Extend sympathy to the brave and courageous while you withhold overmuch pity from those cowardly souls who only halfheartedly stand up before the trials of living. Offer not consolation to those who lie down before their troubles without a struggle. Sympathize not with your fellows merely that they may sympathize with you in return." P. 1766.

410. WE ARE ALWAYS UNAFRAID

"Teach all believers that those who enter the kingdom are not thereby rendered immune to the accidents of time or to the ordinary catastrophes of nature. Believing the gospel will not prevent getting into trouble, but it will insure that you shall be *unafraid* when trouble does overtake you. If you dare to believe in me and wholeheartedly proceed to follow after me, you shall most certainly by so doing enter upon the sure pathway to trouble. I do not promise to deliver you from the waters of adversity, but I do promise to go with you through all of them." *P. 1767.*

411. HOW TO LOOK AT THE BIBLE

"'But the greatest error of the teaching about the Scriptures is the doctrine of their being sealed books of mystery and wisdom which only the wise minds of the nation dare to interpret. The revelations of divine truth are not sealed except by human ignorance, bigotry, and narrow-minded intolerance. The light of the Scriptures is only dimmed by prejudice and darkened by superstition. A false fear of sacredness has prevented religion from being safeguarded by common sense. The fear of the authority of the sacred writings of the past effectively prevents the honest souls of today from accepting the new light of the gospel, the light which these very God-knowing men of another generation so intensely longed to see.'" *P. 1768.*

412. ON BEING "SECOND MILERS"

"When Jesus instructed his apostles that they should, when one unjustly took away the coat, offer the other garment, he referred not so much to a literal second coat as to the idea of doing something *positive* to save the wrongdoer in the place of the olden advice to retaliate—'an eye for an eye' and so on. Jesus abhorred the idea either of retaliation or of becoming just a passive sufferer or victim of injustice. On this occasion he taught them the three ways of contending with, and resisting, evil:

"1. To return evil for evil—the positive but unrighteous method.

"2. To suffer evil without complaint and without resistance—the purely negative method.

"3. To return good for evil, to assert the will so as to become master of the situation, to overcome evil with good—the positive and righteous method.

"One of the apostles once asked: 'Master, what should I do if a stranger forced me to carry his pack for a mile?' Jesus answered: 'Do not sit down and sigh for relief while you berate the stranger under your breath. Righteousness comes not from such passive attitudes. If you can think of nothing more effectively positive to do, you can at least carry the pack a second mile. That will of a certainty challenge the unrighteous and ungodly stranger.'" *P. 1770.* **Lev. 24:20; Matt. 5:41**.

413. MASTERING THE ART OF LIVING

"The more complex civilization becomes, the more difficult will become the art of living. The more rapid the changes in social usage, the more complicated will become the task of character development. Every ten generations mankind must learn anew the art of living if progress is to continue. And if man becomes so ingenious that he more rapidly adds to the complexities of society, the art of living will need to be remastered in less time, perhaps every single generation. If the evolution of the art of living fails to keep pace with the technique of existence, humanity will quickly revert to the simple urge of living—the attainment of the satisfaction of present desires. Thus will humanity remain immature; society will fail in growing up to full maturity." *P. 1772.*

414. WORSHIP AND SPIRITUAL STRENGTH

"This worshipful practice of your Master brings that relaxation which renews the mind; that illumination which inspires the soul; that courage which enables one bravely to face one's problems; that self-understanding which obliterates debilitating fear; and that consciousness of union with divinity which equips man with the assurance that enables him to dare to be Godlike. The relaxation of worship, or spiritual communion as practiced by the Master, relieves tension, removes conflicts, and mightily augments the total resources of the personality. And all this philosophy, plus the gospel of the kingdom, constitutes the new religion as I understand it." *P. 1774.*

415. LEARNING HOW TO FAIL GRACEFULLY

"But life will become a burden of existence unless you learn how to fail gracefully. There is an art in defeat which noble souls always acquire; you must know how to lose cheerfully; you must be fearless of disappointment. Never hesitate to admit failure. Make no attempt to hide failure under deceptive smiles and beaming optimism. It sounds well always to claim success, but the end results are appalling. Such a technique leads directly to the creation of a world of unreality and to the inevitable crash of ultimate disillusionment." *P. 1779.*

416. TRUE SUCCESS

"The career of a God-seeking man may prove to be a great success in the light of eternity, even though the whole temporal-life enterprise may appear as an overwhelming failure, provided each life failure yielded the culture of wisdom and spirit achievement. Do not make the mistake of confusing knowledge, culture, and wisdom. They are related in life, but they represent vastly differing spirit values; wisdom ever dominates knowledge and always glorifies culture." *P. 1780.*

417. TRANSCENDENCE OF THE RELIGION OF JESUS

"The religion of Jesus transcends all our former concepts of the idea of worship in that he not only portrays his Father as the ideal of infinite reality but positively declares that this divine source of values and the eternal center of the universe is truly and personally attainable by every mortal creature who chooses to enter the kingdom of heaven on earth, thereby acknowledging the acceptance of sonship with God and brotherhood with man. That, I submit, is the highest concept of religion the world has ever known, and I pronounce that there can never be a higher since this gospel embraces the infinity of realities, the divinity of values, and the eternity of universal attainments. Such a concept constitutes the achievement of the experience of the idealism of the supreme and the ultimate." *P. 1781.*

418. THE WATER OF LIFE

"On the last day, the great day of the feast, as the procession from the pool of Siloam passed through the temple courts, and just after the water and the wine had been poured down upon the altar by the priests, Jesus, standing among the pilgrims, said: 'If any man thirst, let him come to me and drink. From the Father above I bring to this world the water of life. He who believes me shall be filled with the spirit which this water represents, for even the Scriptures have said, "Out of him shall flow rivers of living waters." When the Son of Man has finished his work on earth, there shall be poured out upon all flesh the living Spirit of Truth. Those who receive this spirit shall never know spiritual thirst.'" *P. 1795.* **John 7:37-39.**

419. LOVE OF RICHES

"Riches have nothing directly to do with entrance into the kingdom of heaven, but the *love of wealth does*. The spiritual loyalties of the kingdom are incompatible with servility to materialistic mammon. Man may not share his supreme loyalty to a spiritual ideal with a material devotion." P. 1803.

420. JESUS THANKFUL FOR HIS ASSOCIATES

"And it was at this time, just before partaking of the evening meal, that Jesus experienced one of those rare moments of emotional ecstasy which his followers had occasionally witnessed. He said: 'I thank you, my Father, Lord of heaven and earth, that, while this wonderful gospel was hidden from the wise and self-righteous, the spirit has revealed these spiritual glories to these children of the kingdom. Yes, my Father, it must have been pleasing in your sight to do this, and I rejoice to know that the good news will spread to all the world even after I shall have returned to you and the work which you have given me to perform. I am mightily moved as I realize you are about to deliver all authority into my hands, that only you really know who I am, and that only I really know you, and those to whom I have revealed you. And when I have finished this revelation to my brethren in the flesh, I will continue the revelation to your creatures on high.'" *P. 1807.*

421. OF MORE VALUE THAN MANY SPARROWS

"'Are not five sparrows sold for two pennies? And yet, when these birds flit about in quest of their sustenance, not one of them exists without the knowledge of the Father, the source of all life. To the seraphic guardians the very hairs of your head are numbered. And if all of this is true, why should you live in fear of the many trifles which come up in your daily lives? I say to you: Fear not; you are of much more value than many sparrows.'" *P. 1820.* **Matt. 10:29,31; Luke 12:6,7.**

422. WHY TARRY IN THE VALLEY OF DECISION?

"'How long will you tarry in the valley of decision? Why do you halt between two opinions? Why should Jew or gentile hesitate to accept the good news that he is a son of the eternal God? How long will it take us to persuade you to enter joyfully into your spiritual inheritance? I came into this world to reveal the Father to you and to lead you to the Father. The first I have done, but the last I may not do without your consent; the Father never compels any man to enter the kingdom. The invitation ever has been and always will be: Whosoever will, let him come and freely partake of the water of life.'" *P. 1820.*

423. WE CAN HAVE THE KINGDOM

"'You are only a small group, but if you have faith, if you will not stumble in fear, I declare that it is my Father's good pleasure to give you this kingdom. You have laid up your treasures where the purse waxes not old, where no thief can despoil, and where no moth can destroy. And as I told the people, where your treasure is, there will your heart be also.'" *P. 1823.* **Luke 12:32.**

424. PROSPERITY NOT A TOKEN OF DIVINE FAVOR

"'All too long have your fathers believed that prosperity was the token of divine approval; that adversity was the proof of God's displeasure. I declare that such beliefs are superstitions. Do you not observe that far greater numbers of the poor joyfully receive the gospel and immediately enter the kingdom? If riches evidence divine favor, why do the rich so many times refuse to believe this good news from heaven?

"'The Father causes his rain to fall on the just and the unjust; the sun likewise shines on the righteous and the unrighteous. You know about those Galileans whose blood Pilate mingled with the sacrifices, but I tell you these Galileans were not in any manner sinners above all their fellows just because this happened to them. You also know about the eighteen men upon whom the tower of Siloam fell, killing them. Think not that these men who were thus destroyed were offenders above all their brethren in Jerusalem. These folks were simply innocent victims of one the accidents of time.'" *P. 1830.* **Matt. 5:45; Luke 13:1-3.**

425. MEANING OF HEALTH AND DISEASE

"'In the matter of sickness and health, you should know that these bodily states are the result of material causes; health is not the smile of heaven, neither is affliction the frown of God.

"'The Father's human children have equal capacity for the reception of material blessings; therefore does he bestow things physical upon the children of men without discrimination. When it comes to the bestowal of spiritual gifts, the Father is limited by man's capacity for receiving these divine endowments. Although the Father is no respecter of persons, in the bestowal of spiritual gifts he is limited by man's faith and by his willingness always to abide by the Father's will.'" *P. 1831.*

426. WOMAN WITH SPIRIT OF INFIRMITY

"Abner had arranged for the Master to teach in the synagogue on this Sabbath day, the first time Jesus had appeared in a synagogue since they had all been closed to his teachings by order of the Sanhedrin. At the conclusion of the service Jesus looked down before him upon an elderly woman who wore a downcast expression, and who was much bent in form. This woman had long been fear-ridden, and all joy had passed out of her life. As Jesus stepped down from the pulpit, he went over to her and, touching her bowedover form on the shoulder, said: 'Woman, if you would only believe, you could be wholly loosed from your spirit of infirmity.' And this woman, who had been bowed down and bound up by the depressions of fear for more than eighteen years, believed the words of the Master and by faith straightened up immediately. When this woman saw that she had been made straight, she lifted up her voice and glorified God." *Pp. 1835-6.* **Luke 13:11-13.**

427. THE PHARISEE AND THE PUBLICAN

"On the way to Judea Jesus was followed by a company of almost fifty of his friends and enemies. At their noon lunchtime, on Wednesday, he talked to his apostles and this group of followers on the 'Terms of Salvation,' and at the end of this lesson told the parable of the Pharisee and the publican (a tax collector). Said Jesus: 'You see, then, that the Father gives salvation to the children of men, and this salvation is a free gift to all who have the faith to receive sonship in the divine family. There is nothing man can do to earn this salvation. Works of self-righteousness cannot buy the favor of God, and much praying in public will not atone for lack of living faith in the heart. Men you may deceive by your outward service, but God looks into your souls. What I am telling you is well illustrated by two men who went into the temple to pray, the one a Pharisee and the other a publican. The Pharisee stood and prayed to himself: "O God, I thank you that I am not like the rest of men, extortioners, unlearned, unjust, adulterers, or even like this publican. I fast twice a week; I give tithes of all that I get." But the publican, standing afar off, would not so much as lift his eyes to heaven but smote his breast, saying, "God be merciful to me a sinner." I tell you that the publican went home with God's approval rather than the Pharisee, for every one who exalts himself shall be humbled, but he who humbles himself shall be exalted.'" *P. 1838.* **Luke 18:10-14.**

428. JESUS CONCERNED ONLY WITH RELIGION

"It was very difficult for the apostles to understand the Master's reluctance to make positive pronouncements relative to scientific, social, economic, and political problems. They did not fully realize that his earth mission was exclusively concerned with revelations of spiritual and religious truths." *P. 1839.*

429. AT THE TOMB OF LAZARUS

"The said Jesus, looking straight into the eyes of Martha: 'I am the resurrection and the life; he who believes in me, though he dies, yet shall he live. In truth, whosoever lives and believes in me shall never really die. Martha, do you believe this?' And Martha answered the Master: 'Yes, I have long believed that you are the Deliverer, the Son of the living God, even he who should come to this world.'" *P. 1843.* **John 11:25.**

430. LAZARUS IS RESURRECTED

"Then went Lazarus over to Jesus and, with his sisters, knelt at the Master's feet to give thanks and offer praise to God. Jesus, taking Lazarus by the hand, lifted him up, saying: 'My son, what has happened to you will also be experienced by all who believe this gospel except that they shall be resurrected in a more glorious form. You shall be a living witness of the truth which I spoke—I am the resurrection and the life. But let us all now go into the house and partake of nourishment for these physical bodies.'" *P. 1846.*

431. HOW WE CAN KNOW GOD

"You learn about God from Jesus by observing the divinity of his life, not by depending on his teachings. From the life of the Master you may each assimilate that concept of God which represents the measure of your capacity to perceive realities spiritual and divine, truths real and eternal. The finite can never hope to comprehend the Infinite except as the Infinite was focalized in the time-space personality of the finite experience of the human life of Jesus of Nazareth.

"Jesus well knew that God can be known only by the realities of experience; never can he be understood by the mere teaching of the mind. Jesus taught his apostles that, while they never could fully understand God, they could most certainly *know* him, even as they had known the Son of Man. You can know God, not by understanding what Jesus said, but by knowing what Jesus was. Jesus *was* a revelation of God." *P. 1856.*

432. KNOWING GOD AS A FATHER

"Jesus is the spiritual lens in human likeness which makes visible to the material creature Him who is invisible. He is your elder brother who, in the flesh, makes *known* to you a Being of infinite attributes whom not even the celestial hosts can presume fully to understand. But all of this must consist in the personal experience of the *individual believer.* God who is spirit can be known only as a spiritual experience. God can be revealed to the finite sons of the material worlds, by the divine Son of the spiritual realms, only as a *Father.* You can know the Eternal as a Father; you can worship him as the God of universes, the infinite Creator of all existences." *P. 1857.*

433. JESUS' METHODS OF MINISTRY

"Jesus could help men so much because he loved them so sincerely. He truly loved each man, each woman, and each child. He could be such a true friend because of his remarkable insight—he knew so fully what was in the heart and in the mind of man. He was an interested and keen observer. He was an expert in the comprehension of human need, clever in detecting human longings.

"Jesus was never in a hurry. He had time to comfort his fellow men 'as he passed by.' And he always made his friends feel at ease. He was a charming listener. He never engaged in the meddlesome probing of the souls of his associates. As he comforted hungry minds and ministered to thirsty souls, the recipients of his mercy did not so much feel that they were confessing *to* him as that they were conferring *with* him. They had unbounded confidence in him because they saw he had so much faith in them.

"He never seemed to be curious about people, and he never manifested a desire to direct, manage, or follow them up. He inspired profound self-confidence and robust courage in all who enjoyed his association. When he smiled on a man, that mortal experienced increased capacity for solving his manifold problems." Pp. 1874-5.

434. "AS JESUS PASSED BY"

"Most of the really important things which Jesus said or did seemed to happen casually, 'as he passed by.' There was so little of the professional, the well-planned, or the premeditated in the Master's earthly ministry. He dispensed health and scattered happiness naturally and gracefully as he journeyed through life. It was literally true, 'He went about doing good.'

"And it behooves the Master's followers in all ages to learn to minister as 'they pass by'—to do unselfish good as they go about their daily duties." P. 1875. **John 9:1**.

435. HOW WE SHOULD CARRY ON

"'And even you, Thomas, fail to comprehend what I have been saying. Have I not all this time taught you that your connection with the kingdom is spiritual and individual, wholly a matter of personal experience in the spirit by the faith-realization that you are a son of God? What more shall I say? The downfall of nations, the crash of empires, the destruction of the unbelieving Jews, the end of an age, even the end of the world, what have these things to do with one who believes this gospel, and who has hid his life in the surety of the eternal kingdom? You who are God-knowing and gospel-believing have already received the assurances of eternal life. Since your lives have been lived in the spirit and for the Father, nothing can be of serious concern to you. Kingdom builders, the accredited citizens of the heavenly worlds, are not to be disturbed by temporal upheavals or perturbed by terrestrial cataclysms. What does it matter to you who believe this gospel of the kingdom if nations overturn, the age ends, or all things visible crash, since you know that your life is the gift of the Son, and that it is eternally secure in the Father? Having lived the temporal life by faith and having yielded the fruits of the spirit as the righteousness of loving service for your fellows, you can confidently look forward to the next step in the eternal career with the same survival faith that has carried you through your first and earthly adventure in sonship with God.

"'Each generation of believers should carry on their work, in view of the possible return of the Son of Man, exactly as each individual believer carries forward his lifework in view of inevitable and ever-impending natural death. When you have by faith once established yourself as a son of God, nothing else matters as regards the surety of survival. But make no mistake! this survival faith is a living faith, and it increasingly manifests the fruits of that divine spirit which first inspired it in the human heart. That you have once accepted sonship in the heavenly kingdom will not save you in the face of the knowing and persistent rejection of those truths which have to do with the progressive spiritual fruit-bearing of the sons of God in the flesh. You who have been with me in the Father's business on earth can even now desert the kingdom if you find that you love not the way of the Father's service for mankind.'" P. 1916.

"'To every one who has, more shall be given, and he shall have abundance; but from him who has not, even that which he has shall be taken away. You cannot stand still in the affairs of the eternal kingdom. My Father requires all his children to grow in grace and in a knowledge of the truth. You who know these truths must yield the increase of the fruits of the spirit and manifest a growing devotion to the unselfish service of your fellow servants. And remember that, inasmuch as you minister to one of the least of my brethren, you have done this service to me.

"'And so should you go about the work of the Father's business, now and henceforth, even forevermore. Carry on until I come. In faithfulness do that which is intrusted to you, and thereby shall you be ready for the reckoning call of death. And having thus lived for the glory of the Father and the satisfaction of the Son, you shall enter with joy and exceedingly great pleasure into the eternal service of the everlasting kingdom.'" P. 1917.

436. ONE DAY WITH GOD IN THE HILLS

"As Jesus was about to take the lunch basket from John's hand, the young man ventured to say: 'But, Master, you may set the basket down while you turn aside to pray and go on without it. Besides, if I should go along to carry the lunch, you would be more free to worship, and I will surely be silent. I will ask no questions and will stay by the basket when you go apart by yourself to pray.'

"While making this speech, the temerity of which astonished some of the nearby listeners, John had made bold to hold on to the basket. There they stood, both John and Jesus holding the basket. Presently the Master let go and, looking down on the lad, said: 'Since with all your heart you crave to go with me, it shall not be denied you. We will go off by ourselves and have a good visit. You may ask me any question that arises in your heart, and we will comfort and console each other. You may start out carrying the lunch, and when you grow weary, I will help you. Follow on with me.'

"Jesus did not return to the camp that evening until after sunset. The Master spent this last day of quiet on earth visiting with this truth-hungry youth and talking with his Paradise Father. This event has become known on high as 'the day which a young man spent with God in the hills.' Forever this occasion exemplifies the willingness of the Creator to fellowship the creature. Even a youth, if the desire of the heart is really supreme, can command the attention and enjoy the loving companionship of the God of a universe, actually experience the unforgettable ecstasy of being alone with God in the hills, and for a whole day. And such was the unique experience of John Mark on this Wednesday in the hills of Judea.

"Jesus visited much with John, talking freely about the affairs of this world and the next. John told Jesus how much he regretted that he had not been old enough to be one of the apostles and expressed his great appreciation that he had been permitted to follow on with them since their first preaching at the Jordan ford near Jericho, except for the trip to Phoenicia. Jesus warned the lad not to become discouraged by impending events and assured him he would live to become a mighty messenger of the kingdom.

"John Mark was thrilled by the memory of this day with Jesus in the hills, but he never forgot the Master's final admonition, spoken just as they were about to return to the Gethsemane camp, when he said: 'Well, John, we have had a good visit, a real day of rest, but see to it that you tell no man the things which I told you.' And John Mark never did reveal anything that transpired on this day which he spent with Jesus in the hills." Pp. 1920-1.

"It was about midafternoon when Nathaniel made his speech on 'Supreme Desire' to about half a dozen of the apostles and as many disciples, the ending of which was: 'What is wrong with most of us is that we are only halfhearted. We fail to love the Master as he loves us. If we had all wanted to go with him as much as John Mark did, he would surely have taken us all. We stood by while the lad approached the Master and offered him the basket, but when the Master took hold of it, the lad would not let go. And so the Master left us here while he went off to the hills with basket, boy, and all.'" P. 1923.

437. DUAL CITIZENSHIP

"There is nothing incompatible between sonship in the spiritual kingdom and citizenship in the secular or civil government. It is the believer's duty to render to Caesar the things which are Caesar's and to God the things which are God's. There cannot be any disagreement between these two requirements, the one being material and the other spiritual, unless it should develop that a Caesar presumes to usurp the prerogatives of God and demand that spiritual homage and supreme worship be rendered to him. In such a case you shall worship only God while you seek to enlighten such misguided earthly rulers and in this way lead them also to the recognition of the Father in heaven. You shall not render spiritual worship to earthly rulers; neither should you employ the physical forces of earthly governments, whose rulers may sometime become believers, in the work of furthering the mission of the spiritual kingdom.

"Sonship in the kingdom, from the standpoint of advancing civilization, should assist you in becoming the ideal citizens of the kingdoms of this world since brotherhood and service are the cornerstones of the gospel of the kingdom. The love call of the spiritual kingdom should prove to be the effective destroyer of the hate urge of the unbelieving and war-minded citizens of the earthly kingdoms. But these material-minded sons in darkness will never know of your spiritual light of truth unless you draw very near them with that unselfish social service which is the natural outgrowth of the bearing of the fruits of the spirit in the life experience of each individual believer." *Pp. 1929-30.*

438. NOT TO BE MYSTICS OR ASCETICS

"You are not to be passive mystics or colorless ascetics; you should not become dreamers and drifters, supinely trusting in a fictitious Providence to provide even the necessities of life. You are indeed to be gentle in your dealings with erring mortals, patient in your intercourse with ignorant men, and forbearing under provocation; but you are also to be valiant in defense of righteousness, mighty in the promulgation of truth, and aggressive in the preaching of this gospel of the kingdom, even to the ends of the earth." *P. 1931.*

439. HOW WE SHOULD LIVE

"Throughout the vicissitudes of life, remember always to love one another. Do not strive with men, even with unbelievers. Show mercy even to those who despitefully abuse you. Show yourselves to be loyal citizens, upright artisans, praiseworthy neighbors, devoted kinsmen, understanding parents, and sincere believers in the brotherhood of the Father's kingdom. And my spirit shall be upon you, now and even to the end of the world." *P. 1932.*

440. WASHING THE APOSTLES' FEET

"'Do you really understand what I have done to you? You call me Master, and you say well, for so I am. If, then, the Master has washed your feet, why was it that you were unwilling to wash one another's feet? What lesson should you learn from this parable in which the Master so willingly does that service which his brethren were unwilling to do for one another? Verily, verily, I say to you: A servant is not greater than his master; neither is one who is sent greater than he who sends him. You have seen the way of service in my life among you, and blessed are you who will have the gracious courage so to serve. But why are you so slow to learn that the secret of greatness in the spiritual kingdom is not like the methods of power in the material world?'" *Pp. 1939-40.* **John 13:12-17.**

441. ESTABLISHING THE REMEMBRANCE SUPPER

"As they brought Jesus the third cup of wine, the 'cup of blessing,' he arose from the couch and, taking the cup in his hands, blessed it, saying: 'Take this cup, all of you, and drink of it. This shall be the cup of my remembrance. This is the cup of the blessing of a new dispensation of grace and truth. This shall be to you the emblem of the bestowal and ministry of the divine Spirit of Truth. And I will not again drink this cup with you until I drink in new form with you in the Father's eternal kingdom.'" *P. 1941.*

"When they had finished drinking this new cup of remembrance, the Master took up the bread and, after giving thanks, broke it in pieces and, directing them to pass it around, said: 'Take this bread of remembrance and eat it. I have told you that I am the bread of life. And this bread of life is the united life of the Father and the Son in one gift. The word of the Father, as revealed in the Son, is indeed the bread of life.' When they had partaken of the bread of remembrance, the symbol of the living word of truth incarnated in the likeness of mortal flesh, they all sat down." *P. 1942.*

"This supper of remembrance, when it is partaken of by those who are Son-believing and God-knowing, does not need to have associated with its symbolism any of man's puerile misinterpretations regarding the meaning of the divine presence, for upon all such occasions the Master is *really present*. The remembrance supper is the believer's symbolic rendezvous with Michael. When you become thus spirit-conscious, the Son is actually present, and his spirit fraternizes with the indwelling fragment of his Father." *P. 1942.*

"When Jesus had thus established the supper of the remembrance, he said to the twelve: 'And as often as you do this, do it in remembrance of me. And when you do remember me, first look back upon my life in the flesh, recall that I was once with you, and then, by faith, discern that you shall all some time sup with me in the Father's eternal kingdom. This is the new Passover which I leave with you, even the memory of my bestowal life, the word of eternal truth; and of my love for you, the outpouring of my Spirit of Truth upon all flesh.'

"And they ended this celebration of the old but bloodless Passover in connection with the inauguration of the new supper of the remembrance, by singing, all together, the one hundred and eighteenth Psalm." P. 1943. **Mark 14:22-25; Luke 22:14-20**.

442. THE NEW COMMANDMENT

"'The time has now come for the Son of Man to be glorified, and the Father shall be glorified in me. My friends, I am to be with you only a little longer. Soon you will seek for me, but you will not find me, for I am going to a place to which you cannot, at this time, come. But when you have finished your work on earth as I have now finished mine, you shall then come to me even as I now prepare to go to my Father. In just a short time I am going to leave you, you will see me no more on earth, but you shall all see me in the age to come when you ascend to the kingdom which my Father has given to me.'

"After a few moments of informal conversation, Jesus stood up and said: 'When I enacted for you a parable indicating how you should be willing to serve one another, I said that I desired to give you a new commandment; and I would do this now as I am about to leave you. You well know the commandment which directs that you love one another; that you love your neighbor even as yourself. But I am not wholly satisfied with even that sincere devotion on the part of my children. I would have you perform still greater acts of love in the kingdom of the believing brotherhood. And so I give you this new commandment: That you love one another even as I have loved you. And by this will all men know that you are my disciples if you thus love one another.

"'When I give you this new commandment, I do not place any new burden upon your souls; rather do I bring you new joy and make it possible for you to experience new pleasure in knowing the delights of the bestowal of your heart's affection upon your fellow men. I am about to experience the supreme joy, even though enduring outward sorrow, in the bestowal of my affection upon you and your fellow mortals.

"'When I invite you to love one another, even as I have loved you, I hold up before you the supreme measure of true affection, for greater love can no man have than this: that he will lay down his life for his friends. And you are my friends; you will continue to be my friends if you are but willing to do what I have taught you. You have called me Master, but I do not call you servants. If you will only love one another as I am loving you, you shall be my friends, and I will ever speak to you of that which the Father reveals to me.'" *Pp. 1944-5.* **John 13:34,35; 15:12.**

443. LET NOT YOUR HEARTS BE TROUBLED

"'Let not your hearts be troubled. You believe in God; continue to believe also in me. Even though I must leave you, I will not be far from you. I have already told you that in my Father's universe there are many tarrying places. If this were not true, I would not have repeatedly told you about them. I am going to return to these worlds of light, stations in the Father's heaven to which you shall some time ascend. From these places I came into this world, and the hour is now at hand when I must return to my Father's work in the spheres on high.'" *P. 1947.* **John 14:1,27.**

444. WORDS OF COMFORT

"Jesus looked down upon them all, smiled, and said: 'My little children, I am going away, going back to my Father. In a little while you will not see me as you do here, as flesh and blood. In a very short time I am going to send you my spirit, just like me except for this material body. This new teacher is the Spirit of Truth who will live with each one of you, in your hearts, and so will all the children of light be made one and be drawn toward one another. And in this very manner will my Father and I be able to live in the souls of each one of you and also in the hearts of all other men who love us and make that love real in their experiences by loving one another, even as I am now loving you.'" *P. 1949.* **John 14:18,19.**

445. THE OLD AND THE NEW RELIGION

"And all this clearly indicates the difference between the old religion and the new. The old religion taught self-sacrifice; the new religion teaches only self-forgetfulness, enhanced self-realization in conjoined social service and universe comprehension. The old religion was motivated by fear-consciousness; the new gospel of the kingdom is dominated by truth-conviction, the spirit of eternal and universal truth. And no amount of piety or creedal loyalty can compensate for the absence in the life experience of kingdom believers of that spontaneous, generous, and sincere friendliness which characterizes the spirit-born sons of the living God. Neither tradition nor a ceremonial system of formal worship can atone for the lack of genuine compassion for one's fellows." *P. 1951.*

446. THE MANSION WORLDS

"'When I have returned to live in you and work through you, I can the better lead you on through this life and guide you through the many abodes in the future life in the heaven of heavens. Life in the Father's eternal creation is not an endless rest of idleness and selfish ease but rather a ceaseless progression in grace, truth, and glory. Each of the many, many stations in my Father's house is a stopping place, a life designed to prepare you for the next one ahead. And so will the children of light go on from glory to glory until they attain the divine estate wherein they are spiritually perfected even as the Father is perfect in all things.'" *P. 1953.*

447. MORE WORDS OF COMFORT

"'And now, as I am about to leave you, I would speak words of comfort. Peace I leave with you; my peace I give to you. I make these gifts not as the world gives—by measure—I give each of you all you will receive. Let not your heart be troubled, neither let it be fearful. I have overcome the world, and in me you shall all triumph through faith. I have warned you that the Son of Man will be killed, but I assure you I will come back before I go to the Father, even though it be for only a little while. And after I have ascended to the Father, I will surely send the new teacher to be with you and to abide in your very hearts. And when you see all this come to pass, be not dismayed, but rather believe, inasmuch as you knew it all beforehand. I have loved you with a great affection, and I would not leave you, but it is the Father's will. My hour has come.'" *P. 1954.* **John 14:26-29.**

448. JESUS' TITLES

"The Master, during the course of this final prayer with his apostles, alluded to the fact that he had manifested the Father's *name* to the world. And that is truly what he did by the revelation of God through his perfected life in the flesh. The Father in heaven had sought to reveal himself to Moses, but he could proceed no further than to cause it to be said, 'I AM.' And when pressed for further revelation of himself, it was only disclosed, 'I AM that I AM.' But when Jesus had finished his earth life, this name of the Father had been so revealed that the Master, who was the Father incarnate, could truly say:

> "I am the bread of life.
> "I am the living water.
> "I am the light of the world.
> "I am the desire of all ages.
> "I am the open door to eternal salvation.
> "I am the reality of endless life.

"I am the good shepherd.
"I am the pathway of infinite perfection.
"I am the resurrection and the life.
"I am the secret of eternal survival.
"I am the way, the truth, and the life.
"I am the infinite Father of my finite children.
"I am the true vine; you are the branches.
"I am the hope of all who know the living truth.
"I am the living bridge from one world to another.
"I am the living link between time and eternity." *P. 1965*.

449. JESUS' SUFFERING IN THE GARDEN

"Jesus' humanity was not insensible to this situation of private loneliness, public shame, and the appearance of the failure of his cause. All these sentiments bore down on him with indescribable heaviness. In this great sorrow his mind went back to the days of his childhood in Nazareth and to his early work in Galilee. At the time of this great trial there came up in his mind many of those pleasant scenes of his earthly ministry. And it was from these old memories of Nazareth, Capernaum, Mount Hermon, and of the sunrise and sunset on the shimmering Sea of Galilee, that he soothed himself as he made his human heart strong and ready to encounter the traitor who should so soon betray him." *P. 1969*. **Matt. 26:26-39. Mark 14:34-42**.

450. "BEHOLD THE MAN"

"Then Pilate led forth this bleeding and lacerated prisoner and, presenting him before the mixed multitude, said: 'Behold the man! Again I declare to you that I find no crime in him, and having scourged him, I would release him.'

"There stood Jesus of Nazareth, clothed in an old purple royal robe with a crown of thorns piercing his kindly brow. His face was bloodstained and his form bowed down with suffering and grief. But nothing can appeal to the unfeeling hearts of those who are victims of intense emotional hatred and slaves to religious prejudice. This sight sent a mighty shudder through the realms of a vast universe, but it did not touch the hearts of those who had set their minds to effect the destruction of Jesus." *P. 1995*. **John 19:5**.

451. THE TRIAL OF JESUS

"Here stood the Son of God incarnate as the Son of Man. He was arrested without indictment; accused without evidence; adjudged without witnesses; punished without a verdict; and now was soon to be condemned to die by an unjust judge who confessed that he could find no fault in him. If Pilate had thought to appeal to their patriotism by referring to Jesus as the 'king of the Jews,' he utterly failed. The Jews were not expecting any such a king. The declaration of the chief priests and the Sadducees, 'We have no king but Caesar,' was a shock even to the unthinking populace, but it was too late now to save Jesus even had the mob dared to espouse the Master's cause." *P. 1996.*

"These shortsighted Jews clamored unseemlily for the Master's death while he stood there in awful silence looking upon the death scene of a nation—his earthly father's own people.

"Jesus had acquired that type of human character which could preserve its composure and assert its dignity in the face of continued and gratuitous insult. He could not be intimidated. When first assaulted by the servant of Annas, he had only suggested the propriety of calling witnesses who might duly testify against him.

"From first to last, in his so-called trial before Pilate, the onlooking celestial hosts could not refrain from broadcasting to the universe the depiction of the scene of 'Pilate on trial before Jesus.'" *P. 1999.* **Matt. 26:57-68; 27:11-14; Mark 14:55-65; 15:1-20; Luke 23:1-5, 13-25; John 18:19-32.**

452. JESUS LAYS DOWN HIS LIFE

"The two thieves crucified with Jesus were associates of Barabbas and would later have been put to death with their leader if he had not been released as the Passover pardon of Pilate. Jesus was thus crucified in the place of Barabbas.

"What Jesus is now about to do, submit to death on the cross, he does of his own free will. In foretelling this experience, he said: 'The Father loves and sustains me because I am willing to lay down my life. But I will take it up again. No one takes my life away from me—I lay it down of myself. I have authority to lay it down, and I have authority to take it up. I have received such a commandment from my Father.'" *P. 2004.* **John 10:15,17,18.**

453. AT THE CRUCIFIXION

"Standing near the cross at one time or another during the crucifixion were Mary, Ruth, Jude, John, Salome (John's mother), and a group of earnest women believers including Mary the wife of Clopas and sister of Jesus' mother, Mary Magdalene, and Rebecca, onetime of Sepphoris. These and other friends of Jesus held their peace while they witnessed his great patience and fortitude and gazed upon his intense sufferings." *P. 2008.* **Mark 15:40,41; Luke 23:49.**

454. THE THIEF ON THE CROSS

"One of the brigands railed at Jesus, saying, 'If you are the Son of God, why do you not save yourself and us?' But when he had reproached Jesus, the other thief, who had many times heard the Master teach, said:

'Do you have no fear even of God? Do you not see that we are suffering justly for our deeds, but that this man suffers unjustly? Better that we should seek forgiveness for our sins and salvation for our souls.' When Jesus heard the thief say this, he turned his face toward him and smiled approvingly. When the malefactor saw the face of Jesus turned toward him, he mustered up his courage, fanned the flickering flame of his faith, and said, 'Lord, remember me when you come into your kingdom.' And then Jesus said, 'Verily, verily, I say to you today, you shall sometime be with me in Paradise.'

"The Master had time amidst the pangs of mortal death to listen to the faith confession of the believing brigand. When this thief reached out for salvation, he found deliverance. Many times before this he had been constrained to believe in Jesus, but only in these last hours of consciousness did he turn with a whole heart toward the Master's teaching. When he saw the manner in which Jesus faced death upon the cross, this thief could no longer resist the conviction that this Son of Man was indeed the Son of God." *Pp. 2008-9.*
Matt. 27:38,44; Mark 15:27; Luke 23:32,33,39-43; John 19:18.

455. LAST HOUR ON THE CROSS

"Shortly after one o'clock, amidst the increasing darkness of the fierce sandstorm, Jesus began to fail in human consciousness. His last words of mercy, forgiveness, and admonition had been spoken. His last wish—concerning the care of his mother—had been expressed. During this hour of approaching death the human mind of Jesus resorted to the repetition of many passages in the Hebrew scriptures, particularly the Psalms. The last conscious thought of the human Jesus was concerned with the repetition in his mind of a portion of the Book of Psalms now known as the twentieth, twenty-first, and twenty-second Psalms. While his lips would often move, he was too weak to utter the words as these passages, which he so well knew by heart, would pass through his mind. Only a few times did those standing by catch some utterance, such as, 'I know the Lord will save his anointed,' 'Your hand shall find out all my enemies,' and 'My God, my God, why have you forsaken me?' Jesus did not for one moment entertain the slightest doubt that he had lived in accordance with the Father's will; and he never doubted that he was now laying down his life in the flesh in accordance with his Father's will. He did not feel that the Father had forsaken him; he was merely reciting in his vanishing consciousness many Scriptures, among them this twenty-second Psalm, which begins with 'My God, my God, why have you forsaken me?' And this happened to be one of the three passages which were spoken with sufficient clearness to be heard by those standing by." *P. 2010*.

"Jesus died royally—as he had lived. He freely admitted his kingship and remained master of the situation throughout the tragic day. He went willingly to his ignominious death, after he had provided for the safety of his chosen apostles. He wisely restrained Peter's trouble-making violence and provided that John might be near him right up to the end of his mortal existence. He revealed his true nature to the murderous Sanhedrin and reminded Pilate of the source of his sovereign authority as a Son of God. He started out to Golgotha bearing his own crossbeam and finished up his loving bestowal by handing over his spirit of mortal acquirement to the Paradise Father. After such a life—and at such a death—the Master could truly say, 'It is finished.'" *P. 2011*. **Matt. 27:45-50; Mark 15:33-39**.

456. JESUS' BURIAL

"When Joseph and Nicodemus arrived at Golgotha, they found the soldiers taking Jesus down from the cross and the representatives of the Sanhedrin standing by to see that none of Jesus' followers prevented his body from going to the criminal burial pits. When Joseph presented Pilate's order for the Master's body to the centurion, the Jews raised a tumult and clamored for its possession. In their raving they sought violently to take possession of the body, and when they did this, the centurion ordered four of his soldiers to his side, and with drawn swords they stood astride the Master's body as it lay there on the ground. The centurion ordered the other soldiers to leave the two thieves while they drove back this angry mob of infuriated Jews. When order had been restored, the centurion read the permit from Pilate to the Jews and, stepping aside, said to Joseph: 'This body is yours to do with as you see fit. I and my soldiers will stand by to see that no man interferes.'" *Pp. 2012-13*. **Matt. 27:57-61**.

457. MEANING OF THE CROSS

"Although Jesus did not die this death on the cross to atone for the racial guilt of mortal man nor to provide some sort of effective approach to an otherwise offended and unforgiving God; even though the Son of Man did not offer himself as a sacrifice to appease the wrath of God and to open the way for sinful man to obtain salvation; notwithstanding that these ideas of atonement and propitiation are erroneous, nonetheless, there are significances attached to this death of Jesus on the cross which should not be overlooked. It is a fact that Urantia has become known among other neighboring inhabited planets as the 'World of the Cross.'" *P. 2016*.

"Mortal man was never the property of the archdeceivers. Jesus did not die to ransom man from the clutch of the apostate rulers and fallen princes of the spheres. The Father in heaven never conceived of such crass injustice as damning a mortal soul because of the evildoing of his ancestors. Neither was the Master's death on the cross a sacrifice which consisted in an effort to pay God a debt which the race of mankind had come to owe him." *P. 2016*.

"Jesus lived and died for a whole universe, not just for the races of this one world. While the mortals of the realms had salvation even before Jesus lived and died on Urantia, it is nevertheless a fact that his bestowal on this world greatly illuminated the way of salvation; his death did much to make forever plain the certainty of mortal survival after death in the flesh.

"Though it is hardly proper to speak of Jesus as a sacrificer, a ransomer, or a redeemer, it is wholly correct to refer to him as a *savior*. He forever made the way of salvation (survival) more clear and certain; he did better and more surely show the way of salvation for all the mortals of all the worlds of the universe of Nebadon." *P. 2017*.

"This entire idea of the ransom of the atonement places salvation upon a plane of unreality; such a concept is purely philosophic. Human salvation is *real*; it is based on two realities which may be grasped by the creature's faith and thereby become incorporated into individual human experience: the fact of the fatherhood of God and its correlated truth, the brotherhood of man. It is true, after all, that you are to be 'forgiven your debts, even as you forgive your debtors.'" *P. 2017*.

458. RESURRECTION OF JESUS

"At two forty-five Sunday morning, the Paradise incarnation commission, consisting of seven unidentified Paradise personalities, arrived on the scene and immediately deployed themselves about the tomb. At ten minutes before three, intense vibrations of commingled material and morontia activities began to issue from Joseph's new tomb, and at two minutes past three o'clock, this Sunday morning, April 9, A.D. 30, the resurrected morontia form and personality of Jesus of Nazareth came forth from the tomb.

"After the resurrected Jesus emerged from his burial tomb, the body of flesh in which he had lived and wrought on earth for almost thirty-six years was still lying there in the sepulchre niche, undisturbed and wrapped in the linen sheet, just as it had been laid to rest by Joseph and his associates on Friday afternoon. Neither was the stone before the entrance of the tomb in any way disturbed; the seal of Pilate was still unbroken; the soldiers were still on guard. The temple guards had been on continuous duty; the Roman guard had been changed at midnight. None of these watchers suspected that the object of their vigil had risen to a new and higher form of existence, and that the body which they were guarding was now a discarded outer covering which had no further connection with the delivered and resurrected morontia personality of Jesus." *Pp. 2020-1*.

"Now is the mortal transit of Jesus—the morontia resurrection of the Son of Man—completed. The transitory experience of the Master as a personality midway between the material and the spiritual has begun. And he has done all this through power inherent within himself; no personality has rendered him any assistance. He now lives as Jesus of morontia, and as he begins this morontia life, the material body of his flesh lies there undisturbed in the tomb. The soldiers are still on guard, and the seal of the governor about the rocks has not yet been broken." *P. 2022*. **Matt. 28:1-8; Mark 16:1-11; Luke 24:1-10; John 20:1-18.**

459. DISPOSING OF JESUS' BODY

"At ten minutes past three o'clock, as the resurrected Jesus fraternized with the assembled morontia personalities from the seven mansion worlds of Satania, the chief of archangels—the angels of the resurrection—approached Gabriel and asked for the mortal body of Jesus. Said the chief of the archangels: 'We may not participate in the morontia resurrection of the bestowal experience of Michael our sovereign, but we would have his mortal remains put in our custody for immediate dissolution. We do not propose to employ our technique of dematerialization; we merely wish to invoke the process of accelerated time. It is enough that we have seen the Sovereign live and die on Urantia; the hosts of heaven would be spared the memory of enduring the sight of the slow decay of the human form of the Creator and Upholder of a universe. In the name of the celestial intelligences of all Nebadon, I ask for a mandate giving me the custody of the mortal body of Jesus of Nazareth and empowering us to proceed with its immediate dissolution.'" *P. 2022*.

"As they made ready to remove the body of Jesus from the tomb preparatory to according it the dignified and reverent disposal of near-instantaneous dissolution, it was assigned the secondary Urantia midwayers to roll away the stones from the entrance of the tomb. The larger of these two stones was a huge circular affair, much like a millstone, and it moved in a groove chiseled out of the rock, so that it could be rolled back and forth to open or close the tomb. When the watching Jewish guards and the Roman soldiers, in the dim light of the morning, saw this huge stone begin to roll away from the entrance of the tomb, apparently of its own accord—without any visible means to account for such motion—they were seized with fear and panic, and they fled in haste from the scene. The Jews fled to their homes, afterward going back to report these doings to their captain at the temple. The Romans fled to the fortress of Antonia and reported what they had seen to the centurion as soon as he arrived on duty." P. 2023.

460. THE WOMEN AT THE TOMB

"As these women sat there in the early hours of the dawn of this new day, they looked to one side and observed a silent and motionless stranger. For a moment they were again frightened, but Mary Magdalene, rushing toward him and addressing him as if she thought he might be the caretaker of the garden, said, 'Where have you taken the Master? Where have they laid him? Tell us that we may go and get him.' When the stranger did not answer Mary, she began to weep. Then spoke Jesus to them, saying, 'Whom do you seek?' Mary said: 'We seek for Jesus who was laid to rest in Joseph's tomb, but he is gone. Do you know where they have taken him?' Then said Jesus: 'Did not this Jesus tell you, even in Galilee, that he would die, but that he would rise again?' These words startled the women, but the Master was so changed that they did not yet recognize him with his back turned to the dim light. And as they pondered his words, he addressed the Magdalene with a familiar voice, saying, 'Mary.' And when she heard that word of well-known sympathy and affectionate greeting, she knew it was the voice of the Master, and she rushed to kneel at his feet while she exclaimed, 'My Lord, and my Master!' And all of the other women recognized that it was the Master who stood before them in glorified form, and they quickly knelt before him." P. 2026. **Matt. 28:5-10; Mark 16:1-8; Luke 24:10,11; John 20:1,2.**

461. DAVID ZEBEDEE HERALDS THE RESURRECTION

"From the tomb David and Joseph went immediately to the home of Elijah Mark, where they held a conference with the ten apostles in the upper chamber. Only John Zebedee was disposed to believe, even faintly, that Jesus had risen from the dead. Peter had believed at first but, when he failed to find the Master, fell into grave doubting. They were all disposed to believe that the Jews had removed the body. David would not argue with them, but when he left, he said: 'You are the apostles, and you ought to understand these things. I will not contend with you; nevertheless, I now go back to the home of Nicodemus, where I have appointed with the messengers to assemble this morning, and when they have gathered together, I will send them forth on their last mission, as heralds of the Master's resurrection. I heard the Master say that, after he should die, he would rise on the third day, and I believe him.' And thus speaking to the dejected and forlorn ambassadors of the kingdom, this self-appointed chief of communication and intelligence took leave of the apostles. On his way from the upper chamber he dropped the bag of Judas, containing all the apostolic funds, in the lap of Matthew Levi.

"It was about half past nine o'clock when the last of David's twenty-six messengers arrived at the home of Nicodemus. David promptly assembled them in the spacious courtyard and addressed them:

"'Men and brethren, all this time you have served me in accordance with your oath to me and to one another, and I call you to witness that I have never yet sent out false information at your hands. I am about to send you on your last mission as volunteer messengers of the kingdom, and in so doing I release you from your oaths and thereby disband the messenger corps. Men, I declare to you that we have finished our work. No more does the Master have need of mortal messengers; he has risen from the dead. He told us before they arrested him that he would die and rise again on the third day. I have seen the tomb—it is empty. I have talked with Mary Magdalene and four other women, who have talked with Jesus. I now disband you, bid you farewell, and send you on your respective assignments, and the message which you shall bear to the believers is: "Jesus has risen from the dead; the tomb is empty."'" *P. 2030.*

462. JESUS APPEARING TO THOMAS

"When the Master had so spoken, he looked down into the face of Thomas and said: 'And you, Thomas, who said you would not believe unless you could see me and put your finger in the nail marks of my hands, have now beheld me and heard my words; and though you see no nail marks on my hands, since I am raised in the form that you also shall have when you depart from this world, what will you say to your brethren? You will acknowledge the truth, for already in your heart you had begun to believe even when you so stoutly asserted your unbelief. Your doubts, Thomas, always most stubbornly assert themselves just as they are about to crumble. Thomas, I bid you be not faithless but believing—and I know you will believe, even with a whole heart.'

"When Thomas heard these words, he fell on his knees before the morontia Master and exclaimed, 'I believe! My Lord and my Master!' Then said Jesus to Thomas: 'You have believed, Thomas, because you have really seen and heard me. Blessed are those in the ages to come who will believe even though they have not seen with the eye of flesh nor heard with the mortal ear.'

"And then, as the Master's form moved over near the head of the table, he addressed them all, saying: 'And now go all of you to Galilee, where I will presently appear to you.' After he said this, he vanished from their sight." *P. 2043.* **John 20:26-29.**

463. JESUS' LAST APPEARANCE

"Early Thursday morning, May 18, Jesus made his last appearance on earth as a morontia personality. As the eleven apostles were about to sit down to breakfast in the upper chamber of Mary Mark's home, Jesus appeared to them and said:

"'Peace be upon you. I have asked you to tarry here in Jerusalem until I ascend to the Father, even until I send you the Spirit of Truth, who shall soon be poured out upon all flesh, and who shall endow you with power from on high.'" *P. 2055.*

"When he had spoken, he beckoned for them to come with him, and he led them out on the Mount of Olives, where he bade them farewell preparatory to departing from Urantia. This was a solemn journey to Olivet. Not a word was spoken by any of them from the time they left the upper chamber until Jesus paused with them on the Mount of Olives." P. 2055. Luke 24:49.

464. JESUS' RELIGION

"To Jesus, mortal life had dealt its hardest, cruelest, and bitterest blows; and this man met these ministrations of despair with faith, courage, and the unswerving determination to do his Father's will. Jesus met life in all its terrible reality and mastered it—even in death. He did not use religion as a release from life. The religion of Jesus does not seek to escape this life in order to enjoy the waiting bliss of another existence. The religion of Jesus provides the joy and peace of another and spiritual existence to enhance and ennoble the life which men now live in the flesh.

"If religion is an opiate to the people, it is not the religion of Jesus. On the cross he refused to drink the deadening drug, and his spirit, poured out upon all flesh, is a mighty world influence which leads man upward and urges him onward. The spiritual forward urge is the most powerful driving force present in this world; the truth-learning believer is the one progressive and aggressive soul on earth.

"On the day of Pentecost the religion of Jesus broke all national restrictions and racial fetters. It is forever true, 'Where the spirit of the Lord is, there is liberty.' On this day the Spirit of Truth became the personal gift from the Master to every mortal. This spirit was bestowed for the purpose of qualifying believers more effectively to preach the gospel of the kingdom, but they mistook the experience of receiving the outpoured spirit for a part of the new gospel which they were unconsciously formulating." *P. 2063.*

465. ENDURANCE OF CHRISTIANITY

"Christianity exhibits a history of having originated out of the unintended transformation of the religion of Jesus into a religion about Jesus. It further presents the history of having experienced Hellenization, paganization, secularization, institutionalization, intellectual deterioration, spiritual decadence, moral hibernation, threatened extinction, later rejuvenation, fragmentation, and more recent relative rehabilitation. Such a pedigree is indicative of inherent vitality and the possession of vast recuperative resources. And this same Christianity is now present in the civilized world of Occidental peoples and stands face to face with a struggle for existence which is even more ominous than those eventful crises which have characterized its past battles for dominance." P. 2075.

466. THE MATERIALISTIC PANIC

"Scientists have unintentionally precipitated mankind into a materialistic panic; they have started an unthinking run on the moral bank of the ages, but this bank of human experience has vast spiritual resources; it can stand the demands being made upon it. Only unthinking men become panicky about the spiritual assets of the human race. When the materialistic-secular panic is over, the religion of Jesus will not be found bankrupt. The spiritual bank of the kingdom of heaven will be paying out faith, hope, and moral security to all who draw upon it 'in His name.'" P. 2076.

467. INCONSISTENCIES OF THE MECHANIST

"The inconsistency of the modern mechanist is: If this were merely a material universe and man only a machine, such a man would be wholly unable to recognize himself as such a machine, and likewise would such a machine-man be wholly unconscious of the fact of the existence of such a material universe. The materialistic dismay and despair of a mechanistic science has failed to recognize the fact of the spirit-indwelt mind of the scientist whose very supermaterial insight formulates these mistaken and self-contradictory *concepts* of a materialistic universe." P. 2078.

"Materialism reduces man to a soulless automaton and constitutes him merely an arithmetical symbol finding a helpless place in the mathematical formula of an unromantic and mechanistic universe. But whence comes all this vast universe of mathematics without a Master Mathematician? Science may expatiate on the conservation of matter, but religion validates the conservation of men's souls—it concerns their experience with spiritual realities and eternal values." P. 2077.

"The very pessimism of the most pessimistic materialist is, in and of itself, sufficient proof that the universe of the pessimist is not wholly material. Both optimism and pessimism are concept reactions in a mind conscious of *values* as well as of *facts*. If the universe were truly what the materialist regards it to be, man as a human machine would then be devoid of all conscious recognition of that very *fact*. Without the consciousness of the concept of *values* within the spirit-born mind, the fact of universe materialism and the mechanistic phenomena of universe operation would be wholly unrecognized by man. One machine cannot be conscious of the nature or value of another machine." P. 2079.

"If the universe were only material and man only a machine, there would be no science to embolden the scientist to postulate this mechanization of the universe. Machines cannot measure, classify, nor evaluate themselves. Such a scientific piece of work could be executed only by some entity of supermachine status." P. 2079.

"The very claim of materialism implies a supermaterial consciousness of the mind which presumes to assert such dogmas. A mechanism might deteriorate, but it could never progress. Machines do not think, create, dream, aspire, idealize, hunger for truth, or thirst for righteousness. They do not motivate their lives with the passion to serve other machines and to choose as their goal of eternal progression the sublime task of finding God and striving to be like him. Machines are never intellectual, emotional, aesthetic, ethical, moral, or spiritual." P. 2079.

468. WEAKNESS OF SECULARISM

"The inherent weakness of secularism is that it discards ethics and religion for politics and power. You simply cannot establish the brotherhood of men while ignoring or denying the fatherhood of God.

"Secular social and political optimism is an illusion. Without God, neither freedom and liberty, nor property and wealth will lead to peace.

"The complete secularization of science, education, industry, and society can lead only to disaster. During the first third of the twentieth century Urantians killed more human beings than were killed during the whole of the Christian dispensation up to that time. And this is only the beginning of the dire harvest of materialism and secularism; still more terrible destruction is yet to come." P. 2082.

469. THE NEEDS OF CHRISTIANITY

"But paganized and socialized Christianity stands in need of new contact with the uncompromised teachings of Jesus; it languishes for lack of a new vision of the Master's life on earth. A new and fuller revelation of the religion of Jesus is destined to conquer an empire of materialistic secularism and to overthrow a world sway of mechanistic naturalism. Urantia is now quivering on the very brink of one of its most amazing and enthralling epochs of social readjustment, moral quickening, and spiritual enlightenment.

"The teachings of Jesus, even though greatly modified, survived the mystery cults of their birthtime, the ignorance and superstition of the dark ages, and are even now slowly triumphing over the materialism, mechanism, and secularism of the twentieth century. And such times of great testing and threatened defeat are always times of great revelation." *P. 2082.*

"Christianity is threatened by slow death from formalism, over organization, intellectualism, and other nonspiritual trends. The modern Christian church is not such a brotherhood of dynamic believers as Jesus commissioned continuously to effect the spiritual transformation of successive generations of mankind.

"So-called Christianity has become a social and cultural movement as well as a religious belief and practice. The stream of modern Christianity drains many an ancient pagan swamp and many a barbarian morass; many olden cultural watersheds drain into this present-day cultural stream as well as the high Galilean tablelands which are supposed to be its exclusive source." *P. 2083.*

"Christianity is an extemporized religion, and therefore must it operate in low gear. High-gear spiritual performances must await the new revelation and the more general acceptance of the real religion of Jesus. But Christianity is a mighty religion, seeing that the commonplace disciples of a crucified carpenter set in motion those teachings which conquered the Roman world in three hundred years and then went on to triumph over the barbarians who overthrew Rome. This same Christianity conquered—absorbed and exalted—the whole stream of Hebrew theology and Greek philosophy. And then, when this Christian religion became comatose for more than a thousand years as a result of an overdose of mysteries and paganism, it resurrected itself and virtually reconquered the whole Western world. Christianity contains enough of Jesus' teachings to immortalize it." *P. 2086.*

470. THE HOPE OF CHRISTIANITY

"The hope of modern Christianity is that it should cease to sponsor the social systems and industrial policies of Western civilization while it humbly bows itself before the cross it so valiantly extols, there to learn anew from Jesus of Nazareth the greatest truths mortal man can ever hear—the living gospel of *the fatherhood of God and the brotherhood of man." P. 2086.*

Part IV: *The Life of Jesus*

471. THE FAITH OF JESUS

"Theology may fix, formulate, define, and dogmatize faith, but in the human life of Jesus faith was personal, living, original, spontaneous, and purely spiritual. This faith was not reverence for tradition nor a mere intellectual belief which he held as a sacred creed, but rather a sublime experience and a profound conviction which *securely held him*. His faith was so real and all-encompassing that it absolutely swept away any spiritual doubts and effectively destroyed every conflicting desire. Nothing was able to tear him away from the spiritual anchorage of this fervent, sublime, and undaunted faith. Even in the face of apparent defeat or in the throes of disappointment and threatening despair, he calmly stood in the divine presence free from fear and fully conscious of spiritual invincibility. Jesus enjoyed the invigorating assurance of the possession of unflinching faith, and in each of life's trying situations he unfailingly exhibited an unquestioning loyalty to the Father's will. And this superb faith was undaunted even by the cruel and crushing threat of an ignominious death." *Pp. 2087-8.*

"The faith of Jesus visualized all spirit values as being found in the kingdom of God; therefore he said, 'Seek first the kingdom of heaven.' Jesus saw in the advanced and ideal fellowship of the kingdom the achievement and fulfillment of the 'will of God.' The very heart of the prayer which he taught his disciples was, 'Your kingdom come; your will be done.' Having thus conceived of the kingdom as comprising the will of God, he devoted himself to the cause of its realization with amazing self-forgetfulness and unbounded enthusiasm. But in all his intense mission and throughout his extraordinary life there never appeared the fury of the fanatic nor the superficial frothiness of the religious egotist." *P. 2088.*

472. PRAYER LIFE OF JESUS

"Jesus never prayed as a religious duty. To him prayer was a sincere expression of spiritual attitude, a declaration of soul loyalty, a recital of personal devotion, an expression of thanksgiving, an avoidance of emotional tension, a prevention of conflict, an exaltation of intellection, an ennoblement of desire, a vindication of moral decision, an enrichment of thought, an invigoration of higher inclinations, a consecration of impulse, a clarification of viewpoint, a declaration of faith, a transcendental surrender of will, a sublime assertion of confidence, a revelation of courage, the proclamation of discovery, a confession of supreme devotion, the validation of consecration, a technique for the adjustment of difficulties, and the mighty mobilization of the combined soul powers to withstand all human tendencies toward selfishness, evil, and sin. He lived just such a life of prayerful consecration to the doing of his Father's will and ended his life triumphantly with just such a prayer. The secret of his unparalleled religious life was this consciousness of the presence of God; and he attained it by intelligent prayer and sincere worship—unbroken communion with God—and not by leadings, voices, visions, or extraordinary religious practices." *P. 2089.*

473. JESUS WANTS US TO BELIEVE WITH HIM

"Jesus does not require his disciples to believe in him but rather to believe *with* him, believe in the reality of the love of God and in full confidence accept the security of the assurance of sonship with the heavenly Father. The Master desires that all his followers should fully share his transcendent faith. Jesus most touchingly challenged his followers, not only to believe *what* he believed, but also to believe *as* he believed. This is the full significance of his one supreme requirement, '*Follow me.*'" P. 2089.

474. THE RELIGION ABOUT JESUS

"But the greatest mistake was made in that, while the human Jesus was recognized as *having* a religion, the divine Jesus (Christ) almost overnight became a religion. Paul's Christianity made sure of the adoration of the divine Christ, but it almost wholly lost sight of the struggling and valiant human Jesus of Galilee, *who, by the valor of his personal religious faith* and the heroism of his indwelling Adjuster, ascended from the lowly levels of humanity to become one with divinity, thus becoming the new and living way whereby all mortals may so ascend from humanity to divinity. Mortals in all stages of spirituality and on all worlds may find in the personal life of Jesus that which will strengthen and inspire them as they progress from the lowest spirit levels up to the highest divine values, from the beginning to the end of all personal religious experience." *P. 2092.*

475. JESUS A WHOLEHEARTED RELIGIONIST

"You would be neither shocked nor disturbed by some of Jesus' strong pronouncements if you would only remember that he was the world's most wholehearted and devoted religionist. He was a wholly consecrated mortal, unreservedly dedicated to doing his Father's will. Many of his apparently hard sayings were more of a personal confession of faith and a pledge of devotion than commands to his followers. *And it was this very singleness of purpose and unselfish devotion* that enabled him to effect such extraordinary progress in the *conquest of the human mind* in one short life. Many of his declarations should be considered as a confession of what he demanded of himself rather than what he required of all his followers. In his devotion to the cause of the kingdom, Jesus burned all bridges behind him; he sacrificed all hindrances to the doing of his Father's will." *P. 2093.*

476. JESUS' FAITH IN MEN

"Jesus led men to feel at home in the world; he delivered them from the slavery of taboo and taught them that the world was not fundamentally evil. He did not long to escape from his earthly life; he mastered a technique of acceptably doing the Father's will while in the flesh. He attained an idealistic religious life in the very midst of a realistic world. Jesus did not share Paul's pessimistic view of humankind. *The Master looked upon men as the sons of God* and foresaw a magnificent and eternal future for those who chose survival. He was not a moral skeptic; he viewed man positively, not negatively. He saw most men as weak rather than wicked, more distraught than depraved. *But no matter what their status, they were all God's children and his brethren.*" P. 2093.

477. MAN'S DIVINE INDWELLING

"Unless a divine lover lived in man, he could not unselfishly and spiritually love. Unless an interpreter lived in the mind, man could not truly realize the unity of the universe. Unless an evaluator dwelt with man, he could not possibly appraise moral values and recognize spiritual meanings. And this lover hails from the very source of infinite love; this interpreter is a part of Universal Unity; this evaluator is the child of the Center and Source of all absolute values of divine and eternal reality." P. 2094.

"This profound experience of the reality of the divine indwelling forever transcends the crude materialistic technique of the physical sciences. You cannot put spiritual joy under a microscope; you cannot weigh love in a balance; you cannot measure moral values; neither can you estimate the quality of spiritual worship." P. 2095.

478. TRUE NOBILITY SPURNS MERE SUCCESS

"Some men's lives are too great and noble to descend to the low level of being merely successful. The animal must adapt itself to the environment, but the religious man transcends his environment and in this way escapes the limitations of the present material world through this insight of divine love. This concept of love generates in the soul of man that super-animal effort to find truth, beauty, and goodness; and when he does find them, he is glorified in their embrace; he is consumed with the desire to live them, to do righteousness." P. 2096.

479. FATHER IDEA THE HIGHEST CONCEPT OF GOD

"And God-consciousness is equivalent to the integration of the self with the universe, and on its highest levels of spiritual reality. Only the spirit content of any value is imperishable. Even that which is true, beautiful, and good may not perish in human experience. If man does not choose to survive, then does the surviving Adjuster conserve those realities born of love and nurtured in service. And all these things are a part of the Universal Father. The Father is living love, and this life of the Father is in his Sons. And the spirit of the Father is in his Son's sons—mortal men. When all is said and done, the Father idea is still the highest human concept of God." *P. 2097*.

www.ingramcontent.com/pod-product-compliance
Lightning Source LLC
Chambersburg PA
CBHW020946230426
43666CB00005B/191